# KRISHNA SMILED

*For Suzanne,
In friendship and fondness
Judith Elkin
Ann Arbor
2010*

*Judith Laikin Elkin*

# KRISHNA SMILED:

*Assignment in Southeast Asia*

SCHOLARLY PUBLISHING OFFICE  ANN ARBOR  2010

Published in 2010 by The Scholarly Publishing Office
The University of Michigan University Library

©1972 Wayne State University Press, © 2001 Judith Laikin Elkin

This edition is reprinted from the 1972 Wayne State University Press edition by arrangement with Judith Laikin Elkin.

Permission is required to reproduce material from this title in other publications, coursepacks, electronic products, and other media. Please send permission requests to:

Scholarly Publishing Office
University of Michigan Library
4186 Shapiro
919 South University Avenue
Ann Arbor, MI 48109

lib.spo@umich.edu
Fax: (734) 763-6850

ISBN 978-1-60785-209-4

*Grateful acknowledgement is extended to the* U. S. Foreign Service Journal *for permission to reprint part of chapter 14, which appeared in a slightly different form under the title "Where She Danced" (January 1956).*

*For Alissa and Susannah*

Foreward

I have a special fondness for this book and its author. I read *Krishna Smiled* when it first appeared and I greatly enjoyed it. Sometime after, I met the author under circumstances that were pleasingly odd. It was at the Detroit Zoo, where we both attended a seminar on elephants. We have been friends ever since, drawn together by a common interest in elephants, and in India.

*Krishna Smiled* is the story of a young woman having the adventure of her life as the Publications Procurement Officer to the US Department of State, accredited to India, Pakistan, Burma, Ceylon, and Afghanistan. The adventure began five years after the Partition (1947) that created India and Pakistan out of British India, and lasted two years (1954 - 56). Her task was to acquire publications in the languages of the region and to send the books to the Library of Congress and other libraries. To do so she had to seek out booksellers and government presses all over the subcontinent. This duty provided a reason to visit to every part of South, or as it then was called, Southeast, Asia.

This moment in history is now receding into the dimness of a past remembered only by the mature. Even the map is unfamiliar. Judith Laikin Elkin visited places which no longer exist, places such as Pepsu, Patiala, Vindhya Pradesh, and East Pakistan as well as the aforementioned Burma (now Myanmar) and Ceylon (now Sri Lanka). It is not a diary, contemporary with that moment, but a memoir of a rollicking adventure recalled in tranquility, written and published more than a decade later, in 1971. It recalls an America ignorant of India and its neighbors, a government needing books about them, and a popular culture as yet untouched by Indian culture as mediated by the Beatles, Allen Ginsberg and the hippies. Its writing is framed by these changes that separate its now from its then, changes it invokes at the beginning and returns to in the magnificent crescendo and coda of the last two chapters.

It predates also the invention of political correctness. It is plain-spoken, irreverent, high-spirited and humorous, good-hearted but slightly tart and sparing of sweetness in a way that makes us like it the more. It is what in diplomat-speak is called "frank", as in the phrase, "a frank exchange of views". It is critical, while being humane; it is humane, without losing its critical sense. Its voice is singular. Its style is bracing, freshly-minted, free of clichés, fun.

As the abstract and brief chronicle of the time, *Krishna Smiled* sketches for us the decolonization movement following Partition when the British and other European empires were being wound up. It gives a picture of the new nation-states of India, Pakistan, Burma and Ceylon shortly after their independence from Britain, when they were hard at work defining what kind of nations they would be, and the kingdom of Afghanistan when British influence had retreated. We hear of the linguistic reorganization of states in India, of the Chinese takeover of Tibet when China and India were leaders of the Non-Aligned Movement and before the Sino-Indian border war, of problems of poverty and the question, much on the minds of American political scientists at the time, whether caste and democracy are compatible.

However, we read the book not to learn about South Asia but to follow the life adventures of this American girl, as she calls herself, summoning her courage and trying her wings. The spreading of wings had two aspects. On the one hand there was the foreign service. The very first sentence of the book signals to readers that Judith Laikin was the sole woman in her class of inductees, entering a service in which men set the norms and *were* the norm. This was before what came to be called women's lib, for which the benchmark work, Betty Friedan's *The feminine mystique* (1963), lay far in the future. Inaugurating her career at the State Department on the far side of that divide, Judith Laikin was given to understand at the outset that the rules were different for women: they could not marry and remain in the service. (Eventually she left the service, and became Judith Laikin Elkin.) Under these conditions, this is the story of a young woman maintaining her independence in the office, so to say, under conditions that today are difficult to imagine.

On the other hand, there was South Asia, which was an especially challenging place in which to do so--which is to say, it was the *perfect* place. Readers will admire her courage and inventiveness as she undertakes travels, some of which would be much easier today, and others of which would be utterly impossible. Afghanistan offered the greatest challenge. On a bus ride to Mazar-i-Sharif she had to decide whether to transform herself into an Afghan girl by donning a chador, or a beardless Afghan boy by putting on a turban. I will not spoil it by telling which way she chose.

Readers are in for an enjoyable ride. I wish them pleasant journey, and I send Judith Elkin renewed thanks for the pleasure this book has given me.

Thomas R. Trautmann
Ann Arbor
25 August, 2010

# CONTENTS

## 1
*In which the President of the United States sends me to lie abroad for my country*   11

## 2
*On the way to Banaras, I fall in with Everyman*   16

## 3
*I fail to procure the Bhilsa telephone directory, but live to fulfill other intelligence missions*   32

## 4
*Awash in Delhi, Pepsu, and Punjab*   44

## 5
*I spend a night in a Moslem graveyard, collecting ephemera for the Library of Congress*   61

**6** *Into the Tower of Babel and out by that same door where in I went* 70

**7** *Inadvertently, I introduce Henry Miller to the Defense Minister of Nepal* 90

**8** *Touching the Untouchable* 96

**9** *Beware the Orakzai, My Son* 108

**10** *Wandering through Pomegranate Bazaar, I eat one seed too many* 123

**11** *Maidens* 130

**12** *I climb a Himalaya and miss a coup d'etat* 147

**13**
*Through Kerala with coir and cashew* 157

**14**
*The good servant, Jesus Christ* 177

**15**
*After two years, I finally acquire some intelligence* 190

**16**
*I become the first American girl to ride the Afghan Mail to Mazar-i-Sharif—and return* 206

**17**
*Holy, Holy, Holy* 226

**18**
*It's a long way to Khajuraho, we'd better get started* 244

*Index* 249

U S S R
C H I N A
Balkh
Mazar-I-Sharif
H I N D U K U S H
Doab
A F G H A N I S T A N
Kabul
Chazni
Ch'angiers
Kandahar
Qala Bist
DASHT-I-MARG
I R A N
Peshawar
J A M M U & K A S H M I R
Pahalgam
Srinagar
Lahore
Amritsar
Rishikesh
Patiala
T I B E T
H I M A L A Y A S
P A K I S T A N
Indus
Delhi
EVEREST
SIKKIM
KANCHENJUNGA
Gangtok
Kalimpong
Darjeeling
Agra
Ajmer
Gwalior
Jumna
Lucknow
Gumti
I N D I A
Karachi
Jhansi
Khajuraho
Allahabad
Banaras
Patna
Ganges
Dacca
E. PAKISTAN (BANGLADESH)
Ahmedabad
Bhopal
Bhilsa
Calcutta
Nagpur
Bhuvaneshwar
Puri
Bombay
I N D I A
Hyderabad
Madras
Mercara
Mysore
Coimbatore
Tiruchirappalli
Cochin
Alleppey
Quilon
Madura
CEYLON
Colombo

# 1

*In which the President of the United States sends me to lie abroad for my country*

"Ah, a rose among thorns," Dean Acheson murmured when he commissioned me a United States Foreign Service Officer. True enough, I was the only girl in the class of twenty-seven who graduated from the Foreign Service Institute that term.

It was 1952, and the United States government, still widely regarded as omnipotent, was about to send me to Southeast Asia as its publications procurement officer.

The assignment was an unusual one in many respects. Diplomats, who are honest men sent to lie abroad for their country, are usually assigned to one particular city, for example, New Delhi. Ambassadors get an entire country, for example, India. But I, a novice, was assigned simultaneously to India, Pakistan, Burma, Ceylon, and Afghanistan.

I had prepared myself for Asian adventure by majoring in Latin American studies at the Columbia University School of International Affairs. After receiving my master's degree,

## Krishna Smiled

I sat for the gruelling, three-day foreign service examination for no particular reason save that it was there. Unexpectedly, I passed, and finding the challenge exhilarating, presented myself for oral examination before a board of five curmudgeons. I recall that one of the questions hurled at me then was to name five cities of India. I could muster only four, and had to throw in Karachi for good measure. Had I but known it, before the next two years were out I would become so intimate with Asian geography that cities such as Nasik, Kalimpong, and Peshawar would have the familiar ring of Akron, Phoenix, or Boston.

Having passed the oral, I was examined by a physician, investigated by the FBI, named by the President, confirmed by the Senate, and dispatched via Pan American Flight 2.

My mission was to collect publications of research value for various federal agencies, primarily the Department of State and the Library of Congress. I was to buy, borrow, or procure in any other way, such overtly available printed matter as political manifestos, forest surveys, telephone directories, communist tracts, street guides, dictionaries, economic surveys, newspapers, magazines, and something called ephemera, all of which I was to ship home to the State Department for transmittal to various client libraries in Washington. There they would be culled, cataloged, and made available to researchers.

I was provided with an unlimited book-buying budget and a free hand at arranging my travel. Since books are notoriously cheap and travel notoriously difficult on the subcontinent, what this meant was that I had full authority to break my neck at practically no cost to anybody.

And so I found myself, at age twenty-one, accredited by my government to five foreign capitals: New Delhi, Rangoon, Kabul, Colombo, and the then capital of Pakistan, Karachi. I boarded my plane bound for the world.

So far as I was concerned, I was catapulting into the unknown. I knew Kipling, but he was dead. I had read E. M. Forster, but I could not make sense of *A Passage to India* until my own passage home from there. On my last night in

## The President sends me abroad

America, friends took me to see *The River*, but Rumer Godden and Jean Renoir were a bit poetic to act as guides in concrete situations.

The general atmosphere provided no clues as to the nature of the nonwestern world. The Beatles were still only larvae over in Liverpool, and consequently the raga had yet to penetrate western music. Hollywood stars had not yet initiated their exchange program with Indian holy men, Allan Ginsburg was a cloud no bigger than a guru's hand, and Svetlana Alleluieva lived on in the Kremlin, unaware of the compassionate nature of Hindu men.

The word *sari* was virtually unknown in the United States, and Indian women strolling our streets were generally taken for gypsies. Nehru jackets were less well-known than Nehru, and psychedelic colors bloomed unheralded in the circular gardens of Rashtrapathi Bhavan. If anyone had told me that fifteen years hence American fashion magazines would be pushing Punjabi tunics, I would have thought he had taken leave of his senses, along with the informant who reported that the United States is now the leading importer of sitars.

India, in short, had not been discovered. It awaited me.

Five years after Partition, in the Year 5 of Independence, the state of the Indian and Pakistani publishing industries was such that two years of tangling with them changed my life permanently. Business efficiency was still an exotic fancy waiting to be imported from the West. Although my client libraries besieged me with demands for catalogs and bibliographies, there were in fact no reliable indications of what books, magazines, or newspapers were being published anywhere. Mail orders were not always filled, and when they were, not necessarily by the desired item. A book one saw advertised today might actually have been published twenty years ago and long since been ingested by the great maw of the Library of Congress. Overloaded government presses conscientiously ground out annual reports of ten years back, while this year's report (urgently desired by one of my libraries) waited its turn to see the light of day a decade hence.

## Krishna Smiled

And although India had a copyright law, requiring a copy of each published book to be deposited in the Central Secretariat Library, the law was as much honored by the presses as by the library; which is to say, not much at all.

As a result I discovered that the only way to acquisition books was to sally forth into the bazaars, find them, and physically possess them. Often, as I prowled the bazaars of Bhuvaneshwar or traced a tip through Tiruchchirappalli, I would think of those poor souls, immured in dusty corridors, who would have the cataloging of the publications which I had the fun of procuring. Their work seemed but a pale reflection of mine.

An additional circumstance which forced me into a life of travel was the existence of so many languages within my area of interest. The State Department had given me a six-week crash course in Hindi. But Hindi is the native language of rather less than half the people of India, the other half speaking 845 other languages, 14 of which have Constitutional status. Pakistan has two major linguistic areas and a half dozen minor ones; Afghanistan has two, Ceylon two, and Burma is a linguistic snake pit.

The literature of any one of these linguistic areas is not generally considered to be of interest in any of the other linguistic areas, even if it is of interest to the Library of Congress, and consequently is not advertised or sold outside its own immediate area. The best of the crop appears in its own script, in job lots, from the press of a dear friend of the author who lives in a town which is the ancient seat of that culture, but which in recent centuries has not been much in the public eye, with the result that the roads into town aren't too good and the railroad never got there. To procure these publications, one must begin by learning of their existence. Then one must find the printing press where the type was set, rouse the owner, and try to buy a copy of the book.

In pursuit of these acquisitions I crossed and recrossed the continent by bus, car, train, boat, plane, foot, and ferry over a period of two years. I saw snow-capped Kanchenjunga, and Quetta at 120°. I stood in the demonic down-draft where

### The President sends me abroad

the Western Ghats fall away to the central plains just above Poona; and hiked forty miles out of Afghanistan's aptly-named Desert of Death. Thousands of miles to the south, I flew over Dhanushkodi, where India trickles away into the sea, spattering little islands right up to the green gem Ceylon, all of it in perfect Mercator projection. Oh yes, I bought maps too.

Imagine me, then, in cotton homespun skirt and shirt, travelling alone through antique lands and unknown languages in search of books I could not read. Over my shoulder, anticipating the hippies, I slung an embroidered bag into which I popped my acquisitions. On my feet I wore sandals made of the hides of cows who had died nonviolent deaths.

A song that was popular while I was in India began "Zindigi, kia hai? eek tamasha." "What is life? a county fair." While filling my bag with books, I stored my mind and heart with memories of a time when life indeed seemed like a county fair, and Krishna smiled.

# 2

*On the way to Banaras, I fall in with Everyman*

**R**acketing through the dusty landscape of Uttar Pradesh, alone in my second-class coach, I was shaken by the apparition of a hand at the window.

Brown and dusty, it reached inside the rattling window of the swiftly-moving train, hauling a face behind it. The sight of my own ghastly white face froze the intruder with his mouth open. Then the mouth yelled, though I could not hear the words, and the hand appeared to be slipping back into the scenery. The lad was in some danger I thought and, grasping his arm, landed him on the floor of the coach with minor injuries.

He had been running for the train, he explained in Hindustani (without a ticket, I added to myself) and lost his shoe . . . and . . . the explanation trickled into silence. For the next thirty miles, till the next station, the boy sat in a corner, suspicious and yet not daring to be suspicious, because I was white and rich, and he was black and nobody. I tried to talk

*I fall in with Everyman*

to him; after all, I was travelling second class rather than first so I could meet people. But my newly-fashioned Hindustani (clearly comprehensible to my teacher) got nowhere with the boy. In Hindustani he answered: "I am sorry, Madam, I do not speak English."

I turned to stare out the window again. It is a long journey from Delhi to Banaras, and a dusty one. The fields are dust; the tracks are overlaid with dust; the peasants plow dust and sow it; great sheets of dust rise up, roll themselves into funnels that pirouette nastily, and collapse in dead heaps on the parched seed. Men baked brown by the sun and oxen bleached white by it spot the land with red turbans and gilded horns. Wells draw the countryside to them. Women haul water from a well, their red-cloaked bodies pulling against the weight. Oxen clatter up and down earthen ramps that lead to wells, lifting leather bagsfull of water for the irrigation ditches. Babies lie swaddled and quiescent in the precious shadow of the ramps. At dusk, men coming from the field stop to bathe at a well, their spare bodies silhouetted against the briefly incandescent sky.

My train traversed the Gangetic plain.

Mud villages are half reclaimed by mud around them. Some hills, perhaps, were once villages. Little girls knead cakes of dung, patty-cake, patty-cake, and plaster them against the walls of their homes to dry in the sun. Then they will be stacked in ricks, from which chips will be taken for fuel. When the manure is burned, the ashes will be used for soap and toothpaste, and to spread on the floor of the home at Dussehra time. And this is one of the tragedies of India, for where else can the farmers find fertilizer for their fields?

The boy without a ticket slipped from the coach at the next station, retreating in the direction of third class, which was really fourth class since there was an "inter" between second and third. Out on the platform, the eternal bazaar of India was in progress. Waiting passengers squatted around a family cooking pot, their weight suspended from uncomplaining knee hinges. Babies lay sleeping in heaps of rags. Water carriers and hawkers of sweets and betelnut and pan-

## Krishna Smiled

cakes and soft drinks picked their way among bodies, calling their wares in the singsong which identifies each product. The pitchmen carried huge trays on their heads, stooping to serve their customers without using their hands to balance the load. Their heads were cushioned in yards of towelling, as were the luggage-laden heads of the railway porters. But the porters wore allover red.

The Anglo-Indian stationmaster, a member of that "inter" class which is neither first, second, nor third and which earns its living by facilitating communication among the other classes, put a whistle to his lips and started us. I was contemplating the precise pleat in his ragged uniform trouser leg, when a man in a tweed suit entered. He was tall for a Hindu, almost as tall as I, with small deep-set eyes and disfiguring pock marks.

"Good afternoon," he said toward the paperback which I had ostentatiously raised to my eyes. "I too am an admirer of Mr. Sinclair Lewis."

I had picked up *Main Street* from a book vendor several stations back, hoping it would provide a buffer against the onrush of strange impressions which was threatening to swamp me. I seemed to need a known point of reference, and yet the last thing I wanted to do was talk about *Main Street*, which bored me. In fact, considering the heat and dust, any conversation would require too much effort. My clothes were stiff with dust; I had an unidentified rash up and down one leg; I wasn't certain where I would sleep that night. Also, it seemed discreet to keep my distance from lone male travellers.

Each car on an Indian train is self-contained. As the train starts up, the stationmaster bolts the carriage doors and there you are, imprisoned along with your companions until the next stop.

On the overnight trip from Ahmadabad to Bombay, I had been locked up with a six-and-a-half foot Sikh with a fiercesome beard. He outweighed me a good fifty pounds. On that occasion I pretended that I was not present at all. But the Sikh saw me, and after an ominous twenty miles of si-

## I fall in with Everyman

lence, said: "Aren't you afraid to be travelling alone with a Sikh? We have very terrible reputations, you know." I replied, "Oh, not at all, Sardarji." (All Sikhs are addressed as "Chief" as a precautionary measure, and I added the "ji" of respect just in case.) "When I saw you I was very glad because I felt that if the train were attacked by bandits, you would protect me."

Our train was not attacked by bandits, though trains sometimes were, so I was unable to test the validity of my statement. But the theory was sound. I slept well and so did my Sikh, and in the morning I watched as he combed out his tremendous beard which had never seen a razor, rolled it over an elastic garter, and snooded his chin with a hair net. The only other word we exchanged was "Goodbye."

Of course, I could have bought a ticket in the coach reserved for women. These were horribly crowded, their tiny windows laced with barbed wire against the attack of predators, animal or human I was uncertain which. Women and children engaged in a continuous round of mewling and puking, which was not surprising considering the lack of air, and the smells which issued from these coaches were death-dealing. Having taken a look at the accommodations Indians reserve for their mothers, wives, and daughters, I decided to lean on my cachet as a foreigner and travel with the men.

I soon discovered that, travelling first class, I met only westernized Indians who persisted in talking about the weather. So I switched to second. I paid conscience money, though: village people never would enter a coach which I was occupying, and thus I increased the congestion in all the other coaches.

Now, on the Banaras train, I was locked up with this type I hadn't identified as yet. I regretted his wanting to discuss English literature. It was a bad sign. There are some Indians for whom everything foreign is estimable, while anything learned at the mother's knee is beneath contempt. If I continued to run into no one but sycophants, I would never learn anything about India. I reflected sourly on the babbittry that made the man wear western clothes, necktie and all, in this heat for which dhotis had been invented. Let him be an Indian!

My companion now introduced himself as an inspector of railway signals, and I had to backtrack. His English and his western clothes were marks of office. Coincidentally, I had a library with a morbid taste in railway publications, which it consumed at a faster rate than the Indian government could turn them out. My library was forever demanding titles which no one in Delhi had ever heard of. It hadn't occurred to me before to look for them in the provinces, but here the inspector had been dropped in my lap, as it were. So I let myself be drawn into a discussion of Sinclair Lewis.

Arrived at the caldron of Banaras railway station, Ram Chand saw me to a cycle rickshaw. He told the undernourished cyclist to take me to the Hôtel de Paris, and offered to accompany me there. Like most people I met in India, he was appalled at my travelling alone.

I declined an escort, but the inspector had not exhausted his hospitality. He whistled up a wizened old man in blue denim pyjamas with a massive scarlet turban and white handlebar moustachioes, who loped over on springy bare feet and nestled on the footrest of the rickshaw. "Hotel-ko ja," ordered Ram Chand, and we set off at a good clip while he bowed goodbye, arriving shortly at the hotel, where the proprietor welcomed me effusively, as I was the only guest. Tika Lall was accepted as part of my baggage, and for the duration of my stay in Banaras, he slept across my threshold.

I spent the next days rooting through Banaras looking for bookstores, which of course I had to locate before I could buy any books. The hotel desk clerk could tell me where *the* bookstore was, but that wasn't the one I wanted, because all of its stock was equally available in Times Square or Tottenham Court Road. The major Indian bookstores leaned heavily on the English publishers, and seldom deigned to carry native writers.

It was Tika Lall who pointed out the street where *my* miserable bookstalls were hidden, stuffed with ill-printed books and flimsy pamphlets which no one at the Department

*I fall in with Everyman*

of State would ever have seen if I hadn't made the trip to Banaras. My smidgen of Hindi enabled me to pick out individual words of book titles, not always accurately. Tika Lall, of course, could not read at all. But I drew pretty good crowds wherever I stopped, among whom there was always at least one college student in clean white shirt and pressed ducks who was eager to exercise his English, heavily flavored with Victorian phrases. Once I persuaded him that I really was looking for books by *Indian* authors, about *India* (apparently an unheard-of request from a foreigner) he would knock himself out helping me to select titles.

Often enough it was Tika Lall who clambered up the rickety, dusty shelves on his good bare feet that had the character of hands, to reach the volumes we wanted. It was also he who carried back to the hotel the books I purchased in a wicker basket on his head, shooing away from us as we went the hordes of children who followed and hooted at the large foreign woman.

Banaras's claim to being the oldest city in the world may be true, judging from the amount of garbage that has had time to pile up there. The bazaar is an enormous midden, the houses and shops collapsing under the weight of their own refuse and getting rebuilt with the same material. Until I saw Banaras, I could not understand how ancient cities had become buried and built over. Now it all came clear to me as the garbage mounted in visibly agitated piles up the door jambs and over the lintels, preparing to engulf the families within.

The atmosphere was of one glorious hullabaloo, the noise and smells of masses of people jangling for attention. Everyone was selling something to everyone else. The contents of shops spilled out onto the dusty, dungy street, while back in dim interiors families ate and slept on top of the merchandise. Out front, women sat barefoot under faucets, washing their groceries. The cloth merchants sat cross-legged on platforms before their shops, tape measures hanging from their necks, and the cobblers, who are Untouchables, tapped-tapped-tapped their lonely lives away on little shelves. A cotton ginner

## Krishna Smiled

passed, carrying his peculiarly musical-looking instrument on his shoulder, twanging the single string. Rickshaw coolies waiting on corners clanked a stone against the metal shafts of their buggies in a distinctively hurried, insistent, rhythm. A snake charmer blew three agonized notes from his swell-bellied pipe. Of all the people on the crowded street, he was the only one with plenty of elbow room.

Only about half the shops were standing in one place; the rest were walking about on racks rigged to their proprietor's backs. The hawker of coal, the man who sells plastic toys, pinwheels, and kites, the sellers of sweets, milk, bread, melons, water are peripatetic, and each has a different call that blends into the cacaphony of the market.

The fastest-moving item in the market was an object I couldn't identify at all. Apparently an emblem of the city, it was represented in a variety of sizes and materials; but nowhere could I see the original. Apparently, no tourist should leave Banaras without one—so I bought one and took it back to my hotel room for scrutiny.

It was an orange-painted cylinder embedded in a concave base not unlike an old-fashioned candleholder, but with a funnel leading from it. To my untrained eye, the object which I held with increasing reluctance in my hand appeared to be a male organ in the process of penetrating a female. This rather took me aback until I recalled purchasing a replica of the Washington Monument while on a schoolgirl visit to our nation's capitol. No country should be without a father! The reference books told me that what I had bought was a lingam, a representation of the god Shiva in his formless manifestation. Shiva creates, Shiva destroys; and I suppose a lingam is as good a representation of that process as anything else.

I could not pay my respects to Shiva in person, as a ban against foreigners was strictly enforced in Banarsi temples, but I did surprise one in the act of making up. I was walking past one of those imposing structures of stone in which he resides, the facade of it alive with sculptured gods and demons. Tides of orange paint had washed over them. The effect was as though a child had taken a bucket of paint and thrown it at God.

*I fall in with Everyman*

As the temple gate was ajar, I glanced inside to see a large courtyard, its cobblestones awash in urine, pulverized flowers, incense, and broken crockery. Across the littered yard a little room, a man crouched with a bucket of paint, and Shiva himself.

He was a sturdy three-foot-high cylinder not unlike the markers we use in the United States to mark the limits of parking lots. I had never thought before that those things might be alive. The god had already been painted orange, and now the man was drawing him a blue face.

"Sh'ma!" I cried in terror. "Hear O Israel, the Lord thy God, the Lord is One!" The lingam did not splinter, Banaras stayed where it was, and the man painted in the other eye. Old Adonai was fooling. He'd known about this place right along.

One morning I hired a barge for a view of the city from the river. We embarked in clear dawn, before the sun should have a chance to beat life back into the dust from which it springs lustily each day. Poled by a tall black man whose dhoti, tucked up around his haunches, revealed knots of muscle on fleshless thighs, we floated between high banks of temples. Some were palaces, others as small as sentry boxes, and they shoulder one another on their way down to the sacred river, jealous of the drops of water that lave one another's foundations. The bullies among them seem to have pushed the weaker ones in. Actually, the changing level of the river undermines them, leaving the smaller temples askew.

Each temple is topped by a conical or a wedge-shaped dome, fantastically carved with gods, men, animals, men-gods, god-animals, and animal-men, writhing in the steaming heat. It is not too hard to imagine all these creatures converging on the waterfront in the flesh for their ceremonial bath. In addition to them, there were probably ten thousand people in the water.

Each man prays for himself, standing knee-deep in Mother Ganges and clasping his hands together or sprinkling water over his shaven head. Some stand and stare into the sun. Prayers finished, a man ties a clean dhoti over the one he has on; slips that out from underneath, washes it, washes the sacred thread that encircles his body from right shoulder to left hip, and climbs back up the ghat. He reapplies his caste marks to face, chest and forearms; horizontal lines for Shaivites, vertical for Vaishnavites.

All this while, groups of women, hopelessly entangled in six yards of sari, contrive to bathe themselves, demurely slipping bars of soap under their clothing, then immersing themselves to the chin. Children run naked in the sun, or dive off the ledges of temple windows streaming suds, unmindful of their proximity to the infinite.

In a recess of a temple wall, a man defecates and washes his privates in the river, ignoring the row of flush toilets standing doorless and open—and vacant—several steps above him. A few feet away, laundrymen and women flail great knouts of cloth against upturned slates. A simultaneous *ugh* arises from them; then the slap of wet cloth upon stone. And this is another Indian tragedy, for people are forever bathing and laundering, and achieving only a redistribution of the dirt.

Some yards beyond the bathing ghat, continuous smoking accompanies the departure from this and all possible worlds of those Hindus fortunate enough to have their remains brought here for cremation. The ashes are then thrown in the river and the soul freed from karma, the inexorable fate that condemns one to countless rebirths as man or animal until the soul shall have purified itself sufficiently to achieve nirvana.

The Ganges runs swiftly and thickly at Banaras, rushing to heave its burden into the Bay of Bengal. For me, its heaviest burden is the continual reminder that, though man be part divine, he is at best part animal.

Landing at one of the ghats, I paid off the boatmen and started up a broad flight of stairs leading between the river and the town. The lepers, forbidden by law to touch anyone, parted their rags for me to see their fingerless joints, their shining stumps of elbow. A baby nursed distractedly from its father's dry teat. In the shadow of a temple wall, another father was teaching his son's arm the shape of beggary. It was the only trade he would ever have. Here lay a woman with a

*I fall in with Everyman*

leg larger than her entire trunk, and insects dwelling in it. And there were two . . . human beings.

A foetus. When he was an infant, his parents, who belonged to the caste of beggars and who therefore could bequeath only the occupation of beggar to their son, had doubled his arms against his breast, drawn his knees against his stomach, and bound him with cord. After some years, the cord was no longer needed. He remained permanently in the foetal position. The only way he could get about was to have someone roll him like an egg.

He found as companion a man whose parents, likewise at their wits' end to provide their son with a trade, had scooped out his eyeballs and left the holes untended. These two humans teamed up so that the blind one could trundle the giant foetus along the ground with his foot. Down below, the seeing one could tell the blind man where in this curiously revolving world, they were going. The trickle from the sewer, the jagged shells, the droppings of men and animals, the cobblestones and curbs and mud must all be rolled through by the foetus; while he who walked erect like a man extended the half of a cocoanut shell to collect rice or alms for them both.

Though the blind man's feet were horny as any in India, the foetus's were soft and pink.

In a courtyard, flower vendors sit, threading sweet-smelling jasmine and peppery marigold into garlands to be hung around the necks of gods.

The flower sellers are Moslem, as are the bangle-makers and brocade weavers. The most famous products of the most Hindu of cities are manufactured by non-Hindus. Difficult to understand, until one realizes that most Moslems are converts at some generations' remove, who sought to escape karma by denying it. As castes essentially represent divisions of labor, and have strong clan ties, it is not too much to suppose that at one time or another whole castes have gone over to Islam, bringing their trades with them.

I was introduced to Banarsi brocade by one Mohammed, the dispossessed son of a weaver. A Moslem and an orphan, he was bitter against this city redolent of Hinduism and the joint family. He used to hang around the Hôtel de Paris preying on the guests, filling them with libels against the Hindus. One afternoon, when I had returned triumphant from a joust with a communist bookdealer, I allowed Mohammed to coax me into visiting the home of his uncle, evidently the man who had cheated him of his inheritance.

Leading on through streets of dust, Mohammed brought me to the weavers' quarters. The hard mud walls of the houses on either side of the walk seemed like a continuation upward of the ground on which we walked, and equally dusty children blended like chameleons into them.

Then we came upon the outposts of the weavers, like Cleopatra's barge upon the sand: rows of stakes set into the ground, from which hung hundreds of yards of silk thread drying luminously in the sun. Startling as a peacock unskeined, scarlet and sea blue, emerald and gold, the threads glistened in the sun like something only recently alive.

Stooping through an entrance, Mohammed led me through a mean courtyard and thence into his uncle's (his?) home.

Coming from the street, at first I could not see. Then I made out the room, which was unlighted, unfurnished, and perhaps ten by ten feet. In a corner, a boy was drawing. Opposite him in another corner, an old man was sitting shrouded and withdrawn, having given up the conduct of business, and of life itself, to his son, who kept the center of the floor.

Seeing me enter, the neighbors came too, and pan was distributed. The betelnut is hard as a rock and tastes like detergent. It is demolished with a hammer before the bits are placed, together with a smear of damp lime, on the center of a green betel leaf. The leaf is then folded into a triangle and held fast with more lime. (By "lime" I do not mean the citrus fruit, but calcium oxide.) When chewed, it is claimed to have a prophylactic effect on the stomach.

Legend has it that maharajahs used to grind pearls into their pan. Ground pearl is reputedly aphrodisiac. I myself

*I fall in with Everyman*

have seen pan eaten with a silver foil wrapping. I do not know about the aphrodisiac qualities of silver. The pan itself gives the system a lift comparable to that obtained in a good Coke.

Now in the weavers' hut large bundles were dragged in. Delicately, Mohammed's uncle undid the grimy knots, and exposed upon the floor the wealth of Ind. Shimmering lengths of silver there were, cunningly intersticed with lapis birds and scarlet ladies; blue silk, gossamer as a dragonfly's wing; pearl grey silk woof, with silver warp so pure the cloth could be burned and the silver retrieved; plain gold—six yards of plain gold—to wrap a princess on her wedding night. All this on the floor of that hovel.

The place was so bare, so innocent of contrivance, I could not believe such craft was worked here. The weavers enjoyed my astonishment and invited me into the second room.

Again, I could see nothing at first. The only light came from a slit in the wall just under the eaves. As my pupils dilated, I made out a monstrous wooden machine struggling in a net of cords that fastened it to a beam in the ceiling. Perched on the beam, a man arranged the cords so as to evolve the pattern which he held between his toes. Below him, in a seated position unusual among Indians, a man worked the shuttle and pressed home the threads. Below him on the floor, a boy on all fours worked the pedals. It was too dark in the room for me to distinguish the color of the cloth.

In this family, the labor of all its members does not suffice to enable them to buy decent clothing, let alone one sari from among the hundreds they have created. It is the banya, the village moneylender, who holds the threads, and pays them out as a fisherman pays a fish enough line to choke itself with. First the banya lends thread and food to the weavers. The weavers produce the cloth while consuming the food. When they deliver the finished work to the banya, he credits the cloth toward payment for the food and thread, and pays a small amount as wage—minus interest on the loan.

The wage, as Karl Marx calculated, is enough to enable

the weaver to work and to reproduce the next generation of workers. The weavers have to go back into debt in order to get more thread and more food so they may continue to work. The brocade sells in the bazaar, at the banya's shop, for prices only the wealthiest can afford.

Generations ago, the weavers tried to free themselves from the unwritten law that keeps them chained, starving, to their looms. The entire weavers' caste embraced Islam, which has no karma and which teaches the brotherhood of man, or at least of Moslems.

Unfortunately, the weavers hadn't identified their real problem. The banyas continue to control the credit. So although the weavers cut themselves free from the doom of reincarnation, yet in this life they remain trapped in the traditional society as surely as their giant looms are trapped in the glorious fabric which they weave.

Every morning, Tika Lall brought me a note from "Master," meaning Ram Chand the railway signal inspector. I do not know how or when the two used to meet, for I never saw Ram Chand near the hotel. But there would be a note every morning on my breakfast tray. Once I found, stacked upon my bedside table, three sets of the railway publications which I had been seeking.

By the time Sunday came, bringing with it an invitation to tea, Ram Chand had acquired some of those aspects of familiarity with which a few days previously I had invested *Main Street*. Accordingly, I accepted.

Ram Chand arrived in a cycle rickshaw, which waited while he rang my room. I hesitated to climb into the rickshaw with him, and was so quickly misinterpreted ("Of course, a foreign lady would not want to be seen riding with an Indian"), that I immediately got in. What was concerning me was that our combined weight was in the neighborhood of three hundred pounds. The cyclist may have weighed ninety. For hauling us around Banaras the better part of six hours, he was later to receive the equivalent of two cents. Having enjoyed the ride, however, I rationalized: if he had not been hired, he would not have earned the two cents.

*I fall in with Everyman*

Through the busy bazaar, in the cool succeeding the setting of the sun, the cyclist drew Ram Chand and me. Lights were being lit as the second round of business began. Merchants open their shops at dawn; close up against the heat of the day; then reopen at dusk to do business through the long evening till everyone has left the streets except for the people who sleep on them.

We climbed a rickety stair to an English tearoom, a retreat in other days for British and Anglo-Indian railway personnel. It was deserted now and looked as though it would soon be engulfed by India.

Over tea, Ram Chand picked up the thread of our conversation on the train a week earlier. Pearl Buck. Ernest Hemingway. Coleridge. Lord Byron. And . . . He hesitated before naming "the greatest author." I wondered who he could be, and why Ram Chand spoke of him with such reverence. I asked him about himself.

He was born, Ram Chand said, in one of those little houses that guard the level railway crossings. His father was the man who lowers the rail when the train is due to pass, and raises it after the train is gone. There is a book fastened to the wall of such houses in which travellers can write any complaints they may have about the service. These are regularly inspected by the railways. Perhaps it was this that instilled an atmosphere of rectitude in the household.

Ram Chand's father was killed at the crossing, and the son received a scholarship in compensation. In due course, Ram Chand entered the railway service too, but he rose higher than his father and spent most of his adult life travelling up and down the lines of Banarsi District. He had never been outside the boundaries of the district.

At twenty, he married a girl of a neighboring village. At twenty-three, he was a widower with two infants. His in-laws offered and certainly expected that he would accept a sister in place of his dead wife, but Ram Chand refused her.

The inspector looked at me, anticipating my surprise. "Why did you not remarry, then?" I asked gently. I was moved by the thought of the two motherless babies. Who

## Krishna Smiled

would marry these girls, if they had never had a mother to teach them the household skills?

"You see," Ram Chand said shyly (he was a big man, and his shyness like his ugliness possessed him physically. How could I have taken him for a sycophant?), "You see, I loved my wife."

I really was surprised. Love is not absolutely unknown in India, but it is a disease which is usually confined to the wealthiest upper-class, who can afford it.

Ram Chand continued. "I have discovered a wonderful man, the greatest writer who ever lived. He is scarcely known. Undoubtedly, you have never even heard of him. He had many things to say about women. Revolutionary things that have not been said before in India. When I married, I tried to put these things into practice, so that my wife would be more than a wife to me, but a woman too, a person. We were very happy."

The unknown writer was Henrik Ibsen. Of course "no one" had ever heard of him. Only the English writers are taught in Indian schools. Ram Chand gave me his copy of the Everyman edition of Ibsen's plays when I left Banaras. The notations he had made in the margins of *A Doll's House* show clearly that Everyman includes an Indian railway inspector held incommunicado in Village Suriawan, District Banaras, Uttar Pradesh.

"Let him be an Indian!" I had thought on first meeting Ram Chand, without realizing that he, like so many educated Indians, was two people. Half of him lived within a traditional society, where everything is foreordained and predetermined, the individual lashed to the wheel of karma by the accident of his birth; the other half has betaken himself upon the perilous journey of Everyman, a journey that can only be made by a free and independent mind.

While all his old friends were standing around in sacred rivers washing their sins off onto one another, Ram Chand set out toward enlightenment, Everyman his guide, and began to blossom into an autonomous human being. But his wife died; and he refused the substitute which the wheel of karma

## I fall in with Everyman

would have thrust upon him. As a result, he experienced bitter personal suffering as well as social ostracism in his village. The penalty for being an individual was terrible: rejection by the only society he knew.

Was the effort worthwhile? I wondered as I parted from Ram Chand at the railway station. Would India emerge into the twentieth century only at the cost of so much ambivalence and heartache?

A basket of mangoes preceded me to my flat in New Delhi. I never had eaten the fruit before, which tastes like a cantaloupe that has been injected with turpentine. Its effect was toxic, and I swelled up like a dirigible.

("It is well known that one does not eat the mango before monsoon," said my friend Bijay, who came from Mysore. "You know little of such things in the south," retorted Jivraj. To me he said, "You must eat only mangoes which come from Saharanpur. These may be eaten either before or after monsoon without heating the blood.")

At the time, it was hard for me to appreciate the note which came with the mangoes. But after my allergy subsided, the words continued to echo.

"I am so happy to have met you," Ram Chand wrote. "Now I know that I was right. Something good becomes of Nora when she leaves her doll's house."

# 3

*I fail to procure the Bhilsa telephone directory, but live to fulfill other intelligence missions*

All my libraries lusted after telephone directories, which they consumed in industrial quantities. Washington researchers dredge through these directories in search of nourishing particles of information in much the same way that giant whales sieve the sea through their baleen in order to retrieve the tiny plankton on which they feed.

It was largely the demand for phone books which drove me the length and breadth of the subcontinent, into countryside I would never have penetrated otherwise. So I am truly grateful to whoever those people were who read my phone books; if indeed they did. I sometimes wonder, since I never received a complaint about Bhilsa. I didn't acquisition that one, and never will, for I won't go back. The good citizens of the town might succeed in killing me the third time 'round.

The post-World War II concept of intelligence requires field agents who are willing to behave like vacuum cleaners, sucking up scraps of information which lie about the landscape either free of charge or for a nominal cost (my first

## The Bhilsa telephone directory

year's expenditure for books was less than $600). These are transmitted through the diplomatic pouch for evaluation by I & R. It is the function of the Intelligence and Research people to fit all this waste paper into a collage, or perhaps I should say trompe d'oeil, from which intelligence forecasts can be projected. For this reason, nothing is too trivial to be forwarded, as long as it falls within the perimeters of general instructions; the merest scrap of printed matter may find its small place in completing an intelligence estimate.

There was one popular Indian general who couldn't believe I was as naive as I appeared to be, and concluded I was Mata Hari. He had me followed around by the secret service, all of whom were his relatives, when I visited his home state of Coorg. But actually, as publications procurement officer, I was not officially encouraged to fool around, and I seldom mixed pleasure with business.

Much of the work was routine, as vacuum-cleaning is apt to be. An order for Bombay telephone directories, for example, could be filled by mailing a request to the Bombay post office, with money order enclosed, in the reasonable expectation that the directories would one day arrive. Very dull.

But occasionally some Washington-based researcher, possibly pregnant, would develop a craving for exotic directories pertaining to towns which no one in the embassy had ever heard of. Towns, moreover, whose postmasters did not answer their mail. A town like Bhilsa had to be spotted on my inadequate map, and as occasion arose, I would try to work it into one of my field trips. I am one of the very few people in the world who ever went to Bhilsa on purpose.

This particular scavenger hunt began in Vindhya Pradesh, in central India. I was probably the only member of the American Embassy to penetrate so far into the interior that year, as the rest of the staff was busy reading the publications I procured. Since I travelled incessantly, I never could take a newspaper subscription and was forced to rely upon firsthand observation of the country, a circumstance which disconnected me from the embassy's interior lines of communication.

Vindhya, for whom this province is named, was the wife

## Krishna Smiled

of Hanuman the Monkey God, who gained the gratitude of Hindus by linking his subjects together in a living monkey chain to form a bridge between India and Ceylon over which Rama was enabled to pursue Ravenna, who had abducted his wife Sita. The romance is recorded in the Ramayana, an ages-old epic poem. Although the events took place a long while ago, monkeys remain enshrined in the hearts of Hindus, who worship them in much the same way that we worship dogs, crediting them with personalities, as well as specie traits such as fidelity and cunning.

Vile-bottomed baboons and hyperactive langurs are draped all over Vindhya Pradesh. They brachiate joyously through the trees, keeping an eye on the humans below who toil to produce the food which they, the monkeys, will eat at their leisure—at the rate of 15 percent of the crop each year. Entire troops will drop down to forage unmolested in the fields for grain, the attitude of the farmers being that, after all, the monkeys must eat too. At the intersections of roads, hundreds of baboons may be seen gathered in convention, making speeches, breaking up into committees, dining, picking lice out of one another's hair, sleeping, suckling, and carrying on with one another's wives. Apparently, monkeys' reflexes are quicker than dogs', for I never saw one flattened by a car.

Coming southward from Gwalior, I was driving too fast. Forty-five mph is too much for a one-and-a-half lane dirt road with no shoulders, covered in a foot of powdery dust. Also, no AAA, no telephone, no garage, no ambulance. But I was exhilarated, for I had just stumbled upon the tomb of Tan Sen, outside Gwalior Fort.

The fort itself left me cold—a monstrous stone heap that must have been the death of thousands of laborers. King Man Singh diverted the River Rai so as to flow through the fort, in order to please his Queen, Mriganayana the Fawn-eyed, who once vanquished a wild buffalo in single combat. She attributed her strength to drinking the waters of the river, and it seems to me that under these circumstances Man Singh would have done all he could to keep her away from it.

*The Bhilsa telephone directory*

The tomb of Tan Sen, on the other hand, is small and homely, overgrown in prickly cactus and thorn bushes. It is said that the poet-composer-singer, who was court musician to the Emperor Akbar, quelled wild animals by his singing, lighted a candle by the force of prayer, and opened heaven so that rain might fall upon a passion-parched lover.

It was the melody of the latter song that I was striving to reconstruct as I drove headily along beneath a canopy of baboons. If I had but known of the tamarind tree that grows beside Tan Sen's tomb, I might have chewed a leaf of it and thus developed a capacity to sing Indian music. Alas, I was back in Delhi before I learned about the musical properties of the tree, and so I was reduced to playing and replaying my 78 rpm until the grooves were worn through and I still hadn't learned to sing the melody, which continues to haunt me.

Ahead of me, the monkeys frolicked, cannily swinging up into a branch just in time to let the car pass, then dropping down again behind me in the space just vacated.

Suddenly, a few yards in front of me, I saw a tiny morsel of baboon, all eyes and fur, sitting on the road staring stupidly as I bore down upon him. I think all babies are cute, but I knew in a flash I was not going to kill myself for this one by going off the road. Inexorably, my Vauxhall closed the distance between us, me not daring to apply my brakes on the powdery sand. At the last moment, a great brown mother swung down from the trees directly in the path of the car, something no sane baboon would do. Scooping her baby onto her abdomen, she swung up and out of the way. I was tremendously relieved, and resolved to write a letter home to my own mother that very night.

Central India is a different India from the India of the north. The north has a thick crust of Islam over it, the major structures are Moslem, and all the ancient Hindu gods have been decapitated and castrated.

But the Moghuls were driven from Vindhya Pradesh in the early eighteenth century, and the victorious Marathas ruled here until they in turn fell to the British. So there has been time for Hinduism to reestablish itself upon the hilltops.

## Krishna Smiled

People here worship on the high places, and every little hill is crowned by its temple. Every temple has its god, every god has his head and his lingam and his half-dozen manifestations. Every manifestation has a ramekin of biographies and names. The Lord X of this town is the Lord Y of the next town over; and the temple dedicated to Shiva by the classical texts is well known by the townspeople to belong to Kali. One simply has to take the temples at skin value, allowing them to enter the nervous system by osmosis, sans intellectual analysis. It all defies reason, logic, and order. One has to shed such westernisms in order to enter a temple.

Once, back in the capital, when the embassy closed for Janamasthmi (the birthday of Lord Krishna) I put on a wine-red sari of the cheapest cotton, draped the tail of it over my face, slipped into leather chaplis and dotted my forehead with lipstick. Then I drove to Old Delhi, parked, walked over to Chandni Chowk, and entered the holiday on what I hoped were honest terms.

As I entered the chowk I was caught up in a current of humanity such as I had never experienced. The crush was so great that I could not direct my own movements. Knees, elbows, feet, pushed, kicked, and gouged while we milled toward the temple. Despite my sari and every attempt to be inconspicuous, I was the object of gibes and lewd remarks, some extremely imaginative. Locked in by the crowd, I could not say whose hand was against me; so I kicked at random all the blank-faced youths behind me.

The police dammed us at the foot of a long stair leading up to the gate of the temple. All the while, new arrivals piled up behind till the crush made it impossible to move in any direction. When the pressure seemed more than I could bear, unexpectedly, a whistle blew, the police leaped aside, and the crowd stampeded up the stair.

Tripping on the unaccustomed sari, I churned up the stair with the others, since there was in any event no way to turn back. We entered a large anteroom where sandals had to be left with the shoe-check boy. Up and on then we were rushed, bare feet squishing on the slushy floor. To fall would

## The Bhilsa telephone directory

mean to be trampled. In the darkened room we now entered, I was pressed up against an iron grill that barred us from the main hall. On the other side of the grill, in jail as it were, Krishna and Radha his wife, idols about the size of five-year-old children, were seated at table. Conspicuous in the corner was a doll-sized double bed with gingham spread covering an overstuffed mattress. Opposite was the hearth, stacked with kitchenware.

At the sound of a policeman's whistle, the human mill-race resumed its onward course, forcing me willy-nilly into the dark interior of the temple. Had there been a way to turn back, I would have done so, for the noise was inhuman. Each person was praying, crying, wailing, singing, chanting to the music of a different star, straining with tremendous effort to make God hear. The result was as if all the elements had been trapped inside a dark tunnel.

The curtain in the second room was drawn, and as we waited for it to open, the young men in the crowd amused themselves by pitching pennies against it and by calling out to me in English: "Good morning, Madam." "Hello, darling." "What time is it?" Intermittently, there were shouts of "Kolo!" —the rude form of "open up!"—directed at an old man in a filthy dhoti who sprawled listlessly on the proscenium, raking in coins with the handle of his umbrella. Meanwhile, the crowd poured in in ever greater numbers, pushing the foremost against the rail. Beside me, a man was singing quietly, hands clasped to his forehead, oblivious to the bedlam around him. Perhaps he was the one who made contact with Krishna.

The cry of "Kolo!" having reached the desired pitch of ferocity, the deacon rose and drew the white flowered curtain aside. Cries of "Ram, Ram," (God) arose and the hail of marigolds and pennies grew thicker. Immediately, the police blew their whistles and commenced shoving the crowd out.

For that one moment we had glimpsed a doll-sized Krishna, his face painted the traditional blue, clasping the hand of one of his wives. Beatific smiles illumined their wooden faces.

A similar display awaited us in the next room, but here

## Krishna Smiled

Krishna was represented as a baby in a hanging cradle, the endearing Balakrishna. Again, the police permitted us only a moment's prayer before whistling us forward.

We now faced the greatest danger: descending the twenty steps to the street. I had counted them on the way up, anticipating the blind rush down. As desperate as the crowd had been to get in, the same people now seemed twice as desperate to get out. Two policemen stood with arms locked across the doorway, permitting only a dozen or so to leave at one time. Each time they broke their grip, the front standers were propelled through the doorway by the pressure of the crowd behind. At one point, several people jammed in the opening. When one man tugged loose, the whole lot tumbled down the flight of stairs into the street.

When my turn came, I tried to anchor myself to the doorway to withstand the initial thrust. Despite my best efforts, I found myself ejected with such force that I barely managed to keep my feet. At the bottom of the stairs I was welcomed by a fresh band of hot-blooded youths with further clever things to say. Struggling upstream to my car, I reflected on what a dismal failure had been my attempt to blend into the scene. I would not have been more conspicuous if I had gone naked.

It was always with relief that I turned toward open country. Even the temples were quiet here, the women padding softly to them in the dawn, the floors clean-swept, the sweet odor of the perspiration of herbivores lingering in the corner closenesses, the field smells coming in through arcaded walls. The city corrupts, and big cities corrupt absolutely.

By contrast, villagers were invariably polite and gentle to me. One time, I was invited to break my journey and turn aside into a village for refreshment. I did, and was offered an immense copper beaker full of milk. When I asked where it came from, a villager pointed to a mountainous black water buffalo which loomed nearby. Straight from the tap. I drank, muttering an incantation intended to ward off undulant fever. I would not have refused for the world: it was my first real Hindustani conversation with people who spoke no English.

## *The Bhilsa telephone directory*

As we chatted—who was I, where was I going, who was my father?—I started to sit down on a charpai. A man stepped forward and touched my elbow. Pulling aside a blanket that lay crumpled on the wooden cot, he revealed a sleeping baby. I apologized, and the man smiled gently at me. It was the smile I had seen on the face of Krishna.

Somewhere between Gwalior and Jhansi, I saw a white herd upon a grey hill. From the road I thought, "white cows." But so still? Then, "a deserted town." But whitewashed? Gleaming against the grey hill of rock and grey sky of cloud, a white town, still, deserted.

I swung off the road, where the gullies end in scrub top and bottom, and followed a cart-track that wound between high hedges, cutting the little town from view. Freshly whitewashed, and deserted? No soul moved up here save peacocks'. I could hear their shrewish call on the wind that smelled of rain. That could be used, too; the dust rose wheeling round the car; my face was caked with it and it gritted under my clothes.

The track gave no hint of where it was going, then suddenly stopped at a neat, whitewashed gate with a freshly painted sign: JAIN TEMPLE. There was no one about, just a large black umbrella leaning in a corner of the courtyard. I borrowed it, leaving three annas and my sandals, and started up the hill as the first drops fell.

The path, steep, stepped among tiny temples. Some were marble and some whitewashed stone, but identical. And miniature. With their elaborate roofs and sculpted arches, they would have been imposing had they been more than four feet in height. Some were no more than cameos. Inside, shadow. About, silence and the snapping of peacocks' fans.

After the fourth, the fifth, I steeled myself to turn aside and enter. If it was a tomb, there would be bats. But I found instead a white marble, clean-limbed Tirthankara, a Jain saint, vigilant, naked and erect in his sanitary shrine.

Square brows, earlobes distended to square shoulders set high above a slender waist, the torso supported on round pillar legs, the feet bare and square. A mating of Hindu and

## Krishna Smiled

Buddhist beliefs created these Tirthankaras upon a hill, forbearing, like all observant Jains forbear, to end the life of plant or animal in order to provide mere clothing. Eighty-eight temples, eighty-eight Tirthankaras, identical.

On up the hill. Its crest had been levelled. Paved in marble, it was a platter for the grey meat of the sky. Under a marble canopy stood an eighty-ninth Tirthankara, against the sky, sky-clad. Perhaps, I thought, he is Mahavira himself, Great Hero.

The marble platter is forecourt to a temple where my eyes cannot see in and so miss the step down. But eyes see out. Rubies pierce the head of Mahavira (now I know that I am seeing Mahavira) rising enormous out of a pit to confront me at eye-level with fire set in ice.

I cannot see the marble vines I know must grow about his feet. He endured all. I cannot hear the gong my scalp detects. He endures all. I cannot smell the jasmine. He endures.

Say yea, say nay: Endure.

I ran outside onto the marble plate. The rain had started. The eighty-nine Tirthankaras sheltered their stainless bodies in their marble huts. An incandescent sky transfixed the shrines like insects in grey amber. Peacocks spread enamelled fans on porcelain roofs. It was their voices charmed the herd of temples on the hill.

Having made a clean sweep of Vindhya Pradesh in terms of publications, I wandered over into neighboring Bhopal where I acquisitioned some little boys' embroidered skull caps and vests which were not to come into fashion in the United States for another fifteen years. Bhopal did better by embroidery than by books, and I got restless after an hour or so. It was then that I looked over the map and saw, with a shock of recognition, the name of Bhilsa, somewhat off the main highway which would take me back to Delhi. Checking my little black notebook, I ascertained that this was indeed one of those miserable towns someone wanted the phone book of, and I thought I might just have time to make it over there before five o'clock closing.

As I set out northeasterly along the country road, the

## The Bhilsa telephone directory

cattle were already returning from the fields. Next to monkeys, who don't use the road itself very much, cattle are the principal travellers of provincial highways. Gaunt and humpbacked, xylophone-ribbed, horns upswept like lyres, they haul their cumbersome carts along, raising clouds of dust in which the road disappears. It is useless to honk; the driver is asleep, the bullock knows where he is going and will not alter course to oblige you. It's into the dust with you, spinning your wheels on the edge of the shoulder. The smell of hay passes gently in the hot air.

The bullocks make up in beauty what they lack in road courtesy. Their eyes, larger and more limpid than cats', pick up your headlights at night, weaving luminously out of darkness. They are gentle, oh so gentle, that a child can control them, and frequently does by bunching up the tail and squeezing it, or ramming a pole up the anus.

Cattle, like monkeys, are sacred, so it is best for a foreigner not to tangle with them. But their exalted status does not keep them from a life of hard labor.

Across the road from a flat I temporarily occupied in Karolbagh, a suburb of New Delhi, there was an open, rocky field with no blade of grass. All night the sound of bawling came from there. The field was a dairy, I learned, and the bawling came from hungry calves tethered away from their mothers so they wouldn't drink too much milk. The cows had to be bred in order to produce milk, but the milk couldn't be wasted on feeding the calves. The result is generation after forlorn generation of starving cattle with a very low milk yield that hardly repays upkeep of the animal. The cows' udders are so small that they are not visible to an observer.

It was getting on toward five as I approached Bhilsa, so I whanged into town somewhat incautiously, to find myself running a gauntlet of somberly drunk men whose faces were painted allover blue, hanging from the closed shop fronts singing, shouting, and banging garbage can lids together in martial rhythm. The street being narrow, two men leaning over from either side could clasp hands in the middle, or throw buckets full of colored water down on the car, which they now did, along with rocks, dust, garbage and anything else that came to hand. I didn't think I should stop to ask the way to the post office, but assuming as pleasant an expression as I could, kept going. Realizing how badly outnumbered I was, men began dropping down from the shop shutters onto the street in front of the car. I figured that if I stopped, I'd had it, and if I went too fast, one of them would have it, so I kept a light but firm foot on the gas.

Some of the more educated fellows now ran and fetched a newspaper, which they applied, wet, to my windshield. Unable to see out, I kept going blindly, tensed to hear the thud which would announce I had run over someone, prelude to my own lynching.

A breeze lifting one corner of the paper showed me that I had come to a triple fork in the road. Undoubtedly one led out of the town and back to the highway, but which one? My forty-mile-to-an-inch road map wouldn't have helped if I had had time to consult it, which I didn't. So I chose the middle course, and dead-ended. In front of the post office, which was closed.

Now I had to back out, toward the crowd which awaited me at the fork. Knowing of course, that the road came to an end, and that missahib must return, they had whistled up more of their jolly company and were ready for me now.

I backed out gently. I still didn't want to be first to draw blood. As I reached the forks, my rear car door was wrenched open. I could almost feel the cold knife striking home. I regretted not having accelerated right into the crowd.

Instead, I heard a voice in schoolboy English saying from the back seat, "Keep going, Madam, I will tell you the way." And he did, with his head out the rear window, between curses at the crowd. "Faster, you may go faster, Madam," the youth said to me, and I took his word for it. As the crowd loped alongside, I accelerated blindly, and left them behind.

I turned to thank my benefactor. But he would let me stop only long enough to remove the newspaper from the windshield and insisted that I drive another two miles to make sure we were not followed by the panting crowd. He of course would have to walk back.

*The Bhilsa telephone directory*

At last, we stopped beside a pasture, got out, and introduced ourselves. Krishna was a student home on vacation from Allahabad University. He apologized for his fellow townsmen: "They are adivasis (aborigines), you know, and they should not drink, but this is their holiday and one cannot stop them."

"How long has the holiday been going on?" I asked him.

"Four days, so far," Krishna replied.

For me, the measure of this young man was not that he had rescued me—saving a damsel in distress might fulfill a raft of romantic dreams—but that he now insisted on helping me to wash the car. "If not," he pointed out, "it will present an invitation to the people in the next town." Students generally do not soil their hands in India, for manual labor declasses one. It can fit into no romantic dream.

After I was miles from there, it occurred to me that, in the line of duty, I might have asked Krishna to buy my telephone books for me when the post office reopened, if it ever did. But that would have been scurvy reward for his gallantry, and I preferred to let the State Department limp along without the directories.

How could one thank such a man? We said goodbye in the pasture and clasped hands a long moment. Bells tinkled on a herd of cattle that pastured nearby, the same bells that are now sold at every restaurant along the Pennsylvania Turnpike. The cows you pass in Pennsylvania dairy country have great drooping bags of milk such as were never seen in India. But nowhere in Pennsylvania can I find a country Krishna, his faced streaked ceremonially blue in honor of the blue Krishna who lives in that god-forsaken temple in Old Delhi. That idol, of course, stands in lieu of the real Krishna, who was a great lover, who lifted a mountain once to let the dairymaids he adored shelter under it from a rainstorm, and whose face was a heavenly blue.

So when I said goodbye to Krishna, I smiled, and I tried to smile the very smile I had seen on the face of Radha.

# 4

## Awash in Delhi, Pepsu, and Punjab

Pepsu may sound like a stomach remedy, but the name was actually an acronym for Patiala and East Punjab States Union, a ramshackle federation of former princely states which were glued together for the purpose of forming a unit of independent India in 1947, and which came unglued ten years later, having lived and died without distinction.

I had to visit the capital city of Patiala in order to start a flow of publications from the Pepsu state government to the Library of Congress. When I learned that the train would leave me for three hours in the middle of the night at Ambala railway station, both coming and going, I mounted my Vauxhall and headed north by road.

Leaving New Delhi at dawn, I passed the regal government buildings, a heritage of the British Raj, which will one day take their place among the rest of India's magnificent ruins. My route lay alongside Yamuna Canal, beside the orchard where Krishna, on a lazy afternoon a year before, had revealed himself to me, smiling. Farther from Delhi, the or-

## Awash in Delhi, Pepsu, and Punjab

chards gave way to fields of reeds fifteen feet high, bearing silvery heads that bent and whistled in the wind, spreading like mercury across brown velvet fields. Crossing the canal, I could see but three feet of water in it, which turned out to be lucky for me.

Now I entered Sikh country, historically Punjab, Land of Five Waters. In the eighteenth century, Guru Govind Singh tried to link Hinduism with Islam in order to heal the breach between India's two major communities. He failed magnificently, bringing forth instead a third, and completely distinct religious community, with its center at the market town of Amritsar in the Punjab. His followers today are distinguished by their brawny build, their monotheism, their untrimmed beards, their swords, steel bracelets, and undershorts (which are *de rigeur*).

I made my home among displaced Sikhs in the Jangpura district of New Delhi. Three and a half millions of farmers, merchants, and warriors fled the western half of Punjab when that was allotted to Pakistan amidst some of the greatest bloodletting of all time. Now, Sikhs were pouring into New Delhi to begin new lives, turning the city's suburbs into boom towns that evidenced more vigor than anything that had been seen around here since the death of the Moghuls.

Jangpura was still building when I moved in. Electricity had not penetrated as yet, and although there were pipes, there was no water. It was hard to tell at times where the desert left off and my house began, for the sand was continually blowing into my bed.

Even without electricity and water, my flat was an improvement over the back seat of my car, which I had been sleeping on since the hotel bills outstripped my pay check. The embassy maintained a well-equipped barracks, with an air conditioner in each room. (It was said that the "Taj" consumed more electricity than the entire remainder of the city of New Delhi.) Rooms at the Taj were available at reasonable rent to embassy clerks, but not to officers (except unmarried males, as determined by the barracks housing committee, composed of the residents).

Late in my stay, the embassy began to provide housing

## Krishna Smiled

for officers, beginning with the highest rank and working on down. The two housing plans met in the middle, which was me, and I was thrown on the local housing market, where I found that I had little to choose between a castle, which I couldn't afford, and a chawl, which I couldn't bear.

It was at this point that Krishna began smiling, having assumed for this purpose the body of a tall, soft-spoken army captain from the Karnatak who was stationed in New Delhi. He was named Krishnamurti, meaning Idol of Krishna, but he was called Kitu. Kitu had won a medal for gallantry in the "police action" by which Hyderabad was brought into the Indian Union, and I believe he killed some people in that connection. But he would not kill animals, and he had never eaten meat in his life. Indeed, in his family tomatoes were not eaten, since when one is cut, it bleeds. How Kitu achieved his magnificent physique on a diet of rice and peas is one of the mysteries of Asia.

Smiling, Kitu taught me several dozen things all at once and endlessly on forever, so that I left India a better woman than I came.

First, there were survival instructions for the westerner stranded in Asia: Take your liquor straight, preferably Scotch, and no more than two chhotta pegs (small shots) at a time; play squash or swim each day, and if that is not possible, perform setting-up exercises; stay out of the noonday sun; and think healthy thoughts at night.

Secondly, Kitu undertook to provide me with decent housing. This was the first mothering I had had since leaving home, and it left me gasping with gratitude. After some preliminary scouting around, Kitu drove me southward out of New Delhi past Purana Qila (Old Fort) whose majestically crumbling walls sheltered refugee families, and suggested I anchor my sheet there with the rest of them. But he continued past the fort, past the open-air cinema which was showing *Aloma of the South Seas,* past the turnoff to Humayun's Tomb and the Ambassador Hotel where the wealthy Americans stayed; past Khan Khanan's Tomb, and turned down Hospital Road, euphemistically named for an eye and ear clinic, to the alley where lived the Delhi truck drivers and their trucks, all Sikhs. Here he again offered to let me out.

About a block behind the truck drivers' alley, we passed a muddy field or a dry river bed, I never discovered which, in use as a public latrine; and stopped finally at Jangpura Extension, an encampment of middle class Sikhs. There, Kitu had found a displaced Punjabi with a second story to rent.

I looked around the house, and it seemed very alien to me. It was U-shaped, built around a courtyard which was Sri Puri's. My rooms were on the second floor, and each one opened onto an outdoor balcony that overlooked the courtyard below. What finally won me over was that each room had a window of its own. Up till then, I hadn't been able to find quarters with windows for the amount of rent I was able to pay. And Sri Puri, my landlord, seemed very decent.

He was a widower who had fled to Delhi with his twelve-year-old daughter, remnant of a large family that had lived for three hundred years in the West Punjab, but now would live no more. He was enlightened; had declined to engage the girl in infancy, and would allow her to choose her own mate when she finished high school. As an interim precaution, he did not let her eat eggs or pulses lest they heat her blood. Since the family was also vegetarian, I do not honestly know what the child ate.

Sri Puri was a strong Congress Party member, and explained to me (after I moved in) that, having refused to pay a five rupee bite to a local official, our water would not be turned on for some time to come. "It was not for the increase of graft that we have achieved our independence, isn't it?" he asked, and I had to agree.

Meanwhile, it was the public water tap for me, or rather for Emmanuel, my bearer, or rather for the bisti (water carrier) he hired to do it for him, for no man will do another's work in India, and take his livelihood away. So the bisti forsook his cow's stomach and accepted the missahib's bucket, which he filled at the public tap, waiting his turn among women washing laundry and babies in toe-deep mud.

In the evenings, the men would come to bathe at the tap,

## Krishna Smiled

stripping to their shorts, soaping all over, and luxuriating under the flowing stream. Sikhs, being omnivorous, present a solid front of sinew to the rest of India, supplying their country with soldiers, policemen, truck drivers, hackies, carpenters, and emigrants to California. Their physiques are great, but I never could get past that waist-length hair dressed in mustard oil.

While the men bathed, the swine of the neighborhood would come down to enjoy the resulting wallow, and there carry out the commandment of their lord to increase and multiply. They were of an enormous size, their bellies armored in grey bristles, pendant from razor-sharp spines. They filled their bellies through narrow questing muzzles, and all in all were the ugliest monsters I had ever seen. Nevertheless, they found favor in one another's angry pink eyes, and were constantly pregnant or in the act of becoming so.

At some distance from the tap there was an animal trough, and here the water buffalo ranged, their black hides glistening with fresh mud or dull with dried muck, for they too wallowed to escape the heat of the sun. Scattered among these were the ivory white bullocks who pull the drays. An occasional horse joined the throng of animals at the trough, but these always looked out of place. Delhi is really too hot for horses, as indeed, it is for human beings.

Around this historic site of the water tap and trough, adobe houses were going up, thick and quick as mushrooms. You never knew where another house might appear. For example, after I'd gotten used to Jangpura, I used to sleep on the roof like everybody else, in order to take advantage of a slight pre-dawn breeze. But one morning, waking with the sun, I found a row of turbaned faces chinning and grinning on my parapet. The house next door had unexpectedly reached the same height as mine, and I was forced to retreat indoors until its construction was complete and the laborers had departed.

The houses in Jangpura were surrounded by thick adobe walls. The narrow street-level windows had bars cemented into them against bandits and kidnappers. Everything looked

## Awash in Delhi, Pepsu, and Punjab

as though it had been built by blind men, and only Sri Puri had planted geraniums in front of his house, in little rows that marched stiffly beside the brick pathway to his door. And I liked him on that account, because he had seen the destruction of everything he owned, yet he still wanted to grow flowers.

That first night in Jangpura, lying in my bed of sand sleepless, fanless, and lightless, I tried to feel at home in India. It was good to have a place of my own. Stripping the mattress and sheets from my charpai, I threw them on the floor and slept on the webbing that was strung across the wooden bed frame. In this way, the air could circulate under my body as well as over it. Freed of the serpent embrace of my bedding, I dozed.

Suddenly, I was jolted from sleep by the most hideous noise I had ever heard. Speeding to my window, I saw donkeys below, tethered next to the bricks which they would resume hauling in the morning. They were browsing and heehawing over the straw that leaked from the bricks.

While I cowered at the curtainless window examining the wildlife below, something which appeared to be a lynch mob turned onto my street. I had no way of interpreting this mass movement of armed men, but they were clearly heading toward my house, which was at the end of the lane. Why had Kitu abandoned me? Sri Puri might have felt called upon to defend his tenant, but he had gone out for the evening. Emmanuel, who was a Methodist but who surely would have known, had gone home long ago. And anyway, it was too late.

Two hundred bearded, sworded Sikhs surrounded my house, brandishing flaming torches. Had I violated some tabu by moving here? Had I defiled someone's food by looking at it, or given the evil eye to a baby? How could I know? I was only looking for a place to live, like everybody else. Was it possible that, in the space of ten hours, I had become known as the Great Anti-Sikh?

As the robust men clustered about my house, chanting ominously, I wished to God that Guru Govind Singh, to whom I render all respect, had not lifted the tabu from meat. Alter-

## Krishna Smiled

natively, I wished all Sikhs in the San Fernando Valley, together with their swords. These swords were real, and clacked in their scabbards, unlike the atrophied little charms which citified Sikhs wear on chains around their necks.

Determined to know why I should have been called upon to die by the hand of Sikhs, I remained crouched below the windowsill trying to make out the words of the chant.

Then, amid the shouting, I distinguished the words *"nikel aje, nikel aje!"* (come out, come out). I relaxed. They would never have used the polite form of the imperative had they meant me harm. A warm rush of gratitude replaced my fear. These wonderful, gentle, men had come to welcome me to Jangpura. I began to prepare my speech, in rudimentary Hindi, which is quite similar to Punjabi except that the one is written in Devanagri and the other in Gurmukhi, which looks like Urdu to me but apparently isn't, because Emmanuel couldn't read it. But the press releases would come later. Now there would be garlands of marigolds.

My neighbor in the other half of the duplex relieved me of speechmaking by stepping out on the balcony to the accompaniment of hosannahs and making one himself. Thereafter, the crowd lifted him from the balcony, beard and all, and carried him off to their temple. He was a Sikh saint.

Mahan Singh, who worked for the embassy as a chauffeur and was a Sikh, but no saint, who changed a tire in three minutes by the clock and opened Coca Cola bottles with his Sikh's steel bracelet, thought I was very lucky to live next door to this unusual person. I agreed. In addition to all the traffic he attracted, his daughter was teaching me folksongs. Mahan Singh thought this was the wrong reason, but allowed as how the sanctity would affect me anyway. The saint's blessing had brought Mahan Singh home safely from Mitzri, where he went to fight Rommel. Oh, those Mitzr—they couldn't fight at all.

The Sikhs had a dual reputation in Delhi. On the one hand, they were aggressive go-getters, more like Americans than anyone else around. Mahan Singh, for example, saved up enough money from his salary to buy a taxi and go into

## Awash in Delhi, Pepsu, and Punjab

business for himself. On the other hand, Sikhs were the Poles of the world of humor. It was alleged that the noonday sun boiled their brains under the thick padding of hair and turban. The observation was fortified when a Member of the House of the People, who was a Sikh, addressed the Speaker of the lower house of Parliament as "Madam." Unfortunately, it was exactly 12 noon.

Northward through Ambala I penetrated deep into Sikh territory, or at least that part of it which had fallen to India in the Partition. I would have to approach the western half of Punjab via Karachi, since border communications were still disrupted. Patiala and East Punjab States Union was composed of the former princely states of Patiala, Nabha, Kapurthala, Jind, Faridkot, Malerkotla, Nalagarh, and Kalsi. It may well be asked what a princely state was, let alone a former princely state.

The British penetrated India during the reign of the first Elizabeth, just about the time that British settlers began to appear in North America. But instead of an unpopulated continent and virgin resources, they found ancient, settled civilizations exhibiting a staggering diversity of cultures. The first contacts were mercantile; but toward the end of the eighteenth century, the British government took a hand in matters. The unequal contacts between technologically superior Europeans and the Indians, who were demoralized by the decay of Moghul government and fragmented by caste, language and religious differences, led to the gradual absorption of India through conquest, purchase, commercial penetration, and treaty alliance with native princes. But despite their long rule, the British never succeeded—any more than the Moghul or Chandragupta or Maratha empires succeeded—in turning India into one nation.

By the time the British left India, they had annexed 55 percent of the country and 76 percent of the people. This territory was organized into provinces administered by the Crown with varying degrees of Indian participation. Some of these provinces, Madras, Bengal, Uttar Pradesh, had huge populations and distinct personalities of their own, including extensive written literatures. They varied from such as the highly literate and politically vocal Bengal, which had produced an internationally recognized body of art and literature, great scientists and a representative legislature; to the Northeast Frontier region, where headhunters held sway, and which was ruled directly by British district commissioners, insofar as it could be ruled at all.

The British provinces were of immensely uneven development not only between themselves, but even within their own borders. Most contained congeries of clans and tribes and cultures which differed radically from the majority population. These provinces were not the result of natural development or growth around a central core, but had been pieced together over the ruins of countless native kingdoms and fiefs. The organization of provinces corresponded to no "nationalist" feeling on the part of the Indians; they were put together to serve the empire's strategic, political, and economic needs. This lack of inner cohesion was to assume importance after independence.

In the British provinces, British standards of behavior were introduced. Schooling followed the British model, elucidated by Thomas Macaulay in his *Minute on Education* in which he advocated creating "a class of persons Indian in blood and colour but English in taste, in opinion, in morals, and in intellect." English was a required subject after the fourth form. Police and army were trained and led by British officers and non-coms; and at later stages, British style legislatures were introduced in order to give those Indians who were considered to have reached the requisite stage of sophistication the opportunity to participate in government.

These provincial legislatures and the political parties which organized them became the basis for parliamentary government in independent India.

As for the remaining 45 percent of the territory and 24 percent of the people who were not under British rule, at the time of liquidation of the Raj these were organized into an amazing 562 independent kingdoms—the "princely states."

The princely states varied in size from Hyderabad, with an area of 82,000 square miles, a population of 16 million

## Awash in Delhi, Pepsu, and Punjab

and an annual revenue of Rs 260,000,000; to the "state" of Vajanoness in Kathiawar, with an area of 0.29 square miles, a population of 206, and revenue of Rs 500 a year, not enough to keep its rajah in betel nuts. Many of the princely states were fragmented: Baroda had, in addition to the area around its chief city, dozens of tiny enclaves embedded among other, equally fragmented states of Gujerat.

In the princely states, Britain operated in only four fields: communications, defense, foreign affairs, and succession to the throne. Unless conditions within a state became anarchic, it was not British policy to intervene between the prince and his subjects. Consequently, the level of enlightenment in the princely states was extremely ragged. There was one state—Mysore—where a start had been made toward the growth of responsible government; but for the most part, the principles of Louis XIV held sway.

The reason for the continued existence of the princely states well into the democratic era lie twisted in the Mutiny of 1857 (or the First War of Indian Independence, depending on which side you were on). When large numbers of Indians, including a goodly percentage of the army, rose against British rule, the Indian princes "served as breakwaters in the storm which would have swept over us in one great wave," according to Lord Canning, then India's governor general. The princes by and large stood fast by the British, for they stood to lose as much through the rebellion as their imperial masters did.

As reward for princely loyalty, the British ceased annexing India directly to the Crown and concentrated on maintaining the little princes on their thrones. Let *them* keep order among their own. So long as the princes kept furnishing troops for the imperial armies and gold for the imperial treasury, the British guaranteed the loyalty of their subjects and kept the princes on thrones that otherwise might have toppled to democratic movements. The result was that, while all over the world feudalism was dissolving in the elixir of nationalism, in India the princely class flourished and grew fat, and India remained divided.

There was no neat cleavage between "British" and "Indian" India. The territory of each lay intertwined and circumscribed by territory of the other. The states lay frozen in a pattern which had been reached by accident and perpetuated by exigency. The Indian peninsula looked as the European peninsula might have, had some superior external military power conquered it during the age of feudalism, annexing counties here and there, but confirming hundreds of petty princelings in their fiefdoms as agents of its paramount control.

This was a nightmare legacy for leaders of the Indian independence movement. As V. P. Menon put it in 1955, in the opening sentence of his book *The Integration of the Indian States*, (a process in which he played a key role): "India is one geographic entity. Yet, throughout her long and chequered history, she never achieved political homogeneity."

When discussions opened on the transfer of British power, the problem was: To whom should power be transferred? The program of the Indian National Congress (Nehru's party) was One India. The Moslem League, led by Mohammed Ali Jinnah, held that Hindus and Moslems form distinct nations and were therefore entitled to form two countries.

From the first point of view, independence would provide the first opportunity in history to create a single, united nation on the entire subcontinent. Mahatma Gandhi in particular believed that communal differences must be sunk in order to achieve this unity.

But many Moslems believed that communal differences ran too deep to be bridged by any mere political process. They perceived Moslems and Hindus as two distinct peoples, with exclusive culture and habits, who had never coalesced despite more than a thousand years of inhabiting the same territory. Since Moslems constituted only a quarter of the population, they foresaw that representative government would condemn them to a perpetual minority position.

It all boiled down to a question of trust. But the history of India, like the history of Ireland, has not been one to engender trust between religious groups. The impossibility of reconciling the two parties—backed up on each side by in-

## Awash in Delhi, Pepsu, and Punjab

flamed religious sensibilities—led to the decision to create two countries: Pakistan and residuary India.

But this did not touch the question of the princely states. The lapse of British paramountcy meant the lapse also of all those treaties establishing special relationships between them and the British. These principalities would now find themselves at loose ends, without legal affiliation to any sovereign state.

It was obvious from the start that an India composed of the former British provinces alone would not be a feasible unit. It was even more obvious that the majority of the Indian states could not stand on their own. Most of them were incapable of governing themselves in a manner adequate to the modern age. Lines of communication ran through provinces and states alike. And defense concerned everyone—a point which became appallingly clear as communal rioting broke out during the Partition.

The fact that most of the princely states were not economically viable helped them to merge peacefully with either India or Pakistan, depending upon their geographic location. The princes had served their historical function as agents of imperialism; when independence dawned, they passed quietly from the scene. Their departure was eased by consummate statesmanship on the part of the successor governments, which pensioned them off liberally in order to prevent the formation of a powerful dissident faction of princes who, in certain areas at least, might have carried their hereditary subjects with them.

Thus passed from the scene the rajahs, maharajahs, khans, sardars, nawabs, nabobs, and nizams of yesterday. The extinction of their states was accomplished peacefully: a crop of dragon's teeth sprang up in only three instances—Kashmir, Hyderabad, and Junagadh. Otherwise, the basis had been laid for the launching of the dual entities of India and Pakistan.

Whereupon, the new governments had to do precisely what the British had done before them: combine fistfuls of little states into viable provinces. The particular mixture which was Pepsu proved ungovernable and ultimately had

## Krishna Smiled

to be divided between its Sikh and Hindu communities. To a traveller from the Delhi plains, the Sikhs were definitely the more prominent figures on the landscape.

For one thing, they wore all green and blue: green sarongs and bright blue turbans. Then there were those swords dangling down behind from a strap worn over the shoulder. Files of men could be seen along the highway; also entire families balanced precariously upon a single bicycle, camels on their way to pull the Persian wheels, ox carts lumbering down the middle of the road with the driver asleep on top of a load of hay. Taken together, they presented some traffic hazards. But they weren't a patch on the truck drivers.

When Sikhs switched from their ancestral profession of war-making and took up truck-driving, they lost none of their élan. They tend to charge their lorries down the center of the road, yielding for neither man nor beast, scorning brakes, rear-view mirror, and other appurtenances of the soft life. Forty years' growth of beard and two yards of gingham turban insulate them from the dust of the road, the curses of other drivers, and the sound of desperate horns behind them. In Delhi, they may have been the butt of jokes; but here in Punjab it was Sardarji, King of the Road!

Every time I tried to pass a truck, my car would slue and slough in the deep ruts it left behind. These ruts, which were a permanent yet ever-changing feature of the road, were particularly troublesome when crossing rivers. That is to say, the road ended at a river bank and picked up again at the other side, leading me to believe that I could drive across. Although the bed seemed dry, the thalveg turned out to be spongy, and it was ridged high between the ruts left by trucks with a wider chassis than my Vauxhall. So I mired like a turtle on its belly, all four wheels in the air. I suppose I was lucky there wasn't more water in the river. I was also fortunate not to have read the current report of the chief of police of Pepsu, from which I now quote in part:

> The Punjabi is losing his national characteristic and is becoming more and more of a thief and a cheat and cowardly

## Awash in Delhi, Pepsu, and Punjab

when dealing with his enemies, and is definitely becoming more of a cheat than a murderer or a dacoit (bandit).

Presumably, the latter two are ancient Punjabi virtues, the cheating is something new.

But I was at the time more concerned about the possibility of flash floods and winding up in the Arabian Sea. A man who was bathing nearby obligingly bound up his hair which had been hanging out to dry, and together we heaved and hawed, but it did no good. I might have been there yet, were it not for the sunny nature of Punjabis, which gives the lie to their old chief of police. A truckload of laborers approached the ford. Seeing me pancaked in the middle of the river, they vaulted out of the van, picked up my car, and carried it across.

I kept blundering into dry river beds all over Pepsu and neighboring Himachal Pradesh. Most maps of India were classified, and the only one I was able to buy was drawn at a scale of forty miles to the inch, not terribly useful for actual contact with the countryside. Also, the cartographer had an aloof attitude toward topography, tending to ignore such features as mountains and rivers, particularly if there was no way over them.

I will say this about dry river beds: they provide a great vantage point for viewing a solitary water buffalo which has wandered over to the twenty-foot high embankment. Foreshortened by perspective, it looks like a hippopotamus.

The road was well travelled despite its rugged features. Each time I stuck, a King of the Road would pull me out. The Sardars were always cheerful about giving me a push, or clearing my fuel line with the aid of a bicycle pump, changing a tire, or showing me how to dry out my plugs. At one point, I stalled trying to pull up onto the top of a riverbank. A driver parked some distance away eating lunch in his cab roared with laughter at the silly missahib and her silly little car, which couldn't straddle the ruts made by his big, masculine truck. Suddenly, he jumped down from the cab, leaped in front of my car which was struggling like the first salamander ever to burst out of its watery home, and tore the hood open. He snatched the turban from his head and clamped it down upon the carburetor, which had set itself afire. After that, he hooked up a winch and pulled me out. All very good humored, but I'll bet he was a cousin of that fascist beast who charged up the mountain on my side of the road the next day and flattened me against a cliff.

After all this, Patiala was a washout, so far as publications went. The state was then at the beginning of its short and bootless history of governmental ineptitude, corruption, and the corrosive religious rivalry which ended by tearing it in two. I doubt that I was able to accomplish anything of lasting significance for the Library of Congress. So the highlight of my visit there must be the bathroom of the State Guest House.

The Chief Secretary had me put up in this dreary large mansion, thus saving me from the dreary small travellers' bungalow. My bedroom measured forty feet (my feet: it was my only means of measuring) in each direction, including, but here I cannot be exact, up. The bathroom was just half that size in its horizontal dimensions, and it contained a sink, a tub, a separate stall shower, an Indian toilet (in the floor, with a water tap beside it), a European toilet (on a pedestal, with paper beside it), and a bidet that spouted from every direction of the compass. It was the most fully equipped bathroom I encountered on the continent, with the exception of the one imported by the Morrison-Knudsen Company and erected in the middle of the desert for the benefit of its men who were working on the Helmand River Valley dam in Afghanistan. And that one didn't have a bidet.

The only other bidet I saw in my travels was torn out of Bahawalpur House in New Delhi when that building was refurbished for embassy use. Though I pleaded with our administrative officer to save it, he sadistically forced it to stand outside in the brutal sun day after day. At first, the women hod carriers used to leave their babies in it. Then someone got the idea of mixing mortar in the bidet, and evicted the babies. The poor thing stood up to this abuse for a few weeks, but one day its porcelain bowl cracked and it shuddered to the ground far from its native soil of Wisconsin. The whole performance was typical of American insensitivity.

*Awash in Delhi, Pepsu, and Punjab*

From Patiala, I pressed on to Bhakra-Nangal, where I made a killing in dam specifications.

The five rivers of Punjab: Jhelum, Ravi, Beas, Chenab, and Sutlej, together with their network of canals, provided the greatest area of irrigated land in pre-Partition India. But India and Pakistan divided on communal lines, the irrigation system was fragmented, and many parcels of dry land were left on one side of the boundary, with the water intended to irrigate it hopelessly on the other side. Indeed, though India received 45 percent of the population of the province, she got just 28 percent of the total irrigated area.

Bhakra-Nangal, projected to be the largest hydroelectric system in Asia, was intended to repair some of the damage. I refused to believe it could do this when I first laid eyes upon the construction site. Hundreds of thousands of men, women, and child laborers were crawling up and down a mountainside, carrying platters of dirt and rock upon their heads. All the mechanical ingenuity known to Ramses II was obviously being employed here. Only the great-grandchildren of these workers, it seemed to me, would live to enjoy the waters of this dam. For the record, the dam at Bhakra now stands as the highest straight gravity dam in the world (740'), has 652 miles of canals and 2,200 miles of subsidiaries, in addition to numerous smaller dams and hydroelectric stations.

The project was being supervised by an American named Harvey Slocum who had learned his trade toiling on some of the great dams of the world. Having dropped out of school at age twelve, he provided a wicked contrast to the dam's P.R. man, a Bengali whose B.Sc. in civil engineering from the University of Michigan had failed to overcome his brahminical distaste for manual labor. It was a peculiarly disjointed world at Bhakra-Nangal: the lowly hod carriers and the mighty American engineers all immersed in the strain of great physical exertion—yet separated by a cultural gulf so deep there seemed no chance of bridging it. And the Bengali, the educated elite, who scorned physical labor, but who would inherit its products. I wondered whether, in that human chain conveying platters of dirt up and down the mountainside, there lurked an Indian Slocum.

## Krishna Smiled

My return to Jangpura Extension was a joyous one. There was a wedding in progress down the block, and it remained in progress three days longer, with two bands and a victrola hooked up to a loudspeaker system that was the granddaddy of the one later employed at the Electric Circus. Emmanuel had prepared a special dinner for me: peahen, shot not by Kitu, who couldn't bring himself to do it, but by a soldier under his command. There were bushels of flowers on the table, Tan Sen's prayer for rain was on the phonograph, and seated on the divan was Krishna himself, in his human manifestation.

# 5

*I spend a night in a Moslem graveyard,
collecting ephemera for the Library of Congress*

**M**y tour of India was a success in that I managed to avoid the Taj Mahal. The Taj-Imagined is a ravishing poem to immortal love. The Taj-Arrested-in-Marble, with German tourists in lederhosen at work with their cameras, and the Air India swami bowing beside the lotus pool, seemed sure to be intolerable.

I was not alone in this sentiment. A girl at our embassy gave up a perfectly acceptable Nawab solely because, on arrival at Agra for some hanky-panky, he sent out for ice-cold coke. It is depressing to go in search of India, and find oneself in America.

I preferred the homelier monuments anyway, such as Fatehpur Sikri, an improbable fortified castle not far from the more celebrated Taj. Its medieval walls humpback up and down several hills, enclosing what is left of the Emperor Akbar's pleasure dome. Akbar took it upon himself to marry the world's major religions, and he ordered to be built here sumptuous apartments, each individually styled to the religious and ethnic tastes of one of his wives. From my observation, this eclectic approach is rather more typical of India than is the monogamous love commemorated over at the Taj.

At any rate, I was going through my own sari phase when I visited Fatehpur, because there is a little of the eclectic in me. Consequently, I was swathed in six yards of brilliant and highly unmanageable purple silk when I climbed the ruined walls above the Moslem wife's quarters. So it was inevitable, and I knew it was inevitable, that having achieved the top of the castle despite the best efforts of my sari to throw me, an American tourist should dart out into the courtyard below and furtively—because she didn't want to infringe my caste rules—snap a picture of me.

So I am enshrined in some midwestern living room, in the photo album underneath the end table, as "a Hindu woman visiting Fatehpur Sikri."

The North Indian plain is littered with the remnants of the Moghul Empire, which had its stronghold here. On either side the highway that runs between the seventh and eighth cities of Delhi ("Old" and "New" we call them now, but there are others older, older) stand twin relics. To the west is the Jamma Masjid, its triple onion domes ballooning above the squalid Moslem sector of the city. To the east is the Lal Qila, the Red Fort of Shah Jahan, who built the Taj Mahal.

Along this road one day passed a procession of villagers. By the look of their dusty dhotis and turbans, the blankets and pots slung across their shoulders, they had trekked a long way. They were evidently headed for Nizamuddin.

To a foreigner, Nizamuddin is a garish modern suburb to the south of New Delhi. Its houses, functional, unsightly and luxurious beyond the dreams of 99 percent of the population, sit uncomfortably upon the countryside, as though they had been dropped there by some absent-minded roc. Behind Nizamuddin was my less fashionable suburb of Jangpura.

From my front window, in the middle distance, I could see the tomb of Safdarjung, in whose shadow lies the airport.

## A night in a Moslem graveyard

Taking off, planes fly over the Nizamuddin of the Moslems, their twentieth-century roar drowning out the rather antiquated howl of hyenas which sometimes come from the cemetery.

Studded with tiny houses of the dead in ruin and disrepair, the Durgah of Nizamuddin lies obscured by scrub brush and a farm for retired cows. The vanished Moghul aristocracy is buried here, but their tombs (since most of the Moslems were driven out in the riots that accompanied Partition) seem important now only to bats and browsing goats and scorpions which shelter in them from the broiling sun. Most are just large enough to accommodate an oblong gravestone. A few are two stories high, with a cellarful of fetid air, and towers at each corner. By night, their domed roofs blot the full-starred sky like voluptuous breasts.

So far as I knew, no one went there to stir up the crazy old shammus who kept the place. I was all the more surprised to learn that the trekkers I had seen were headed there. I had once made the mistake of talking to the shammus, and from then on he would visit me occasionally, bringing me loathsome pies with unknown substances baked into their interiors. It got to the point where, when I saw his fez coming down the street, I would lie on the floor of my living room until he quit leaning on the bell and went away. Unable to overcome my fear of what exactly this keeper of the cemetery was baking into his pies, I avoided the whole neighborhood and generally couldn't have cared less what was going on over at the Durgah.

The trekkers were something else again, however. So many people might mean books; or possibly ephemera, as the Library of Congress wanted me to call those insignificant throwaways they so loved. The thought of cataloging these ill-printed sheets undated, unnumbered, and unnamed, in dim-lit dusty stacks at the end of grim corridors once again made me realize how lucky I was to be out acquisitioning them instead.

The newspaper informed me that this day was the 500th anniversary of the death of the poet Hazrat Nizamuddin. In

## Krishna Smiled

a bid to improve Indian-Pakistan relations the government of India had dropped passport restrictions, thus enabling Moslems to come in over the border for the celebrations. These were the trekkers.

After dinner, I drove down the familiar road past the open acreage which was used by the neighborhood as a latrine, past the spigot where women lined up with their bulbous brass and clay jars, to the entrance of the cemetery where a large crowd milled. Men only, as one would expect among Moslems. I parked where rickshaw coolies and tonga-wallas (drivers of horse-drawn carriages) vied for space under the eye of a laconic policeman and the chauffeur of a Cadillac, who was above all this.

Dark came, and the crowd moved down a funnel of light cast by Coleman lanterns hung from trees. I looked for the adorable clay figurines which are always offered for sale at Hindu fairs. But, of course, there would be none here as Moslems are forbidden to mould the human likeness.

Wooden shacks bearing signs such as KHAN HOTEL, LAHORE GUEST HOUSE, and WELCOME, bade the travellers make themselves at home among the tombstones. Shills lured the bearded men over for food and a draught on the water pipe. Pancakes big as cartwheels were sizzling in enormous cauldrons of ghee; orange-colored sweets that looked like french-fried onion rings swung from sticks; kebab was roasting on long iron pikes; and everywhere the panwalla did big business.

Most of the fair-goers looked exactly like the rest of the Delhi population. There is no cultural or ethnic difference between the Moslems of the northern provinces who became Pakistanis, and those who remained Indians. Nor is there any obvious physical distinction between Moslems and Hindus native to the same area. Of course, we may rely on time and war to create differences where none existed before, as each side assumes the burden of hatred appropriate to its citizenship.

In addition to the olive-skinned, slight men of north central India, there were darker men in the black caps

## A night in a Moslem graveyard

characteristic of Bengal; and large-boned semitic types from the North-West Frontier Province. These Pathans, rough and surly-looking, shoved among their smaller brethren holding one another's hands like schoolgirls.

The crowd between the lanterns moved slowly forward, and suddenly I emerged through the wall of darkness that rose abruptly at the end of the path. I was alone. I could not see. I appeared to have left the fair behind. Then I stubbed my bare toes against a stone sill. Beside me a repulsive voice requested me to remove my sandals. It was the shammus'.

Clutching my sandals in my hand, I stepped through an aperture in the thick stone wall, aided by that dreadful hand. Then—to be sure, I had seen the cemetery before, that thorny field of monuments—but nothing I had seen in daylight could be related to what I was seeing now. Lanterns hanging from trees and tombs illumined the grandeur of a decaying mosque, made that decay entrance and dance, till the mosque seemed to be melting. In the inconstant light, pyjamaed men roamed the courtyard or slept in companionable heaps. Their families, asleep in chambers hollowed out of the walls, appeared to me like marionettes left jumbled on their little stages after the audience has left the theater. Here and there, at irregular intervals above the ground, a campfire was lit and pots stewed, and women huddled together. Only the very young and the very old lifted their burqas to peep at passersby.

At midnight beneath the trees beside the tomb of Nizamuddin, the people seated themselves on stones and steps, with musicians in their midst—a blind singer, a drummer with his two clay pots, and a flutist.

A moment's stir was caused by a young Sikh student who placed his sandals upon the ground. A clean-shaven man reached over, placed the sandals on the Sikh's lap, and smiled a cautionary smile. Religious passions were not going to flare here, thank God.

I climbed the stair and sat down on the marble floor of the tomb, which is a filigreed cockleshell of white stone, through which I looked out as a Spanish lady might peer through her fan. The tomb smelled of marigolds the pilgrims

## Krishna Smiled

had strewn on the marble sarcophagus, where an oil lamp flickered. Mumtaz, who lies buried at thirty-three in the Taj Mahal, caused these lines to be engraved above her:

> Let no candle burn here
> lest some moth, venturing too near
> should, like myself, meet
> untimely death.

Just outside my tomb, facing inward, burqa thrown back, an old woman was reading the Koran. She was the only Moslem woman I ever saw read.

I could have gone on enjoying the scene and the singing all night; but now the shammus glided to my side. I wasn't going to share a tomb with *him*, if I could help it.

"How do you like it here? It is our little birthday party," he said in tones that suggested he had some interesting postcards to sell.

"It is very nice, very nice indeed," I replied.

"You are American, isn't it? do you like what you see here? you are American? you are alone? you are not married? where is your father? do you like our little birthday party?"

"Yes, yes, yes" I gasped, holding my breath. I knew if I once smelled him I would never get him out of my nose. The shammus closed his eyes in bogus religious ecstasy, raised his scabrous face to the candlelight, and joined his voice in the song the devotees were singing outside our tomb. I took the opportunity to flee him.

Threading my way out among the singers, I left the square by a passage cut through the thick wall of the mosque. Here the grasping hands of beggars rose up out of the dark to clutch the ankles of fleeing wealth. Casting my shadow on the walls of the cave, I fled from there and arrived at a huge square tank where lights were reflected in water like tennis balls that have stopped rolling in wet grass. Mud underfoot. I buckled on my sandals and headed for the roadside lights near which I had parked my car.

But as I walked, a thought struggled to make itself

*A night in a Moslem graveyard*

known to me through the flood of impressions that swamped me.

The dance! The dance! Where were the dancers?

Or, more accurately, the trekkers? Where were the long processions of villagers I had passed earlier in the day? The pilgrims were expected to sleep at the cemetery: witness the signs . . . too many signs for so few customers. And the thousands of Moslems who live in the shadow of the Jamma Masjid? It was too early for them to have returned home. Yet the courtyards I had passed through were nearly deserted.

Reluctantly, I turned back. To find publications, I must first find the public. Stepping back over the stone threshold, I found myself once more at the tank with its depth of stagnant water that was once the liquid heart of some caliph's pleasure dome. A wall. I ran my forehead against it in the dark. Groping toward a ray of light, I came to an arched gateway in the centuries-old stone.

Beyond the wall, thousands of men were seated on the ground. They sat so quietly that I had been unaware of them from ten paces away. Their black eyes were upturned toward the speaker, a man I knew very well. It was the Afghan Ambassador, the owner of the Cadillac.

I was moved by this evidence of the universality of Islam. A common language, a common culture. The organizers of Nizamuddin's birthday party had invited a distinguished foreigner to speak. Yet, he was no foreigner.

I wished desperately that I could understand what the Ambassador was saying. Usually I had no such problem. His Excellency was equally at home in English, French, and Persian, and was well-versed in Judaica as well. We had whiled away many a boring diplomatic-do discussing the Babylonian Talmud and Martin Buber, subjects he understood quite a bit better than I. But here at Nizamuddin I could not penetrate his Persianized Urdu.

I supposed he was praising the art of the poet. But were these students? Surely not, by their clothes. Their faces and hands were work-worn. They were farmers. What could hold them so intensely?

## Krishna Smiled

Was His Excellency extolling Islam? The speaker was a secular man, not a mullah. Wait! Did I catch the word *Pukhtoonistan*?

Pukhtoons (Pathans) have some of the attributes of nationhood, but their traditional homeland is split by the Afghan-Pakistani border. There was strong division of opinion as to whether or not any nationalist sentiment existed among them, but every once in a while someone would reprint a hoary old story to the effect that an independence revolution was brewing among the Pathans of Pakistan's North-West Frontier Province. Should that ever happen, it would be a toss-up as to whether Pukhtoonistan would attract the southern provinces of Afghanistan to itself; or, what is far more likely, Afghanistan would end by absorbing Pukhtoonistan. The example of Texas may be remembered. Since India was wooing Afghanistan's support in her growing quarrel with Pakistan, it made sense for her to support Pukhtoon separatism, leaving the ultimate disposition of these people to time and the Afghans.

My job being to collect literature, I strained to see if there was any lying about. There was, quite a lot. Some yards away, against the inside wall, were stacks of pamphlets and newspapers, displayed on a tarpaulin in which they had probably been brought. I could not tell whether they were reprints of Nizamuddin's poems, essays on soil conservation, or a call to arms on behalf of the people of Pukhtoonistan. The people back at the Library of Congress would have to figure that out.

Crouched on the rocky ground, I scrunched slowly over to the stack of publications. What the hell would I do if Khan Najib-Ullah stopped in mid-sentence and called me by my name? Stealthily, I loaded my shoulder bag and both arms. Then, of course, I could not scrunch out again. I had to stand and saunter to the gate hunchbacked. This I did, my ephemera clutched to my bosom. The weight of large quantities of ephemera is not ephemeral.

At the roadside, the kerosene lamps still flickered. The coolies slept in their rickshaws, awaiting passengers home.

*A night in a Moslem graveyard*

Policemen in their khaki shorts and red-rimmed socks leaned angularly against the night on their six-foot staffs. The enigmatic Cadillac was being polished by the chauffeur.

As I drove home, my headlights picked up a strangely ruffed beast with vicious eyes, that not so much fled from my car as skulked away from it. Puzzled by it, I called the embassy's science attaché the next morning and described the phenomenon.

"That animal," said the doctor, "is called a hyena."

I thought that it was very nice to have a definite name by which to call things. Once having been told the animal was a hyena, everything fitted into place, including the oft-heard fact that hyenas skulk.

But what to do with a phenomenon like Nizamuddin? I had passed it every day for a year, and thought I knew it. I had visited it once by day, and thought I knew it. Now I had peered into its liquid heart by night, and I would never know it.

What, in fact, had I seen?

# 6

*Into the Tower of Babel and out by that same door where in I went*

**D**ictionaries are the seeing-eye dogs of research. The field of Indian studies is a veritable obstacle course of languages, which can defeat the most intrepid researcher unless he possesses suitable dictionaries to use as guides. So I bought word-books no matter how primitively compiled or printed. When my budget was down to the last few pice, I spent these on dictionaries.

Sometimes I wished for a dictionary of dictionaries. Strange new languages were constantly thrusting themselves at me, looking quite self-assured in their well-tailored scripts, and confident that they belonged there, as indeed they did. As I am no linguist, each new language I encountered launched me on a scavenger hunt of continental proportions.

One of my libraries once asked me to procure a title which was picturesquely sent me in the script of the language itself. Across the page of the State Department memo rolled a neatly penned line of *ohs* and *ahs*, dragging their tales be-

*Into the Tower of Babel*

hind them. There was no doubt in the mind of the person writing that this was a language, though he might have taken the time to identify it. I could find no one at the embassy nor among my acquaintances who would hazard a guess as to what the name of the language was, let alone the name of the book. It looked a little like Burmese, but comparison showed it was not. And then, French "looks like" Rumanian, but one would not normally go to Bucharest in order to purchase a book published in Marseilles. I was a little embarrassed to query my home office; it seemed like the sort of thing I ought to know. So I stapled the memo into my little black book and hoped for the best.

Some months later, being in Bhuvaneshwar, I was delighted to recognize the script on storefronts in the bazaar. Whipping out my little note, I confirmed that here indeed was my mystery language, all wrapped up in its mystery script.

Striking up conversation with a bookdealer—in English, of course—I purchased what may have been the American government's first acquisitions in the Oriyan language. I even found my wanted title, by comparing it *oh* for *oh* and *ah* for *ah* with my ordering memo. I then bought some Oriya-English dictionaries, just in case the recipient of this order should be as puzzled by the language as I was.

I had trouble getting through at the post office, however, as English is spread a little thin in Bhuvaneshwar, and Hindi (or at least my Hindi) failed to wash, whatever professional linguists may say about the two languages being related. So I had to carry the books back to New Delhi with me to mail. There I handed them over to my secretary, who was a Kashmiri Brahmin and by definition a scholar.

"Whatever language this is?" he marvelled as he accepted the books.

So much for Oriya and its thirteen million speakers. It was rather as though an educated Italian had never heard of Portuguese; or a Russian being ignorant of Polish.

The languages of India constitute a great romantic epic and repay any amount of study. Sir George Grierson worked for thirty years compiling the nineteen volume *Linguistic Survey of India*. It reads like an oriental *Gone with the Wind*. In 1903 Grierson wrote that a man walking from Assam to Saurashtra (straight across the broadest part of the subcontinent) would be unable to identify any place where the language changed—he would imagine himself to be hearing the same language on the entire course of his journey. Yet, taking cross-sections of speech located a hundred miles from one another, he would find them mutually unintelligible.

Fourteen languages are recognized by the Constitution of India. They account for the speech of 95 percent of Indians. Thereafter one must confront the ineluctable fact that there are 47 more languages spoken by 100,000 people or more; and—hang onto your dictionary—720 languages spoken by fewer than 100,000 people each. Many of the smaller groups are located in Assam. There the Nagas, some of whom are still headhunters, lay claim to greater autonomy on the basis of their linguistic precocity.

Pakistan was set up with Urdu, Punjabi, and Pukhto components in the West, and Bengali in the East, a combination which proved to be indigestible. Then there are the people who live within India and Pakistan but who speak languages indigenous to areas which lie mainly outside their political boundaries; such as Baluchi and Persian on the northwest boundary, Tibetan on the north, and Burmese and Karen on the northeast.

Placing the point of a compass in New Delhi and drawing a circle round it, you can enclose all the modern Indian languages which are descendants of Sanskrit. These include Hindi, Urdu, Hindustani and Punjabi, Rajasthani, Bihari, Pahari, Kashmiri, and Gujerati. These relate to one another approximately as do French, Spanish, Italian, and Portuguese to one another.

At a somewhat further remove in derivation, and in distance from Delhi, there is an outer circle of Sanskritic languages which includes Bengali, Oriya, Assamese, and Marathi. These languages are first cousins to one another and second cousins to the first group. Taken altogether, they are

## Into the Tower of Babel

collateral relatives of all the languages of Europe except Finnish and Hungarian, which are not related to anything but each another.

The Sanskrit, Slavic, Teutonic, Celtic, and Romance languages all find a common ancestor in a language putatively spoken 5,000 years ago by people who inhabited an area south of the Ural mountains. In successive migrations, these hypothetical Aryans invaded and populated Europe, to the west; and India, to the southeast, bringing their victorious language along with them. Naturally, the language underwent modification whenever it came in contact with tongues already in use elsewhere. Then, developing in isolation from one another, dialects diverged even more, which accounts for the strong differences among them today.

By train from Delhi, it takes three days to escape the world of Sanskrit. Heading southwesterly, I travelled on through miles of Hindi variants until I reached Bombay. The second day was spent wading through Gujerati and Marathi. The night was given over to Urdu while I crossed old Hyderabad. On the morning of the third day I woke to find I had left the world of consonants behind and entered the mellifluous world of Dravida. I had also left behind the burning plains and starved-out vegetation of the north, exchanging them for the greenly undulating hills and palm trees of Mysore.

It was to this area south of the Deccan, where India narrows drastically, that the original inhabitants of India, the dark Dravidians, were allegedly pushed by the invading Aryans. Here the Dravidian languages survive, totally unrelated to all other Indian or European languages.

In 1948 the Dravidian language groups stuck with the north to create independent India (Partition occurred within the Hindi-Urdu and Bengali language groups). But the moment the country was free, voices were heard saying that the people would not really be free so long as they were dominated by the Hindi speakers of Delhi. In particular, Telugu speakers launched a violent campaign for the formation of a distinct state within the Indian Union.

## Krishna Smiled

The campaign was climaxed by the self-immolation of an elderly gentleman who could no longer abide sharing his citizenship with speakers of Tamil, from whom he was in many ways indistinguishable. His sacrifice was validated insofar as it forced the government of India to form a Telugu-speaking state of Andhra Pradesh out of what used to be the Madras Presidency, later adding to it much of Hyderabad as well. Far more importantly, the style had been set for a generation of political activists.

Taking their cue from Andhra, other linguistic groups began nationalist agitation against the capital and forced several redrawings of state boundaries to conform to the patterns of speech. Thus Gujeratis and Marathis convulsed and split old Bombay Presidency; and Malayalam speakers tore away bits of Madras, Mysore, and Travancore-Cochin to create Kerala.

Within a decade, the Indian map was redrawn to correspond to major linguistic divisions. (Of course, it is no more possible to draw a neat line of cleavage between Tamil and Telugu, Gujerati and Marathi, Malayalam and Kannarese, than it is to draw one between French and German, Italian and Swiss, Slovene and Slovak. Whenever one language of a multilingual area is recognized as the official one, millions of other people are automatically placed in the minority. For each group whose language is privileged, there is another which is handicapped.)

Pakistan was in the same manner forced to yield Bengali equal status with Urdu. Observers tried to predict whether these concessions to linguistic nationalism would ensure the respective unities of India and Pakistan, or undermine them.

It is not unreasonable to refer to these language groups as nations. They share a collective sense of national identity and have historically been settled in well-defined territories which they regard as their homelands. Some of these regions have larger populations than do many independent countries. Compare Egypt's 31 million with Tamilnad's 33 or Andhra Pradesh's 36 million. Ghana, after all, boasts a bare 8 million people. Indian Bengal has 35 million, and the former East Pakistan (largely Bengali-speaking) over 70 million.

*Into the Tower of Babel*

India attempted to bring order into the Tower of Babel by adopting Hindi as its national language. But taken together with Urdu and Hindustani, this is the mother tongue of only 40 percent of the population. These languages must be taken together because they share a common vocabulary and grammar. But they are written differently: Hindi in the Devanagri script from left to right; Urdu in Persian script from right to left; and Hindustani, so far as I could make out, not at all.

Hindi is the modern incarnation of Sanskrit, and opens up the great Hindu classics such as the Mahabharata and the Ramayana. It thus links India to the Hindu and Buddhist cultures farther east, particularly those of Burma and Indonesia.

Urdu is a kind of switchboard into which Arabic, Persian, and even Pukhto can, in emergency, be plugged, connecting the Moslems of India and Pakistan with their co-religionists in the Near East, Africa, and Central Asia.

During the campaign for independence, Hindu patriots sponsored attempts to "purify" the language by purging Arabic and Persian elements and delving into Sanskrit for the new words which were necessary to update the language. The campaign carried a message for Moslem patriots. As Persian script fell from favor, dictionaries began to appear in Devanagri. It was in its latter form that Hindi became the national language of India; Urdu was made the national language of Pakistan.

I had studied Hindi in its Sanskrit form for six weeks at the impatient knee of the Foreign Service Institute in Washington. I was also taking lessons from a munshi when I was in Delhi, which wasn't often. As a result of my spotty education, I could ask about train schedules, read book titles, and make primitive conversation with friendly persons who were willing to meet me halfway. I was only semi-literate, and often could not understand what I managed to read.

My bearer, on the other hand, could understand what I read out loud but he couldn't read much of anything that was useful to me even though he was literate. His mission school had taught him Urdu, which was now going into discard.

While I was in Delhi, All India Radio took to using extremely sanskritized Hindi for its broadcasts. Emmanuel, who was a native speaker of the language, complained that he could no longer understand the programs. He was, nevertheless, closer to the national linguistic standard than 60 percent of the population.

Urdu lies like a blanket over the many tongues of India. The British used it as an instrument of imperial rule, as the Moghuls had before them. It was the language of administration, law courts, and the army, with the result that five years after independence it was still spoken by every taxi driver, hotel clerk, civil servant, railroad official, soldier, former soldier, teahouse proprietor, and airline stewardess (except the Goan girls, who had a language all their own).

After independence, the Paks naturally started housecleaning too, evicting Sanskrit words to substitute Persian ones. So these languages which, like a revolving door, facilitated entry into a joint Hindu-Moslem culture, may be expected to rigidify into something more like a fire-door with crash bar.

At any given moment, either of these languages may be referred to as Hindustani. Like all great languages, this one is a bastard. Out of Sanskrit by Persian, it accepts all loan words freely. Taking on the coloration of its locale, Hindustani can be used, as I used it, selectively from the Soviet border on the north (where the matey at the State Guest House at Mazar-i-Sharif conducted me to the bathhouse in it) to the island Ceylon on the south (where a moneylender of unknown ethnic origin changed my currency for me in perfectly acceptable Uttar Pradesh-type Hindustani), making it the language with the third widest distribution in the world.

It should be clear by now why dictionaries were important, and why I had to travel to find them. Perhaps I have given some indication of the ferocious administrative problems which exist for any national government of India or Pakistan, of whatever stripe. Just holding the country together on a routine basis is difficult, and when local nationalism becomes inflamed, administration breaks down.

In many ways, the British approach was simpler. They

## Into the Tower of Babel

ignored all Indian languages (except for their scholarly interest) and concentrated on English. In the bad old days of the British Raj, if you wanted to get along, you learned Urdu; if you wanted to get ahead, you jolly well learned English.

English imposed on India the first unity it had ever had. For the first time in history, a northerner could talk to a southerner without an interpreter. And both could talk with the outside world. A person who spoke English could conduct a government office or transact business in any linguistic area. As a *lingua franca,* English facilitated trade, made possible a national civil service of high calibre, enabled the ruling class to ally with the British, and opened India's windows on the world.

For a language, after all, is far more than a system of sounds. It is a storehouse of culture. When English was introduced into India, it brought along the Renaissance, the Reformation, and the concept of self-government; the worlds of science, technology, and rationalism; Locke, Shakespeare, Darwin, Einstein, Marx, Freud, and Jesus Christ. The Indian who learns English transcends the provincial world of Malayalam or Baluchi, and the spiritual concerns of Hinduism or Islam, and becomes the inheritor of the western world as well.

The British realized this, and they made English a required subject from the fourth form on. They thought they would educate an endless supply of clerks and subalterns who would be able to smooth the process of administration, under British command, of course.

What the British did not foresee was that the European inheritance to which India now fell heir included nationalism: the idea that nations of distinct culture have the right to govern themselves. Once Indians became literate in English, they studied not only general accounting procedures but the *Declaration of Independence.* In one of the great dialectical shifts of history, nationalism was injected into the colonies through the efforts of the imperialists themselves, and the medium which carried the message was English.

Ultimately, Indian nationalism (combined with the weakening of England through two major world wars) brought the empire crashing down. But when the dust cleared and the British were gone, the English language remained.

Many Indians and Pakistanis wished to retain English as the official language. The entire educated class knew it already; it was neutral coinage in the interchange between Sanskritic north and Dravidian south; between Urdu west and Bengali east. And English would keep the continent in touch with the rest of the world. In fact, English was the perfect language for all practical purposes.

But at an emotional level, English was unacceptable. How could newly independent states adopt the language of their former master? Many patriots who knew English better than I, and with a better accent, refused to speak it.

English had one fatal flaw. It was foreign. Nationalists argued: so long as we speak the imperialists' tongue, we will think his thoughts. How can we be free until we drive this language out of our minds as we drove the English out of our land? To the argument that successive generations of Indians would lose contact with the rest of the world, nationalists returned the classic reply of the patriot: our own culture is superior. What has England to offer?

Both India and Pakistan retained English for substantial periods of time in order to give people time to learn the national language. When the Indian period of grace was up, all hell broke loose.

The speakers of Dravidian languages wanted to hang on to English. They had always regarded Hindi as a weapon of (north Indian!) imperialism, dating back three millennia to the Aryan invasion. The adoption of Hindi meant that a Dravidian child would have to learn Hindi at school; if he wished to enter a profession, he would then have to master English as well. At a rational level, the three-language requirement handicapped southern intellectuals. At an emotional level, they hated Hindi. It was a foreign language.

Widescale rioting broke out all over South India in 1965, causing millions of dollars worth of property damage and sixty deaths, some from self-immolation and others from murder, police or otherwise. Since it was obvious the language

*Into the Tower of Babel*

was splitting the country instead of uniting it, a compromise was reached: the national standard (as observed in examinations for civil service posts) now requires that each candidate show proficiency in two languages besides his own. One must be English. The other, for a Hindi speaker, must be a Dravidian language; for the speaker of a Dravidian language, it must be Hindi.

This formula stopped the rioting and arrested the drift toward separation. It also reinforced the principal that, if a section of the country wanted something badly enough, it could force the national government to accede, through the threat of violent secession.

The classic instance of a nationalism that would not be contained is Bengal. It can be argued that the Bengali language area has suffered more vicissitudes than most, despite the fact that its national character is most clearly defined. The British split Bengal in 1905. They did it to increase the efficiency of administration; but they also no doubt intended to curb the influence of militant Hindu nationalists who were most active in Calcutta. By cutting off the eastern provinces which held a slight Moslem majority, the British provided the kind of electoral breakwater which Moslems demanded as protection against the Hindu majority. The Hindu nationalists of West Bengal never forgave the British for this exercise in divide and rule, even though Partition was reversed in 1911, which naturally alienated the Moslems.

Probably, the 1905 partition itself came to be a factor in the growth of Bengali nationalism, which, sparked by terrorism and the brilliance of its leaders, stoked the fires of the entire Quit India movement. When independence was won in 1947, many Bengalis, Hindu and Moslem alike, were devastated to learn that freedom would renew the partition of their homeland.

West Bengal, containing the city of Calcutta, fitted easily into the Indian Union. East Bengal had a harder time getting along with Pakistan. With its factories and port cut away, East Bengal was left with only jute fields and the farmers who cultivated them. With no cities of any size, no industry, and no known resources, there was no productive base onto which to graft the hordes of refugees who poured in from Bengal, Bihar and Orissa. In the sixties, a United Nations Commission reported that "the problems of economic development posed by East Pakistan's rapidly growing population are of a kind and dimension hardly encountered in any other part of the world."

The East Pakistanis blamed the West Pakistanis for their problems. Contributing more than their share in tax revenues, they believed themselves to be discriminated against in the allocation of federal funds and appointments to civil service positions. When the expected benefits of self-rule failed to materialize, the Bengalis turned to the time-honored Indian remedy: religious persecution. Unutterable numbers of persons were expelled from both Bengals and forced to find refuge behind their own religious lines. But twenty years of communal riots failed to change the facts: the truncated economy of East Pakistan could not function, and the area was becoming less competent to feed or to govern itself with each passing year.

Heading into Dacca by plane, I looked down to see old Ganges mate with Brahmaputra, spawning rivulets, streams, brooks, and the river Padma. The unbelievable amount of water—reinforced periodically by tidal waves and daily by one of the highest rates of precipitation on the face of the globe — has created a vast swamp. This swamp contains the densest concentration of farm people to be found anywhere in the world: 1,073 per square mile. Considering that much of the land is under water much of the time, that doesn't leave much farm per family.

Dacca itself was a cloaca through which swirled the refuse of a continent on its way to find an outlet to the sea. The city was a recent growth, a product of Partition chaos, and it lacked the organization, the energy, the leadership, or the capital to make anything of itself. All it had was people and water.

Largely because no other publications procurement officer had ever gotten his gorge up sufficiently to visit the city,

*Into the Tower of Babel*

I was able to obtain bales of literature there and arrange for its transmittal through our consulate. I then got out as quickly as I could, but Dacca stayed with me as the absolute nadir of human existence. After seeing it, I too was ready to quit India.

Had I known that in 1971 India and Pakistan would go to war over East Bengal, I would have assumed each was fighting in order to force the enemy to keep the godforsaken place.

During the sixties, East Pakistanis concluded that self-rule was a chimera, that they were in fact being ruled by their Urdu-speaking co-religionists over in the west. Religious affiliation, it turned out, was not sufficient to define a nation, particularly where that nation was split into regions so distinct from one another in other ways. The seething of the dissatisfied easterners grew beyond the powers of the Pakistani government to control, and led first to the abandonment of Dacca as provincial capital, then to the downfall of the national government. Nationwide elections in which the Bengali candidate gained a majority posed the possibility that now the West would be governed by the East; so the elections were disavowed and the winner jailed. This led to civil disorder, brutal repression, and the flight of ten million refugees into India.

India's response was conditioned by all that had happened since the first partition of Bengal in 1905. Still persuaded that Bengal was one nation, and fired by the militant Hindu revivalism that has been so characteristic of Bengali nationalism, India invaded and snuffed out Moslem sovereignty in East Pakistan.

Is Bangladesh to be absorbed into Mother India, so that 1905 may be completely reversed? Or will Bangladesh herself act as a magnet, pulling its western half away from India in order to complete Bengal as an autonomous nation? To put the question another way: will the centrifugal force of Bengali and other nationalisms overwhelm the centripetal force of Indian union?

The question can be asked of many linguistic areas. An

## Krishna Smiled

interesting comparison can be made with Coorg, which is one area with a history of sticking to the Union. Throughout the Mutiny of 1857 its people remained loyal to the British, and under the Disarmament Act which followed, they were the only clan permitted to retain personal weapons. Yet today, while Bengal is resurgent, Coorg has disappeared from view. I think it is because it had no dictionary.

I clanked into Mercara, capital of Coorg, aboard a moribund bus one rainy afternoon and stepped out under a banner reading WELCOME, which turned out to be not for me but for the Commander-in-Chief of the Indian Armed Forces, who was coming home on leave. The Kodagus, who claim to be the original settlers around here, still provide India with some of her most distinguished soldiers. Apparently unrelated to other ethnic groups, Kodagus form a separate caste only partially within Hinduism, and retain unique traditions, social customs and dress. Among other peculiarities, the women wear their saris backwards. Naturally, when I heard of them I felt I must obtain a dictionary of their language.

After handshakes all around from the welcoming committee, who were really rather surprised to see me instead of the Commander-in-Chief (he arrived a few minutes later, by jeep) I was invited to stay at the palace of Tipu Sultan.

This palace, which contains the jail, the press, most government offices as well as the guest house, must be seen during the monsoon to be properly appreciated. That means about any time of year, for this part of the coast benefits from all the monsoons India can conjure up, regardless of season.

The fortress's grey stone walls are covered with slime from incessant damp weather; the windows are small and suitably defensible. In the courtyard, stand twin reminders of Tipu Sultan's humor.

It was the custom in the Sultan's court to waken the monarch each morning with a blast from his favorite elephant. One night the Sultan caroused late and left orders not to be disturbed, but no one informed the elephant, who appeared in his accustomed way. As he knelt beneath the Sultan's window, his trunk raised in loyal salute and a cheerful reveille

## Into the Tower of Babel

bursting from his heart, His Majesty, who was hung over, shot the beast and went back to bed. But remorse seizing him upon awakening, he caused the elephant and his mate to be immortalized in stone.

Looking out my bedroom window on one side, I could see the ill-fated elephant lovers. On the other side, I could see down into a smaller but equally grey courtyard which was also occupied by something of an elephant.

This one was upright, potbellied and sloshed with orange paint: Ganesh, or Ganapati as he is sometimes known. As I understand it, this god once enjoyed human form even as I or you, but was decapitated by his father Shiva. Thereafter, in response to the mother's pleas, Shiva seized the first head that came along, which happened to be an elephant's, and placed it on the child's neck. Ever since, this haphazard god goes galumphing through the Hindu pantheon quite happily. Ganesh is sagacious and wise, remover of obstacles; people pray to him before starting out on a new enterprise. He is also a roly-poly gourmand.

Anyone named Judith has a natural interest in decapitation. I knew Ganesh's story better than some others. One night, he was returning home on mouseback from an orgy with friends when he slid off his gaadi and fell into a puddle, splitting his trousers. The moon, who happened to be looking, forgot to show the respect which is due the gods, and laughed. For this, Ganesh cursed him. Ever since, it has been bad luck to look at the moon on the night of Ganesha Chaturthi.

As luck would have it, that is the night on which I landed at Tipu Sultan's palace. When the moon rose, about a hundred worshippers crowded into the tiny courtyard below my window to wreathe the idol in chains of marigold, ring bells, burn incense, and ostentatiously refrain from looking at the moon.

Child of the West as I am, I was curious to learn whether Ganesha Chaturthi coincided with some natural phenomenon (I had already realized that Hindu Holi coincided with Jewish Purim, and the ten days of Dusserah run from Rosh Hashonah to Yom Kippur). I naturally looked at the moon. It looked like any other moon, but I knew I had drawn upon myself the curse of Ganesh. I could be freed from the curse only by being slandered.

I spent the following day dodging a host of men named Appiah who darted out from dark corners of the fort each time I tried to leave it, holding vast black umbrellas over me and protesting that I must not expose myself to the inclement weather. Whatever else you can say about Coorg, it sure isn't clement. Politely but insistently I was kept incarcerated in my room until afternoon, when I had an appointment to see the Chief Commissioner, who ruled the state on behalf of the central government. It was clear that I would not be allowed to move without his approval. So I sat and listened to the shouts from the women's prison, spied on an army recruiter at work up the hall, and watched the rain ooze down the sides of the two massive black elephants below my window.

The Chief Commissioner, to my surprise, was a Sikh; somewhat far from home, I thought. We spent the afternoon sparring over whether or not I would be allowed to buy any books in Coorg. He claimed there were none published there; but I was not to be permitted to find out for myself, since our embassy had not notified him, through the foreign ministry, that I was coming. Someone else had, however: the Dancing General whose tête-a-tête I had fled some months earlier in Delhi was of course a Coorg, and he had sent advance warning of Mata Hari's arrival. Presumably this was why I was being sequestered. It did no good to explain that I wanted only to buy such harmless items as a dictionary of the Kodagu language and copies of the local newspaper. I had wounded Coorg's amour propre, and it would take a while to recover from the blow. Meanwhile, would I come to dinner that night?

A banquet was being given by the CC in honor of the C-in-C, to use the language of the area, largely composed of initials. This was precisely the kind of event I usually tried to avoid. But it seemed preferable to hanging around the fort all

## Into the Tower of Babel

evening. Anyway, I was practically ordered to appear, presumably because the people keeping an eye on me wanted to go to the banquet themselves. I fretted because I had left my luggage in Mysore (beautiful, happy, cheery, green Mysore!) and travelled up to Mercara in a sensible suit and oxfords, never dreaming I would hit the cocktail circuit here, of all places. There was no railroad, no airport, no telephone, only one all-weather road. But there were cocktails.

I need not have worried. During siesta, the wife of the Deeyem (after some time I realized this was Coorg for District Magistrate) appeared with servant. Opening a box, she displayed a complete outfit for me, including red powder to rub in the part of my hair. So I went to the banquet wearing a gorgeous red, pink, orange, and red sari, a garment which covered me as amply as it did her. The lady wrapped it round me Kodagu style: gathering it at the back of my waist, she wound it tightly upward so as to flatten my bosom, pinning it tightly at the shoulder in the way a gift wrapper at a department store adds the final bow. She topped me off with a little kerchief bound too tightly round my head, which subdued my hair that had frizzed up in the rain but did nothing for my ears. I tried to poke these inside the scarf but the DM's wife disapproved. Perhaps ears were sexy here, as bosoms elsewhere.

The banquet got underway lugubriously beneath a great tent that had been erected on the palace grounds. It looked to be a dull affair. The C-in-C resumed our conversation about the weather where we had left off in the gardens of Rashtrapathi Bhavan. I wondered where the witty CC could be. Late to his own party.

I was happy to see a platoon of bearers descending upon us with drinks. Coorg not only had continuous monsoon, it had Prohibition as well, and so managed to be both sopping wet and howling dry. The DM had kindly provided relief for us, since he gave out the drinking licenses around here. Naturally, under the circumstances, everyone felt honor-bound to drink as much as possible.

When all the guests were seated, the air rang with the

## Krishna Smiled

flourish of imaginary trumpets and in swept what looked like the royal family of Yehupitz. It was the CC himself, Colonel Daya Singh Bedi, or else it was Ronald Colman pretending to be Daya Singh Bedi. His turban rode high on his head, its starched tail stiffly erect and its silver tinsel showering out behind him as he marched. Waxed moustachioes framed a most aristocratic sneer of the kind you seldom see any more. In his wake glided the heir apparent, followed by a morbidly beautiful girl in gold.

Daya Singh Bedi rearranged the seating so as to place me on his right. Ignoring the C-in-C, he proceeded to talk to no one but me, paying me the most effusive compliments. Suddenly, he switched to Hindustani and, calling across my lap to the C-in-C referred to me as *"esa larki"* ("this maid") with all the mixed connotations the English phrase has. It was clear he was socially isolated, and easy to understand why.

I turned to my host and asked him why he was living in the south, among people who didn't care for him too much. The Kodagus, after all, are a distinguished warrior caste with an ancient lineage, and might not care to be governed by a Sikh.

He smiled his winsome smile, which made him look like a boy of twelve: "True enough, but how can I return home? I would surely be hanged."

The banquet proceeded through pilau and curry, with yoghurt to cool the flames and cardamum seeds to extinguish the fumes. Our table was lined with scholarly-looking gentlemen wearing black tunics over white pantaloons, curved daggers thrust into their wide sashes, and neat red and white turbans which they bound evenly over their brows. I always found it difficult to talk to a man who wears his hat straight on, like the lid of a pot. So I turned to a man seated across from me who was wearing a western suit and no hat.

He had recognized me, for we once spent the night together. Air India used to arrange its schedule so that at 3 A.M. planes zeroed in on Nagpur, Central India, from the four major cities of Delhi, Bombay, Calcutta, and Madras. While the planes refuelled, passengers played musical chairs, dis-

*Into the Tower of Babel*

embarking from the plane which had brought them and boarding the one which had just come from their destination. Then the planes turned around and went home.

The arrangement usually worked well, and when it broke down, travellers had the opportunity of meeting anybody who was anybody, because all cross-country traffic funnelled through Nagpur. Of course, since these encounters occurred in the middle of the night, you didn't always carry away a clear memory of them.

This was a newspaperman, however, and he had total recall. "I was about to read your hand, Laikinji," he said. (A mental image of the mists lifting from Nagpur airport, the last bushels of pan being hoisted aboard, hurried goodbyes and exchange of addresses.) "May I see it now?"

The proposal was met with interest by others seated nearby. Palmistry is a science; people assumed they would learn real things about me, and of course I was as much an object of curiosity for them as they were for me.

I had no fear, regarding palmistry as a harmless parlor game. So I extended my palm, and the journalist read the truth from it easily and accurately.

"You came close to death within your first three months of life. You have five different given names. You resemble your father's family more than your mother's." He hesitated, then continued. The leap into the future. "After returning home, you may go to England. You will probably marry when you are thirty-one."

There was a gasp from the DM's wife. "That is not a nice thing to say to Judy," she said. The other women nodded agreement when the prophesy had been translated. In this country, a woman who remains unmarried to that age is a social disaster. They felt I had been slandered.

But I was quite happy with the prophecy. Being "slandered" relieved me of the curse of Ganesha Chaturthi, incurred by looking at the moon the night before. And so far as the events which were foretold, everything came off on schedule.

I left Mercara in the usual driving rain, travelling down

the mountain with my bag no heavier than when I'd gone up the mountain three days earlier. The CC had seen to that. He had prevented me from buying any books in the Kodagu language, if indeed any existed. The whole damn place measured eighty miles by thirty, and I shed not a tear when its cockleshell of state got zapped in the 1956 states reorganization.

My experience in the Indian Tower of Babel persuaded me that you can diagnose a case of nationalism by counting the number of dictionaries in print. Where there is no dictionary, there is no nation: Coorg slipped wordlessly off the map despite the ancient lineage of its founding clan.

The situation was quite different in Pepsu, where the citizens dismembered their state along lines imposed by competing Hindi and Gurmukhi dictionaries, each side then retiring into the privacy and spoils of its tribal dream. Their languages had always been heroic, but now they felt called upon to demonstrate that fact. The linguistic rupture was even more traumatic in Bengal, where the secession of Bangladesh called into question the very survival of the rump state of West Pakistan.

A new era of self-celebration begins when dictionaries make language accessible to all. Universal languages such as English or Latin are scorned, and vernacular artists praised. Native encyclopedists burst into print, proudly displaying the tribe's heretofore secret artifacts to the sunshine of world opinion. Native poets extoll la belle Patrie, or female circumcision, or the goddess Kali. Bengali literature has been famed for at least a century; during much of that time, Bengalis have been staggering through havoc toward self-determination. Nationalism begins with dictionaries, goes on through poetry and song, and proceeds by way of cracked skulls and burned-out homes to independence.

The question of identity was at hazard from the first moment of creation of India and Pakistan. Could these new states create a sense of national identity which would be strong enough to override the powerful nationalisms crammed within their borders? Or would the regional nationalisms with

*Into the Tower of Babel*

their roots in language and historical association overpower the newer concepts of India, of Pakistan?

Pakistan, starting from a weaker position, has not been able to withstand the centrifugal pull. May she not try to console herself in Kashmir for the loss of Bengal (and of Hyderabad before Bengal)?

India has met successive tests brought on by dissidents from within and by a series of confrontations with Pakistan and China. She has remained intact and even extended her influence among Bengalis and Pukhtoons. None of her linguistic or ethnic groups has utilized periods of stress to bolt the Union.

But we have not seen all the spin-off yet. There are languages still to be heard from, dictionaries yet to be published, anthems yet to be composed. Only when all the myriad language groups of India and Pakistan have roused themselves to awareness, will there be a lasting answer to the riddle of the Continent's unity.

# 7

*Inadvertently, I introduce Henry Miller to the Defense Minister of Nepal*

I am unclear just which General SJBR was Defense Minister of Nepal in 1953, but perhaps the right one will read this and send me back my autographed copy of *Tropic of Capricorn*. Although I have never met the General, I rely on his taste: he can see for himself that this book is not the sort of present likely to be sent to him by the United States Library of Congress.

The ploy by which Henry Miller was introduced to the reigning family of Nepal through the facilities of the Library was the result of the determined one-up-manship of my British friend and fellow bibliophile, Thackeray.

Thackeray was one of those detached Caucasians who, unable to bear the loss of Empire, continued to float about the Orient for no discernible reason. I believe he was at that time retained by the University of the Wittwatersrand to investigate the influence of altitude on extrasensory perception.

His researches led him quite naturally to Nepal. This

## I introduce Henry Miller

was in the palmy days before Cinemascope and hippies had reduced that kingdom to a series of commonplaces. At that time, Nepal was almost inaccessible, and Thackeray bicycled in, or something, across the mosquitoed plain and trackless jungle, making good his boast that with his inoffensive physique and devious mind, he was indistinguishable from an Indian.

He didn't die of malaria, and he did meet the General, one of the Shumsher Jung Bahadur Rana generals, and a good man with a palm leaf. The SJBRs have been prominent in Nepalese politics for centuries, making and breaking kings with word and sword much in the manner of the Medici maneuvering the Papacy.

Thackeray, with his keen nose for rumor, managed to get in and out of the country during one of those lulls in the processes of government formation which periodically reduce the numbers of the clan who are available for cultural activity.

Later, sitting over a lemonade at the Delhi Gymkhana Club, Thackeray expressed to me his complete satisfaction with his Nepalese excursion. Not only had he conducted a series of controlled experiments (on sherpa guides who, he thinks, developed extrasensory perceptivity through centuries of communicating with one another from mutually isolated Himalayan peaks. It was like Swiss yodelling, or the whistling of Basque shepherds); but . . .

Thackeray went on to describe the market place at Kathmandu, which he claims is overlooked by a magnificent pair of purple eyes mounted on a tower. These eyes look directly into the living room of that General SJBR who was Nepal's Minister of Defense at the time of Thackeray's visit. The two of them became friendly, and it seems they spent a great deal of time on the floor sorting palm leaves.

The palm leaf is Nepal's answer to papyrus. It is dried and accordion-pleated before being inscribed, so that, as Thackeray showed me, each manuscript looks rather like a tongue depressor. These particular manuscripts dealt with science, history, and astrology, all of which are related in the sight—or insight—of those great purple eyes.

## Krishna Smiled

Forgetting just how expert a Lifeman Thackeray was, I allowed my empathy to run away with me, and therefore merited no better than to be selected for carrying out that act of retaliatory generosity without which Thackeray could never have persuaded himself to accept the palm leaves as a gift from General SJBR.

Evidently, Thackeray passed these along to the United States Library of Congress, and arranged for the library to send the General a fifty-foot shelf of books for his birthday in exchange. But I knew nothing of the arrangement, having lost track of Thackeray when he left Delhi.

I continued peaceably about my business buying books, and eventually wound up sightseeing along the Ganges with a bookdealer named Kapur, who wanted to make sure I hit all the architectural high spots before leaving Banaras.

It turned out that his favorite spot was the Temple of Love, built some centuries ago by a compassionate Nepalese prince who considered Indians unimaginative, though admittedly they functioned all right. The tiny building, insignificant as it appeared from the river bank, proved on closer inspection to be swarming with miniature stone voluptuaries disporting in convivial groups of three and four.

Having ordered the boatman to dock, Kapur urged me up a disused stairway cut out of rock and shored up by chunks of stone. When we arrived before the Temple of Love, a hefty young monk crawled (literally) through a low doorway of it, dragging his pointer behind him. With his grizzled beard and torn orange sarong, he looked as though he had been lost in the temple for some weeks.

Hefting his ten-foot pole at the overhanging eaves, he pointed at the elaborate carvings, intoning a text imperfectly memorized and partially obliterated by the passage of years.

Ignoring the religious aspect of the sculptures, the monk got right down to business.

Monk: "Here, two lady, one gentleman, bftsk wallag-mala."

Kapur: "Gentleman is taking enjoyment of one lady, while other lady holds lantern for them to see."

*I introduce Henry Miller*

Monk: (moving on to next tableau) "Here, three lady achabatnaguptaghy."

Kapur: "Fat lady in middle is not satisfied with passion of husband, so two ladies, one each side, with bamboo sticks . . ."

When the recital was finished, the monk offered to show me his giant lingam for ten rupees. I declined, not knowing whether the lingam was alive or not, and dragged Kapur back down the rocky steps to the relative safety of the river.

Kapur, in a mood of religious elevation, persisted in explaining the temple tableaux to me all the way to the railway station. Once there, we had a final set-to about a compendium of neo-Sanskritic anatomical terms which he was trying to pawn off on me, and then the train started.

Waving somewhat exaggeratedly, I thought, he tossed a book through the window onto my lap, where a note fell out reading "Come back soon to Banaras." It was a lovely book, the pages still uncut except for the autographed frontispiece, and the soft Swedish cover so seductive that for a moment I honestly regretted that I would never come back to Banaras.

That was how I acquired the unexpurgated *Tropic of Capricorn* back in the primitive days before *Roth v. U.S.*, when Miller was proscribed in his native land. I read it on the trip back to Delhi, but it seemed quite tame after Banarsi temples.

One acrid June day a yoke of oxen carted an immense crate up to my doorstep in Jangpura Extension, and made as if to dump it on Sri Puri's geraniums.

There was not then, nor at any future time, a bill of lading, and not being gifted with extrasensory perception, I seized upon the excellent opportunity offered by the bullocks and had the crate drawn and quartered.

There were books inside—one hundred of them. As near as I could make out, they were a tribute to me from the Library of Congress. This was puzzling, since the library had up till then displayed no particular affection for me. They were willing enough to shelve my acquisitions, but we never reached the point where we shared intimacies.

## Krishna Smiled

My neighbors took a utilitarian view of the books, and soon came round asking when the "library" would open. It seemed the books could serve no better purpose, so I set up a card index and opened another front for capitalism.

The doubt which lurked in my mind was activated by a telegram from the library six months later, asking whether the "representative collection of Americana" (I thought then, and still think, this an extravagant description at cable rates) would reach Kathmandu in time for General SJBR's birthday, by inference a day on which he was likely to miss his palm leaves. The date they gave me was one week later.

Thackeray was by then among the Basques, so I consulted Flagstaff of the American Express. He was a conscientious fellow; had sold me a plane ticket once, and the train I had intended to take fell into a gully. Flagstaff confirmed that there was no easy way into Nepal. The automobiles Thackeray had reported seeing there had been dissected and carried up the Himalayas on the backs of porters. Clearly, I would have no time for this sort of thing.

There was still Jaya Narayan, my dancing friend at the Nepalese Embassy. I always thought of him as my dancing friend because it was his invariable custom, whenever our crowd went nightclubbing, to wait until the food was served and then invite me to step out onto the floor. I owed many cold dinners to his love for the dance, which he executed abominably, his round face resting on my shoulder, his ear attuned to the music of distant gongs.

J. N. informed me that His Highness King Tribhuvan of Nepal was accustomed to flying down to Calcutta for the weekend, and if I could get the crate across country by Friday, he would make sure it got on the royal plane for the journey back to Kathmandu.

The next morning I went on a raiding party, beating up the streets a house at a time, seizing from terrified and non-English-speaking women the books their husbands had borrowed from me. Most of my neighbors were refugees from the partitioned Punjab, and there is no telling what scenes of violence and looting were recalled to their minds as I pounced on my books.

*I introduce Henry Miller*

Eventually, I was only one short, and throwing in my own cherished volume of Cotton Mather's *Sermons*, I summoned the carpenter, the cartman, and the bullocks. The books were crated and started on their six-mile journey to the railway station. It would take them six hours to get there. I hesitated to calculate the time to Calcutta, a distance of nearly a thousand miles.

That was the last I saw of the representative collection of Americana, and incidentally also of Henry Miller. Presumably he got into the crate and was smuggled into Nepal by the King, who would have handed him over to the Defense Minister, who, if my history is right, is a lineal descendant of the prince who built that cunning little temple in Banaras.

The way I feel is that this particular gentleman is unlikely to be upset by *Tropic of Capricorn*. Nevertheless, misrepresentation has taken place, and I believe the library would not want to include the book in its birthday presentation. So if someone will pay my way, I'll go up to Kathmandu and retrieve the book myself.

# 8

## Touching the Untouchable

I was returning from a successful raid on Bombay with a carload of books. At 120° Fahrenheit, I kept the car windows closed. To open them was to open a blast furnace. Nevertheless, the car was inches deep in dust, grey powdery dust that found its way into my palate, my inner ear, my navel, and my nerves.

As dusk began erasing all those milestones which had not yet been uprooted by the government in accordance with its pledge to extirpate English from the countryside, it seemed best to find a place to spend the night. I felt fortunate when, at the outskirts of Dhulia, I came upon the Khan Hotel.

It wasn't much of a hotel as those things go, but I rented a room and set the water to running deliriously cold from the spigot which was set at knee height in the wall above the slimy concrete floor of the washroom. I stripped my clothes off, and then I heard a cough outside my door.

*Touching the Untouchable*

The cougher was Emmanuel. In all the months he had worked for me as my bearer, he had never come to my door uninvited. His demeanor was most circumspect. Once when I came upon him smoking, he swallowed the cigarette. So when he coughed audibly, I figured the hotel must be on fire.

I got back into my blue jeans and hair shirt. I didn't have anything else to put on because the lock of the car trunk had jammed, depriving me of clothing, toothbrush, and five pounds of Viennese chocolate which I was importing into the Delhi desert. When I got back home and had the trunk pried open, I laid the whole sticky suitcase tenderly in the refrigerator. My clothes were a total loss, but I had what was the largest chocolate bar ever seen east of Suez.

"Is the hotel burning?" I asked.

"Missahibji," said Emmanuel, shifting his bantam weight from one foot to the other, hands clasped behind his back, meaning he was going to ask a favor, "is better go."

I closed the door on him and returned to the washroom. The spigot shined in the dark like Parsifal's vision of the Holy Grail. But as I turned the water on once more, Emmanuel made distressed sounds from behind the bathroom door itself.

"Missahibji, is better go. Go to Hindu hotel."

This interested me, for I had never known that Emmanuel had a preference for Hindus. In fact, I believed his family were originally Moslems before they became Methodists. Again, I put on my jeans and shirt and went into the bedroom.

"Why?" and I fixed him with what I hoped was an imperious stare. He wasn't going to get me back out into that dustbowl again without a pretty good reason.

"This Moslem place," Emmanuel kept on, giving me half a thought at a time and letting it sink in.

"It looks clean enough," I said, and indeed it did, especially since I had asked the hotel sweeper to remove the chamberpot full of urine that had been standing on the windowsill when I arrived. At the time, I wondered whether the urine was placed in the pot before or after the pot was placed on the sill.

"I went down kitchen, Missahibji, speak to cook for your dinner. Cook smoking pipe with sweeper. Is better go to Hindu place."

I sat down. "Jesus Christ, Emmanuel! Is this what Christ died on Calvary for?"

Emmanuel knew me for the two-faced cad I am. He had never seen me go to church. But he looked uncomfortable enough for me to follow up my advantage with a lecture on the Brotherhood of Man, the Iniquity of the Caste System, and Emmanuel's personal duty as a Christian to help break down the barriers that separate man from man.

At the end of the lecture, Emmanuel shifted his weight back to the other army-booted foot and said, with more than usual outspokenness, that I was missing the point. If the cook shared his pipe with the sweeper, then the two men would eat together too. That meant the sweeper ate in the kitchen.

"Oh, Lord, Emmanuel, he *should* eat in the kitchen. He's a human being, you God-damned Indian."

"While he eat in kitchen, sweeper help Cook peel potatoes."

I began to feel a tiny doubt. "Yes?"

"Sweeper peel potatoes. But every day he go clean chamberpots. And he no have soap, Missahibji." Smiling shyly, Emmanuel scooped up imaginary faeces from an imaginary pot with his hand and plopped them softly on the ground. Then he wiped his hand on his trouser leg.

We went out and found a Hindu hotel, where chamberpots are also in use, but where the people who clean the pots are untouchable. Not just their presence, but their *shadow* is untouchable. No caste Hindu would allow an Untouchable or his shadow into the kitchen. No matter how I felt about caste, I was less likely to contract amoebic dysentery, liver flukes, jaundice, or hookworm among Hindus than among casteless Moslems.

Reclining in the upper branches of the caste system is very pleasant. You need never bother about waste disposal, not even to diaper your own baby, because there are untouchable people to do it. They enter your home by a special door

## Touching the Untouchable

and leave by that same door where in they went taking your excreta with them. You don't ever have to worry about plumbing. Your toilet may not run, but your Untouchable will. He's been running for centuries.

It takes awhile for an American to realize that an Untouchable really is untouchable, no matter how democratic the American may be. We are accustomed to prejudices which evaporate when confronted with reality; "contact and acquaintance" is our social workers' prescription for eroding social barriers.

But Indian prejudices turn out to be based upon reality. Fantastically inhuman reality.

An American Embassy officer, recently arrived in India, was stalking some new construction being erected for the embassy. The entire exterior of the building was scaffolded, with women and children clambering up and down bearing heavy baskets on their heads. Bill deplored child labor, and the caste system which decrees that certain little girls are born to be hod carriers and toilet cleaners. He called over a little worker of seven or eight years of age and patted her on the head. Then he smelled his hand and peered into the basket, which was wicker and leaking. She was thoroughly untouchable, a veritable pradigm of the sociologist's self-fulfilling prophecy.

In India, human beings take the place of plumbing. In the absence of the latter (which you can't afford), you use the former (which are plentiful and cheap). But you don't pet your sewer pipe, or act as though it were human.

I never acquisitioned any literature on the caste system. This may strike the reader as a strange omission. But it is as difficult for a Hindu as for a Scotch Presbyterian to see himself as others see him, and what was written about the Indian social system while I was in India came mostly from foreigners who were not themselves hobbled by the system they were writing about. This is not surprising: Americans, in search of an adequate conceptualization of our racial dilemma, commissioned a Swede, Gunnar Myrdal, to carry it out.

Caste determines what a person is: what he may eat or

## Krishna Smiled

not eat, whom he may eat it with, what clothes he wears, whom he may marry, what job he will hold, and where he may live. No matter what a man's merit, he may not rise to a higher caste in this life, nor sink to a lower one through bad luck.

As an adjunct to this system, millions of people have no caste. They are outcastes, untouchables, or as Gandhi called them, Harijans, Children of God. In some areas, Harijans could not walk the streets of their home towns. The only jobs they could hold were loathesome ones such as scavenging and leather tanning. When they sallied forth to work, they had to announce their contaminating presence in a loud voice. They could not draw water from the village well, nor eat with caste persons, nor attend school, nor enter a temple to pray. Nor has there ever been a way for a man to acquire caste. The most he could hope for was that if he played his cards right, he might be rewarded by a better birth in his next incarnation.

There have been instances in which Harijan groups have adopted the customs of caste Hindus, moved out of their "polluting" occupations, and successfully projected themselves into the caste hierarchy. It is also not unknown for a caste to move into a more prestigious occupation and, by its collective efforts, rise on the social scale. Efforts to climb the hierarchy, of course, are predicated on the legitimacy of that hierarchy.

My experience with caste and outcaste persuaded me that, whatever "democracy" may mean to us, it cannot mean the same to an Indian. The rigid social compartmentalization and hierarchic relationships blessed by religion are as far removed as one can get from the American ideal—breached, it is true, but the ideal—of equality.

Yet India has been working a representative system of government for more than two decades. One way to understand this apparent anomaly is to see caste associations as interest groups which enable their members, many of them political illiterates, to participate in electoral politics in a meaningful way.

## Touching the Untouchable

Chauvinists sometimes claim it was the British who imposed caste on India, following their policy of divide and rule. The claim cannot be supported historically. It is more likely the result of an ages-long process which had completed its evolution long before the British had heard of India.

According to the most likely theory, the original, dark-skinned Dravidian inhabitants of India were overwhelmed by successive waves of light-skinned Aryans from the north. Defeated in war, the Dravidians were pushed to the southernmost tip of their peninsula (where their languages survive today) and likewise to the bottom of the social system. In short, they were enslaved; bound in some cases to the land, in others to particular trades. Thereafter, the conquerors kept them in check through a system of rigid rules determining all aspects of behavior, and stabilized the system by giving it the sanction of religion.

Untouchability was outlawed by independent India. Harijans were enfranchised along with everybody else in 1948 and guaranteed their rights as equal citizens before the law. It is a crime now to enforce caste rules. But as every American knows, establishing a legal claim to equality, and enforcing that claim, is a man of a different color.

I never took kindly to criticism of American racism as levelled by an Indian. As contemptible as it may be to refuse service to blacks at lunch counters, I know of no one who has regarded his food as polluted through the shadow of a black falling across it. Nor can segregated bathrooms compare in viciousness with denying people access to the village's only source of water.

Although the question is boggled in India, I formed the impression that caste is also a matter of race. Upper castes tend to be light-complected, lower castes dark. In fact, the Indian social system is like a poorly dyed garment—the top has faded, draining all the color to the bottom. The lower you are in the social scale, the darker your color is likely to be. There are, of course, enough exceptions to prove the rule.

I had an acquaintance who was Undersecretary to one of the ministries in the government of India. One day while

## Krishna Smiled

we were having tea at the Swiss Coffee House on Connaught Circus, he told me he was planning to marry. He was thirty years old, well above the age at which most Indians have founded their families. Naturally, he would consider marrying only within his own elite caste, and preferred a girl from his ancestral village.

But Shyam Lall had been cut off from his home by Partition. Now that things had calmed a bit, he planned to go to Sind on his annual leave and bring a bride back to Delhi. He had already written to the village elders asking them to scout up some suitable candidates.

I wished him luck, and told him I would be very happy to see him back in Delhi soon, decently wed. And Shyam Lall did, in due course, return to Delhi, but without a bride.

There were very few single girls available of the right specifications. I commiserated. Not even one? Well, perhaps one. She was literate, the right age, and the dowry would have been sufficient to enable him to study in U.K. for a year . . . . Shyam Lall's voice trickled off into uncertainty.

"Why didn't you marry her?" I prompted. "She sounds perfect."

"She was very dark," Shyam Lall replied.

I couldn't bring myself to look at him. On the surface of the black formica table top where I looked instead, my face appeared reflected as a dull blob. There was nothing but a shadow of Shyam Lall, for he was black, as black as the formica.

In the centuries-long process by which caste has become linked to color, it is apparent that the British and the Aryans had some help from the Indians.

Some change is taking place: as landless farmers migrate to the cities, as workers on factory assembly lines rub shoulders, as children crowd into city schools, caste rules blur over. And as in our own country, the weight of law makes a difference.

The first week of my stay in India, a Harijan was arrested for attempting to enter a temple. During my last week in India, a similar incident occurred. But in the later case, the

## Touching the Untouchable

Harijan complained and the complaint reached the Chief Minister of Bihar. Gathering the entire cabinet about him, the Minister commenced to walk from the State House to the temple, gathering Harijans behind him as he went. Knocking at the temple gates, he demanded admission. The priests refused to open the gates, whereupon they were arrested.

The story should sound not unfamiliar to us now, but it happened in India before it happened in our own South.

How does a person who is without caste find his place in a caste society? How does one sniff out barriers in order to avoid them, and at the same time retain one's status as an acceptable guest? Caste was here before I was. And of course, a diplomat's mission is not to reform, but to make contact with the society in which he finds himself.

I was standing on the Mall at Darjeeling, when my friend Shankar, a former Chief of Intelligence and a Kashmiri Brahmin, sailed up to me in his Cambridge boating jacket and his paisley cravat. We fell into conversation about Indian ethnography. Shankar claimed that he could look at any man or woman in India and spot his caste and where he came from, within a radius of twenty miles.

Studying geography in people's faces was a hobby of mine too (one that was to get me into trouble later in Afghanistan), so I readily accepted instruction from Shankar who, God and the British knew, was an authority.

First he picked a Bhutia—close-cropped Mongolian head, calf muscles as big as my waist, bulky yellow and red kimona. Next, a covey of Buddhist monks in saffron robes on a pilgrimage to some holy glacier a hundred miles into the mountains. Then a train of Tibetan yak wallopers, big smelly swagmen swinging down through the passes to trade their gewgaws in Delhi.

The majority of people passing by were sherpas, the beasts of burden of the Himalayas. Men, women, and others who elsewhere might have been children, labored up and down the mountain with loads the size of their own bodies strapped to their backs, saddled cruelly round their foreheads. They wore rags of no nationality, and they all looked alike in the way that cattle all look alike. There was a deadly uniformity in their gait and a tremendous *nothing* in their eyes. You looked at them and *nothing* looked back at you. For them there was no beauty in the mountains, which were their doom and which I had travelled a thousand miles to see. All they saw was the spot eight inches in front of them where they had somehow or other to put the other foot.

Then this Mona Lisa appeared, mincing along in a grey nightgown sort of thing with a striped apron over it. As cool as Kanchenjunga, I thought to myself, and as inaccessible.

"That," said Shankar, "is a Lepcha." Not: "She's a Lepcha," or "What a remarkably handsome woman, isn't it?" or anything else to indicate she was human, but "that" as though he were back in the police station among his files. I began to realize how aloof Shankar felt from these costumed natives, he in his Cambridge boating jacket and properly tied cravat. He had photographs of all of India's fantastic variety of humanity cataloged and filed in his orderly brain; and each photograph was stamped "Wanted."

Darjeeling is one of those Ararats of privilege which were left protruding when the British tide receded from India. It fronts on a stupefying range of the Himalayas, placed there by a beneficent Raj to shield Europeans from the summer of the Indian plains. Every street seems to run slambang up against the flank of Kanchenjunga, only Kanchenjunga is fifty miles away.

The monstrous overstuffed hotel where both Shankar and I were staying had fine vantage points for painting the mountains without getting in the way of the breeze that comes from the shanty town below the Mall. You could still be borne along this Mall at a trot by six uniformed Indians with bells on their feet that jingle quicker than the mules' bells do as the caravans pick their mountain way at a pace less likely to kill the animals.

In the days of the British Raj, hill stations such as Darjeeling, Mussoori, Simla, Shillong, Ootacomund provided the exiled administrators and their families with a refuge from India. There they built little cottages right out of Teddington-

## Touching the Untouchable

on-Thames and stone churches that were pure Stowe-in-the-Wold. God was generally believed to be still alive, and the monarchy certainly was. Billiard tables and polo ponies were ever at the ready, and only on Sunday was curry served at the Club.

The receding tides of Empire left the hill stations stranded like Noah's Arks. A few of the old inhabitants lingered on, afraid to go home because their money wouldn't go as far in England, and besides, they had been so long away that "home" was nearly as strange to them as India was.

So the half-empty grand hotels were home to the survivors of the flood of independence: herds of old warhorses and army mules, giant panda lady missionaries who still used the word "native," bilious giraffe-like planters wandering morosely about buying drinks for anyone who would listen to their labor problems, and the British Colonel (Ret.) and his lady, complaining about their livers loudly over dinner: the hippopotamus and his mate.

These creatures were remnants of the old ruling caste, and "caste" must be taken seriously in this country of caste. The western visitor must decide upon arrival whether to throw his lot in with them or go over to the unknown, to the Indians.

Going over to the Indians is not easy, because then the whites write you off. The white man who has never before thought of caste may panic at the prospect of losing his. And for what? The Indian Indians won't trust you anyway, and the Kept Indians have been admitted to the Club.

It is very trying to be white in Darjeeling. You feel guilty of some terrible crime. But you look around, and there is no crime. Just these beautiful mountains which no one can climb. Practically.

A man approached the point where Shankar and I were standing. He had the blunt, bronzed face and squared-off hands of a sherpa; he wore western trousers and a zipper jacket. His clothes were not in themselves so unusual that one would pick him out because of them. Nevertheless, Shankar and I noticed him at the same instant. My friend, the

## Krishna Smiled

former Chief of Intelligence, scrutinized him. Then, dismissing him with a gesture of the hand said, "That man is a Nepalese."

"Don't be silly!" I replied. "It's Tenzing." It wasn't his nationality I was talking about—Tenzing is a Nepalese and a Sherpa—but the man was transcendantly Tenzing.

He walked erect, his arms swung out unencumbered, his eyes moved brightly from point to point, and when I smiled at him, he smiled back. In order for a sherpa to look one brightly in the eye, there had to have been an act of God in his life. The sort of act of God that hauls a man to the top of Mount Everest and places the arm of his white, educated, wealthy, European, sophisticated, simple brother around him. It was Tenzing all right.

Tenzing headed toward us—though Shankar hadn't admitted yet that it was he. I sensed his dilemma. If the man was Tenzing, he was a sherpa and practically an Untouchable. Gandhi had called Untouchables the Children of God; Brylcream and Rolex had plastered photos of Tenzing all over the countryside; and my friend of the intelligence was educated at Cambridge.

But how in the name of all that's holy could he shake hands with a sherpa? So he said it wasn't Tenzing at all; Tenzing was in Delhi.

Tenzing wasn't in Delhi, and here he put his hand out. I shook it and reassured myself superfluously: "You are Tenzing, are you not?"

He smiled a tremendous smile whose beauty erased the impression of duplicity instilled by the ads, and said he was. Shankar also shook hands. We asked him how he was, and Tenzing asked us how we were. Then he invited us to tea.

I was overwhelmed. Tea with the conqueror of Everest! We accepted and arranged to meet later in the afternoon at his mountain hut. Tenzing looked at his Rolex watch and moved off.

"Shall we go together?" I asked Shankar. "Oh," said the former Chief of Intelligence. "I shan't go. Whatever would I say to the fellow?"

*Touching the Untouchable*

He smoothed his silky white hair back from his handsome face that had almost the features of a European, and said good afternoon.

After Shankar left me—he was due for billiards at the Club—I stood there with my elbows on the railing of the Mall that deceives one into thinking that Darjeeling is a pleasure ship in the trough of gentle waves. From the Mall I could see Kanchenjunga without straining myself. From a nearby hill, I might have seen Everest itself, if I had gotten out of bed in time.

Only two men since Creation have trod the nakedness of Everest, and one of those two had just invited me to tea. You know, I couldn't have invited Tenzing to the hotel; they wouldn't have let him in. And I: did I belong in Tenzing Norkay's hut? or at that dreadful Noah's Ark of a hotel with Shankar, sifting through his bushels of cephalic indices?

I would like to know what Tenzing saw from the top of Everest. Was it dangerous?

I couldn't figure the whole thing out, and allowing myself to get engaged in bookstalls, teatime passed and I did not go to Tenzing's.

# 9

*Beware the Orakzai, my son*

One night, as I was hiking barefoot out of Afghanistan's Desert of Death, a monstrous mouldering mud ruin rose hulking against the earth's curve, across the dry bed of the Helmand River. It was all that is left of Qala Bist, the Twentieth Fort that Alexander built on his march from the Oxus to the Ganges. Now there was a march! Above the fort's miles of thick mud walls, Orion lay stretched out upon his side, his dagger as ready as ever the Macedonian's was to pierce the night now settling down upon the Hindu Kush.

We had left the jeep with its nose buried in a sand dune, and our Pathan scout Faqir-jaan hanging loose on the back seat with his rifle across his knees. We would have to hike back to Ch'angiers. It was twenty-six kilometers across the desert as the vulture flies, and there were plenty of them flying. Others just hunched about expectantly, looking as though they remembered us. Earlier in the day, when the jeep was still operable, Ransom had charged a distant vulture, not

## Beware the Orakzai, my son

knowing, or not caring, that the giant birds need a fifty-yard run before they can get airborne. The result was that the vulture rapidly closed the distance with us, getting bigger as he neared, and only just cleared the top of the windshield when he took off, spraying his filthy reek all over us. Was it possible that same bird was watching us now, ready to challenge us to another game of chicken?

All this had happened before the motor shook itself loose from its moorings and left us stranded miles from anything but Alexander's ghostly fort, and without the two-way radio which everybody else had sense enough to carry along. There was nothing to do but walk, leaving Ransom's man behind to prevent the jeep from falling salvage to wandering tribesmen.

The night was clear and dark. There were no cities within a thousand miles, and without their reflected glow, the sky took on an aspect which western man has not seen since the Industrial Revolution, but which Afghans are privileged to see every night. Unbelievable cascades of stars lighted the sky; occasionally there came an answering sparkle from underground rills which emerged momentarily to the surface of the desert, then flung themselves once more under the sand. The water was conducted here by the Persians thousands of years ago, no one knows how, and it is sweet and safe to drink. What would pollute it but man? and here there are no men.

Just one. A figure appeared on the track ahead of us, his rifle bumping against the starbright sky. A man would no more go forth in Afghanistan without his weapon than he would without a certain other, less detachable feature of his anatomy, which he uses as readily.

Ransom shifted his own hand to the pistol in his belt. I hoped he was getting ready to follow rule number one, which is to hand over your gun on request. Afghans shoot straighter than anybody, and a gun is the thing they will shoot you for quickest. (The others are zar, zan, zamin: gold, women, land. We had neither gold nor land, and I had no illusions that Ransom would die protecting me. All things considered, it seemed best to give up the gun.)

## Krishna Smiled

The figure drew abreast of us, uttered the words "salaam aleikum" to which I had the wit to reply "aleikum salaam," and melted into the magical night behind us. Suddenly I understood those words for the first time: "Peace be with you" is a declaration that you do not intend to shoot.

Now a more pedestrian problem assailed me. My feet were being flayed by the shoes custom-made for me in Peshawar by a Chinese communist (I know he was Chinese: I assume he was some kind of degenerate). I took them off and walked barefoot in the ankle deep dust. The November day had been hot, but once the sun went down, the heat quickly dissipated and the dust was as cool and soothing as talcum to my raw sores. The air began to grow rather chilly, and I wondered just how cold the night was likely to get.

Then we hit gravel. I walked till I couldn't take another step, goaded by Ransom's observation that the women of the Coochies, Afghanistan's nomads, go barefoot all year round. These fantastic women, unveiled and breasty, march the length of the country from spring to fall, and then from fall to spring they march it back again, driving herds, loading and unloading camels, pitching and unpitching tents, cooking over open fires, bearing babies by the roadside and hurrying to rejoin the line of march which never waits for them.

While he talked, Ransom slashed my shoes fore and aft, lashed them to my feet by means of strips which he tore off his shirttail. "You would have made a lousy Coochie," he said. "Coochies make lousy Coochies," I answered. "Have you ever seen an old woman in their caravans? The ones you think are old are twenty-two."

I don't know where the Coochies draw their strength from, but I drew mine from my disdain of Ransom. He had done nothing all week but bitch about being saddled with a woman, though it was my understanding that he had agreed to my coming along on the trip. He never thought I could make it over the rough spots, and was always ready to extend a sardonic hand, which I was equally ready to bite.

Machismo was Ransom's long suit, and he wore it like a hermit his hairy shirt. But nothing is more offensive to me than the cult of masculinity, which poses with rifle in hand

## Beware the Orakzai, my son

and its foot upon the neck of a woman. Ransom was in his element among Pathans, to whom the attitude comes naturally.

Ransom and I met through no fault of ours when our charge d'affaires in Kabul told him to pick me up at the hotel in Peshawar on his way up. Transportation in and out of Afghanistan was pretty chancy, the British diplomatic courier had been shot up the week before and his secrets scattered over the mountainside with the largesse of the illiterate. The embassy tried to provide escort service for all official Americans coming into the country.

Ransom and I took an instant dislike to one another despite the fact that there was a limited selection of American bachelors around. He hated my independence, which seemed to threaten his superiority; and I hated his superiority, which threatened my independence. We maintained a state of warfare throughout my stay in Afghanistan. He was demonstrably stronger than I, but I was quicker witted. Each time he lost a battle, he would sic Faqir on me, who was smarter than he was. I worried about that at first. Faqir was on his home territory, and he was a bit more than six and a half feet tall. But the Pathan knew a winner when he saw one, and soon began to side with me against his boss. That was when I began using the second half of his name, which means something like "dear heart." Faqir-jaan made all the difference between my killing Ransom and my not killing him.

From Peshawar, Ransom and I set out northward through the Khyber Pass, which turned out, to my surprise, not to be a large oaken door fitted between two mountains. Somehow, that is how I pictured it all through my childhood reading of Kipling. The pass is thirty-two miles long and follows the meandering Kabul River as it cuts through the mountains of the Hindu Kush. It is a beautifully engineered all-weather highway, and at all the places where the road bends and bulges out above the valley, there are rock cairns with little flags poked in them, graves or shrines of Moslem saints. It was from behind these that Kipling heard the telltale rifle snick that comes a moment before the bullet's whine.

At Landi Kotal the twentieth century stopped, and

abruptly we were riding on an unpaved track that crosses the southern ranges of the Hindu Kush to Kabul. The mountains are rugged and bare as the face of the moon, rock and sand and dust unrelieved by vegetation, or anything reminiscent of life on earth. By jeep, it is a twelve-hour journey of arduous climbs, sudden descents, and close steering between whitewashed rocks that are all that differentiate the road from the wastes around it. Camel caravans traverse this stretch in a week or a month; how long the pedestrians take, and there were a good many of them, is a matter for conjecture. Who among them would care to measure it?

Like a dirty, buff-colored rug heaped carelessly on a scarred cement floor, the Hindu Kush rises convoluted and riven by erosion. The road follows the mountains' contortions where it can, and bridges ravines where it must. Strewn across the infrequent plateau, rounded boulders attest to the flash floods that tear down without warning from the mountains to engulf, briefly, the plain; and sieve themselves into the sandy soil leaving no trace of green.

These mountains shield India from the warlike and nomadic tribes of Asia, who traditionally make their living by looting the bucolic plainsmen to the south. The passes are crucial: whoever holds them controls the fate of India. While the British ruled India, there were continuous border skirmishes, since immortalized by Shirley Temple as Wee Willie Winkie.

At the time of my visit, the borders were quiet. The government aimed to keep things that way, and that was the major reason, apart from poverty, that there were no paved roads in the country save for the one through Khyber and another that ran from the center of Kabul out to the King's Palace. As one government official put it to me, "Why should we build highways? So the Russians can march through?"

Times change. With Soviet assistance, the Afghans have now laid paved roads all over the place, spoiling the terrain for future writers.

The view from Lataband Pass had not changed much since the British stood there—or Alexander, for that matter.

## Beware the Orakzai, my son

Kabul lies in its saucer depression, a hive of mud houses, each with its own protective mud wall with a chute that empties the latrines into the street.

The Kabul River curves through town, and the townsmen sit on its dike sunning themselves, gloriously unoccupied save for gossiping and polishing their rifles. Afghans are great fighters, and this leaves them little to do in time of peace.

A traveller who passed through Kabul in 1333 wrote that the city is inhabited by a tribe of Persians called Afghans: "They hold mountains and defiles, possess considerable strength, and are mostly highwaymen."

And so they are: in a country without natural wealth, and where constant invasions raise doubts that a man may live to reap what he has sowed, the people began to harvest their invaders. This is dangerous business, and no one ever accused the Pathans of being pantywaists. They are great guerrilleros, and one of the problems of modern government is to acclimatize the citizens to peaceful occupations.

The Pathans believe themselves to be the lost tribes of Israel. Unlike their decadent relations, they retain their tribal organization. Nevertheless, their names are not so well known to history as are those of the sons of Jacob, so a poem has been devised as an aide memoire:

> 'Twas Ghilzai and the Yusufzai
> Did Dir and Wazir on the way
> All mimsy were the Qizilbash
> And the Mohmands are grey.
>
> "Beware the Orakzai, my son,
> Durrans that snick, Baluch that Swat,
> Beware Afridi and Mahsud,
> The frumious Khatak!"

A man's whole loyalty is absorbed by his tribe. Against this claim, neither considerations of family nor patriotism toward the sovereign state Afghanistan can make much headway. Rather, it is a matter of the loyalty of one tribe to another, and to the throne. Despite the considerable amount of propaganda generated by the government press-and-trash department, I found no evidence of a separate Pathan nationalism. The romance of Pukhtunistan (to be carved mostly out of Pak territory) seems to have been hoked up by the Afghan government with the connivance of India.

Likewise divided into warring tribes were the European types in which the city abounded. These were people who had opted at the close of the second World War more or less willingly for the Free World, whatever that could possibly mean in relation to Afghanistan. They imparted a continental flavor to the provincial scene, adding a touch of weltschmerz to the shish kebab. Every single one of them would have departed on a moment's notice, if he had had anywhere to go and a visa to get him in.

There were a number of Free Poles, so free they didn't know what to do with themselves. Mostly they tutored the children of wealthy Afghans. Armenians there were, refugees from both the Russians and the Turks. Personable young German engineers who had fought in the Wehrmacht, never in the SS, and had had no idea what terrible things the Nazis were doing. ("Do you know what is going on in your prisoner of war camps in Korea?" one asked me.) Americans, Germans, French, Poles, Russians, we were all Europeans, no matter how terrible recent history had been; and we have so much in common in an alien and barbarous land, nicht wahr? Hans, stocky, virile, good-looking, smelled of death.

There were Jews, too; but I took care not to meet them. Their situation was precarious enough, without being contacted by foreigners. Two weeks before my arrival, the bodies of two Jewish men were found stuffed down a well. The system of justice had not yet raised itself from the tribal level. But Jews do not participate in Puktunwali, the tribal code by which Pathans extract an eye for an eye, a life for a life. So there was no one to avenge their deaths nor apprehend their murderers. The Jews just went silently about their daily lives, only more silently than before.

Kabul wears quickly. Not because it is small, nor because it is drab. The city has charm, and we know that the

*Beware the Orakzai, my son*

Emperor Babur on his peacock throne at Delhi mourned his Afghan capital. The difficulty which Kabul presents for the foreigner is that there seems to be no way of establishing contact with people. The mud walls and burqas have been there so long, that they have taken root in people's minds.

Even those foreigners who had lived a long time in the city told me that nothing was published here. But the embassy interpreter, he whom I dug out from under the newspapers of yesteryear, found me a bookshop and helped me buy a pretty good assortment, which can now be consulted at the Library of Congress.

But when my acquisitions had been bundled and sent out by plane (there were no railroads nor any road to the sea), my previously vague sense of frustration crystallized. Walking dusty streets hemmed by dusty walls, I saw a door open at the end of a lane. A man, perhaps six and a half feet in height, a sombre man but wearing a brilliant orange turban wound around a skull cap sewn with golden sequins, stood poised in the doorway. Then, closing his home behind him, he strode off the dusty stage and into his world. For me, all doors seemed closed. As so often in this country, I remembered Omar Khayyam:

> There was a door to which I found no key:
> There was a veil past which I could not see . . . .

Perhaps things would be different outside of Kabul. Everyone agreed that city Afghans were but a pale reflection of their country cousins, who exhibited more of the virtues and fewer of the failings of primitive man. I was at a loss as to how to justify further travel, however, since, with government control of the presses, I was fairly certain I would find nothing in the provincial towns that differed from what I had procured in the capital.

But our charge d'affaires was one who thought it a good idea in principle for officers to see as much territory as they could, regardless of any immediate profit to be gained thereby, and suggested a trip to Ghazni. I quickly accepted, even though it mean putting up with Ransom and more machismo.

As agricultural attaché, Ransom's purpose in making the trip was to estimate the size of the wheat crop. That was how I got to see village Afghanistan. We drove in a southwesterly direction out of Kabul, never beyond sight of mountains. Sometimes they were just a purple rim on the horizon; sometimes, crowding in close, they squeezed the road between them.

The villages stand fortified and withdrawn a discreet distance from the highway. Their mud walls are slotted for firing through, and at each corner of town there is an observation tower. I didn't see any provisions for pouring down molten lead, but I wouldn't have been surprised to see them.

Ransom would pull the jeep in through the village gates (open during the day, but barred at night against raids of neighboring clans), and in a moment we would be surrounded by the men of the village who, it seems, have no work to do since women do it all. Ransom would engage them in a discussion of the crops, through the medium of Faqir-jaan. I would remain inside the jeep, sitting aloof and akimbo, one of Faqir's turbans on my head.

Women's faces are an obscenity here, and the penalty for indecent exposure was instant death. None of us was sure how much latitude might be allowed a foreign woman. Ransom wanted to find out, but I didn't think the effort was worthwhile. Nor would I have gone under a burqa, even as a joke. It was no joke to me. The alternative was to face the world like a boy.

In one village, an elderly man invited us into his home for tea. Passing between mud walls, we found ourselves on a pleasant verandah overhung by grape vines. The crowds of children with skin as tough as elephant hide and coated all over in excrement were shooed away. Only one young boy remained to serve us, a pretty, well-cared for lad who poured water for us to wash our hands by. He was apparently the old man's mistress. We were served tea and a bowl of fruit, including the most voluptuous melon I have ever tasted; then Ransom ordered us out and on to the next village.

*Beware the Orakzai, my son*

Judging from the presence of children of all ages, there must be women living in Afghan villages. I never saw any. They don't even have the right the camels and donkeys have, to walk free in the sun.

Along the road, Ransom felt compelled to shoot at every bird that flew by. Since he also insisted on driving, and the road was bumpy, he wasn't having much luck.

I offered to drive, because I could see that if he didn't shoot anything he was going to go into an awful pet. But the S.O.B. wouldn't yield the driver's seat; it was beneath his dignity to let a woman drive. Instead, he bade me steer from the passenger side. So, trundling along at fifteen miles an hour, I held the wheel while he bagged a few see-see. These are tiny fowl about the size of cornish hen, except that Victor Borge wasn't along to disembowel and process them and we got to do that ourselves. We roasted and ate them along the roadside at whatever hour Ransom happened to feel hungry. It was pathetic to see how happy he was.

The result of all this lolly-goggling was that we pulled into Ghazni late at night. This town was built a thousand years ago atop a 7,000 foot high conical mountain; it was once one of the magical cities of the world; but it is my duty to report that things have gone downhill since. The precipitous streets are more like walls than streets, more ruin than wall, as the bricks which pave them have worked loose over the course of centuries. Ghazni has, in fact, largely fallen apart and rolled down the mountain.

At midnight the streets were deserted, as well they might be, and a cold wind whistled down them, cutting us to the bone. From a speaker mounted in the market place, a radio blared as though warning the soundless night to stay out of town. I recognized the music right away: it was whatever Aram Khachaturian listened to with his inner ear that caused him to write the "Sabre Dance."

There reputedly was a hotel in Ghazni, and Faqir questioned a pair of policemen about it, out patrolling their beat with Russian rifles on their backs, the barrels stuffed with cotton wadding. Yes, there was one, sort of. The Hotel Addams, we named it when we found it. There was one room,

## Krishna Smiled

a large anteroom, and a raft of servants. Ransom ordered them to pull one cot into the bedroom (for himself) and one into the anteroom (for me). I countermanded the order. There were just too many unknown characters around for me to sleep in that anteroom, and too many windows and doors (all windowless and doorless) for them to come in by. I was going to sleep with either Faqir or Ransom, I didn't care which.

So Ransom and I continued our war of nerves in the bedroom, which had just one door that needed watching, and Faqir gratefully moved into the anteroom. Ransom didn't need watching. He was the kind of man who likes limp women with wispy hair and no mind.

I was the first to wake next morning, and ordering the servant to bring me a bucket of water from the jooie (the gutter which supplies both intake and outlet for Afghan towns), splashed around a bit to start the sap running. We breakfasted on hot tea, boiled eggs (chicken, I suppose) and yesterday's nan. Then I put on Faqir's turban once more and went out into the bazaar, while Ransom sat down on a rock to clean his rifle. He was immediately surrounded by a crowd of admirers, all eager to show off their own rifles, largely handmade: rifle-making is a sort of cottage industry in Afghanistan.

Ghazni is the town where Sultan Mahmud reigned in the eleventh century, turning his court into one of the great intellectual and artistic centers of the East, a gathering place of poets, artists, historians, and philosophers. In between poetry readings, Mahmud invaded India sixteen times, accomplishing his work of destruction with such energy that he became known as the Idol Breaker. He was immortalized a generation later by Omar Khayyam, who dedicated the *Rubaiyat* to one of Mahmud's successors, and incidentally gives the old rogue honorable mention. Today, I am sorry to say, the lion and the lizard keep the court where Mahmud gloried and drank deep.

I found no clue here to the greatness that was Ghazni. Only the bazaar stalls were still busy, selling sugar cane and

## Beware the Orakzai, my son

silver and wheat and sheepskin jackets and karakul (persian lamb) skins and spices and turbans and burqas and camel dung to tribesmen muffled in skins and cloaks and cloths and padded Tartar kimonas. I could have looked and touched and smelled and listened for days without tiring.

But Ransom had said one hour: the great man wanted to hit the road for Kandahar and shoot his idiot gun again. Since he was quite capable of going off and leaving me stranded, I kept an eye on the time. I did manage to buy myself a sheepskin jacket with the fur side inside and the leather side fancifully embroidered. Then I hightailed it back to the hotel, just in time to catch the last jeep for Kandahar.

Fifteen years later, this jacket appeared on the cover of Harper's Bazaar, even more fancifully priced. Soon the psychedelic clothing shops were filled with them. But even after they had become a cliché of the fashion-ridden, I could not put mine on but that I would smell camel dung burning, grate my feet against ancient brick, and see a lone rider on a high-stepping mare come out of the desert, a beautiful child perched like a bird behind him, her eyes as empty as her world.

Kandahar is supposed to have been founded by Alexander the Great. Later it became the center of the Gandhāra school of sculpture that wed Greek and Buddhist traditions. In the twentieth century, it graduated to factories. Now it was the base of operations for Morrison-Knudson Afghanistan, under contract to build dams for the Afghan government. With typical American brashness, the company advertised that it had moved more earth than anyone else since time began.

Quite possibly it has. Near Kandahar, at a place called Kajakai, you drive through miles of dry-as-bone mountains, rocks, brambles, thorns, no blade of grass; then up a hill, through a canyon at the end of which is a mammoth cement wall, just tacked to the mountains. You drive up on top of that wall, and over on the other side of it is the bluest blue lake that ever was, water where no water could ever be, rising step-by-step up the sides of the mountains, burying hills, creeping through gullies, and finally washing up against little subsidiary barriers. So blue, it should have been a mirage, except real ducks were circling it, and Ransom shot one for our lunch.

We pushed farther west, Ransom investigating reports that the filling of the dam had increased salinity in the soil, rendering it useless. Every few miles now we mired in sand—dust, rather—as we penetrated the Dash-ti-Marg. Each time, Ransom managed to free us by means of the winch on the front bumper and a chain attached to—what? That was always a problem, for there were no trees. Usually, it meant digging a pit, throwing the spare tire into it with a chain attached, and covering it with sand and boulders; then engaging the winch and slowly pulling the car out, me steering and the two men pushing. In this way, we ultimately reached the Morrison-Knudsen camp at Ch'angiers. It was worth the effort.

The camp was filled with hardworking, healthy American proletarians who walked in dignity, grease-stained and smelling of sweat. They talked bluntly and with honesty to one another and to me. Isolated in this vast desert, they made me homesick for all those splendid hardhatted fellows walking steel beams back home, who whistle when a girl goes by, not because she's pretty but because she's there and life is good.

How long it had been since I had seen a working man who was not servile! An Indian worker is scum. He is treated like scum, he lives like scum, he believes himself to be scum. American dam builders in India resisted hiring Indians in managerial posts, whatever their academic accomplishments, because they would not soil their hands. They were afraid of becoming scum. The Indian worker has no dignity. And without dignity, what is a life of labor worth?

The Afghan, on the other hand, is full of dignity, but he does not work. To be a Pathan and to hold a job is a contradiction in terms. Men are for fighting; women or other inferior tribes do the work.

At Ch'angiers I was stunned by the sight of a man wear-

## Beware the Orakzai, my son

ing trousers, shirt, hat, and shoes, carrying a piece of heavy equipment on his shoulders. Why was such a rich man working?

Having been reminded that the laborer is worthy of his hire, I had to take my whole world apart and put it back together again. It was a reminder I sorely needed, for caste is contagious.

There wasn't a single American woman within miles of Ch'angiers, and when word got around that I was not Ransom's property, the men threw a square dance. They scared up an accordian, a ukelele, a caller from Iron Mountain, and as much wine as we could hold.

The wine was by courtesy of the company's chief mechanic, a paisan of superb moral fiber who couldn't bear to see good grapes go to waste. It was an offense to the gods to eat them raw, as the Afghans do. Louis had put together a winepress and a still, with the help of an inner tube and a feather pillow, so that we had both wine and grapa, which is a kind of Italian slivovitz. The band tuned up, we filled our cups, and in the fires of spring the wintry garments of repentance flung. Omar, you were right: wine tastes sweeter out here in your desert!

Ransom retired early with a good book. He couldn't stand seeing me behave like a girl when I hadn't allowed him to patronize me. So the next afternoon he dragged me away from my new friends to tour the surrounding countryside and we broke down near Qala Bist.

I have always been glad we did. One must walk the earth in order to become real, and I walked a good bit of it that night. I had flown over that desert once before in a DC-6, and the heat waves rising above the contoured earth bounced the plane so that the ceiling came down and hit us on the head, then dropped us into a bottomless pit. The pilot vomited at the controls, the rest of us at our seats. It was all a maniacal amusement park ride, but I never felt it had anything to do with Afghanistan or with life on earth.

Walking the desert on my bare feet, following along beside the dry bed of the Helmand River, I felt more alive than I have ever felt before or since. My feet were on an age-old track; my safe arrival subject to my own control—my endurance, my wits, my courage, my stupidity. I thought of Alexander, dead with all his legions; Timur the Lame, Genghis Khan, and all the rest who harried this land. Over at Bamian, giant Bodhisattvas stand rooted to the mountainside, their noses knocked off by Moslem iconoclasts. Whatever else intruders have wrought, they have proved that, in one area of the world, the sword is mightier than the pen.

Sighting dead Qala Bist bearing Orion on its battlements, a song of myself arose within me and will not be quelled until I die. I am I, I sang wordlesslessly, and though the mountains didn't care and the desert did not respond, it was all that mattered to me.

# 10

*Wandering through Pomegranate Bazaar,
I eat one seed too many*

Lack of a Pukhto dictionary constituted an intolerable lacuna in the Asian collection of the Library of Congress. It didn't seem right to slight the Pathans. Not only are they the dominant people of Afghanistan and the North-West Frontier Province of Pakistan; they are the only people in Asia who look like me.

The most accurate and comprehensive Pukhto dictionary was published in Lahore in 1877 and sold out at once to all those stalwart, Pukhto-speaking officers upon whom the Empire depended. It was hard to see how anyone could take up where Kipling had left off, without a good dictionary.

But I never came close to one in over a year of searching my territory, including Afghanistan itself where of course only trash could survive the total government control of the information media.

A possibility opened up when Ramamurthi, my bookdealer in Delhi, told me that when he fled Lahore in 1947 he

## Krishna Smiled

had left behind his entire stock of books. His brother Gopal stayed on in the old university town and in due course reopened the store. Perhaps Gopal, I reasoned, would be able to locate a copy of the dictionary in the very city where it had been published.

So I went to Lahore, something which Ramamurthi himself had not done since Partition. But even Gopal was unable to turn up a copy, though he did sell me a set of gazetteers. These must have held the secret of the lost Atlantis, for I received a special commendation from the Secretary of State for having acquired them.

That came months later. At the time, I was depressed. I wandered out through Anarkali, Lahore's famous Pomegranate Bazaar. This city had had the most tightly-knit Hindu and Moslem communities of pre-partition India. The multi-religious fabric came unravelled in 1947. In some sectors, not a stone was left on a stone, nor a book upon a shelf, as neighbor slaughtered neighbor in a fraternal bid to liberate the city. The wreckage was still being offered for sale by sidewalk vendors.

Anarkali yielded a splendid catch of books, scavenged from the scorched remains of other people's libraries. Lahore, the ancient seat of culture, had been turned into a slaughter house and then a bargain basement by its loving inhabitants. Here was I to profit from the destruction, and lured on by the richness of the offerings. I plunged deeper and deeper into the old city until I lost my way.

The streets were no help. Instead of heading in a specific direction, they dissolved witlessly into one another or allowed themselves to be devoured by tenements that ravened around them. The houses were windowless for six feet up, but their second stories bulged with balconies which met above my head. As the afternoon heat waned, the prostitutes came out to display themselves just above the heads of the pedestrians. They sat on their balconies fanning themselves, chattering six to a dozen, their bulls-eyes of kohl set wide in faces streaked red with pomegranate juice.

I stopped at a cloth shop where a Sikh was sitting tailor

## Wandering through Pomegranate Bazaar

fashion (how else?) among his bolts of cotton, measuring tape draped around his neck. Where, I asked, was Kashmiri Gate? The gate led, I hoped, to the cantonment (modern Lahore), where I had a room at what was recognizably a hotel. Confidently, the tailor pointed west. A few blocks later, a second Sikh pointed east. I was lost. Possibly so were they. I thought I should throw away the pomegranate I was munching on. If I had to remain one month for every seed I ate, I would spend half my life getting out of this place.

From behind mud walls, musicians began to tune their instruments—or, for all I knew, were already playing. There was some question in my mind concerning the forms of Indian music; but I responded like a snake to its rhythms. Somewhat mesmerized, I walked the narrow street, imagining the sixteen-stringed sitar, prostrate on its master's knee, the tabla responding to the stretch of its skin and the beat of calloused fingers. Now, the first courtesan began to sing. It was the song the sirens sang to Ulysses.

Months before, in Karachi, I had persuaded Hashmi to take me to see the nautch girls. Hashmi had been very kind to me since my arrival in Pakistan. He was now ready to draw the line somewhere, but wasn't sure just where. I had ejected myself from a rickshaw, leaving the seat of my dress behind; and Hashmi took me to his mother's dressmaker. I wanted to bathe in the Arabian Sea; and Hashmi took me fifty miles across the trackless desert to see the turtles lurch up out of the sea to lay their eggs by cold moonlight. I wanted to see the ruins of Mohenjo-Daro; and Hashmi changed five tires along the way.

But nautch girls! This was too much. Only when I threatened to ring in Jehangir did he consent. Hashmi was a city man, the inheritor of civilization (and a sizable fleet of taxis). Jehangir was a Pathan, without civilization or scruple. He would stuff me into a burqa and carry me off to Fort Sandemann. So Hashmi took me to the Peshawar Tearoom. (The Peshawar Tearoom is in Karachi. The Karachi Tearoom is in Lahore, the Lahore Tearoom is in Delhi, and the Delhi Tearoom is in Peshawar.)

## Krishna Smiled

From behind beaded curtains, the proprietor sized us up. In the old days, he would have gratified us with ghazals, those haunting Urdu sonnets dedicated to the fleetingness of life and love. Nowadays, no one knew the difference. With one of those crazy American women present, it would be sufficient to parrot the latest film hit. He would send Sultana out first.

Sultana, adjusting her voluminous white satin pyjamas over her billowing hips and pulling a pink tunic down over all, enters. She is barefoot, and has learned the weighty walk of elephants. Around her ankles are leather straps sewn with bells, which jingle provocatively when she walks, and turn a man's spine to jelly when she stamps. Sultana's hair hangs loose, framing in thick black clouds her enormous kohl-encircled eyes, which she rolls violently.

Without caring that Mohammed Ali Jinnah, Father of Pakistan, glares down upon her from the wall, she opens her betel-red mouth. A banal film song burbles forth. Around the room, men lounge on canvas mats, coax bubbles through their water pipes, sigh, and remember the Moghul Empire.

It was thanks to Hashmi's kindness in taking me to the tearoom that I was able to recognize the sounds when, six months later, I lost myself in Anarkali. This time, Hashmi was not around, however. And as I had bought as many books as I could carry, it really seemed time for me to get out of here, if only I could find the gate.

Around the corner came a wedding procession, tangling with the flow of pedestrians who already filled the narrow street. Musicians marched before, and the family came after. Between them sat the groom on a hired white horse, a sword in his belt, his head smothered in a fall of jasmine. Riding pillion behind him was a little boy. He was a decoy: a kidnapping must not prevent the groom from reaching his bride's house. The smell of jasmine overwhelmed us.

Behind, along, and between the marchers flitted a madwoman, attracted by the noise and lights. Barefoot and in rags, her hair starched upright with filth and her eyes wide staring—"Bibi!" she called to me. "Princess!" and danced her crazy dance around me while the procession laughed.

## Wandering through Pomegranate Bazaar

White horse, musicians, wedding party, and beggar disappeared around another corner, led offstage by their acetylene torches. Their noise disappeared with them, and the quiet street now seemed ominous. The day too had passed, as though it were a marcher in the procession. There was a quiet moment; then through an open window above my head, I heard once more the strangled song of the nautch girl.

I came to a place where the walls of two opposing buildings bulged into the street, looking as though they were, like giant paramecia, about to mate. At the same moment, a small English car appeared at the other end of the passage. I flattened myself against the betel-stained wall to let it pass.

A handsome head leaned into my abdomen and asked: "I say, may I give you a lift?"

"No, thank you," I replied, comparing the fire of the street with the frying pan of the Austin.

"Don't be a fool. Get in," Handsome Head said.

Once in the car, I discovered two other heads, less handsome, in the penumbra of the back seat. It is always a mistake to enter a car without checking out the rear first. However, in this case, the street had been so narrow that I was physically unable to bend down and look in the windows first.

Number One Head introduced me to Heads Two and Three as a friend from Karachi. We had met at a dance. I was grateful for the respectable introduction; it augured well. By coincidence, I had been in Karachi last June, though I hadn't gone dancing.

I nodded and smiled toward the rear. "Yes, wasn't it a pleasant evening?" I simpered in cocktail party jargon. I must establish myself as part of the In crowd, so they would know my presence would be missed if I failed to return to the hotel. I wondered how I would look in a burqa, whether I could survive the heat of the North-West Frontier Province behind mud walls, and how I could smuggle a message to Jehangir . . .

Heads Two and Three got out at Kashmiri Gate, which I immediately recognized since I had passed it twice already. I suggested that I might now be released.

"Karachi, in June, at a dance," the young man repeated, as though he believed it. I was equally certain we had never been introduced, but determined to keep the conversation friendly until I was back at my hotel.

"What on earth are you doing here anyway?" my abductor asked, in flawless Etonian. Another point in his favor, surely. I explained that my employer was languishing for lack of a dictionary with which to translate some letters he had received, and had sent me here to look for one. I always stuck pretty close to the truth in these matters, without feeling it necessary to intimidate people by mention of the United States government. This was even more the case since my recent visit to Peshawar, where I had let it be known I was collecting books for the Library of Congress. I then heard myself denounced on the radio as an intelligence agent of Congress (meaning the Congress Party of India). In a region where nightly rifle fire still proclaims the settling of family feuds, this was not a good reputation to have.

"Well," said Malik, for by now we had introduced ourselves, "this is certainly a harebrained scheme, sending a young girl to Anarkali to fetch a book. Hasn't he any peons? Tell me what it is you want, and I shall get it for you."

The specifications having been noted, we arranged to meet at my hotel the next afternoon. Malik did indeed appear, with two copies of the Pukhto dictionary, one well-worn, the other with the pages yet uncut. Apparently one British officer had done his homework, while the second had found other things to do in Anarkali.

By this time, we were good friends, and Malik took me to see the Mirror Palace, where there is a stone that never grows cold. "Just like a heart that is true," he said predictably as we sat in a marble gazebo over a stream that flowed through the Shalimar gardens. He was certainly not original, but dark and handsome he was, and with a better accent than I had. He owned a few thousand acres somewhere near Quetta, which wasn't saying much, since I had seen Quetta once rather by accident, when an ancient DC-3 failed to fly me from Karachi to Kabul and let me down there instead, gently, Praise be to Allah! No books for sale there, either.

Like all Moslems I met, he confided that we (meaning

## Wandering through Pomegranate Bazaar

Jew and Moslem) had far more in common with one another than either of us had with Christian or Hindu. Out here in the desert, it was easy to agree.

In fact, Malik was a most agreeable companion in many ways, the chief one being that I never knew whether he had a wife. One could assume he did, being of age, but if she existed, she lived in that same limbo to which I had committed my fiancé, who was said to be alive and well in New York City. These shadowy figures could be called upon for aid, when needed; but at the same time were conveniently impalpable.

At the races that night (Malik's horse won) he took up an old theme. Why did he have to dress up in pretty words what had essentially been a pick-up?

"Karachi, in June, at a dance," he repeated with good humor.

"June," I answered, "was Ramadan, the month of fasting." (How well I remembered Hashmi racing his taxi through Karachi streets at three in the morning shouting, "Get up! Get up! It's time to eat!!" It was Ramadan all right, or some glorious scenes of chaos had gone for nought.) "There were no dances in Karachi in June."

"Ah," said Malik, "unfortunately there are some people who would dance at any time, at the very brink of the grave, one might say. But you should stay away from them; you will get a bad name."

"I beg your pardon?"

"Peshawar Tearoom," Pluto said, offering me a bite of pomegranate.

# 11

*Maidens*

**M**y first few months in Delhi, until the money ran out, I lived at the Maidens Hotel in a clean, cool room with exposure fore and aft, overlooking a nicely landscaped courtyard. Like any new "European" (i.e. non-Asian) girl, I was quickly sucked into the social whirlpool whose vortex was the nightclub on the main floor of the hotel. There in the heart of Old Delhi one could dine on chicken Kiev, coquille St. Jacques, or steak Chateaubriand, prepared by the former chef of the former Emperor Bao Dai; and dance to the latest hit tunes as perpetrated by a band of renegade Goans only partially under the control of a Sicilian bandit. They were fond of the songs of Piaf and Trenet, which they played between showings of the newest and the oldest nightclub acts from the Continent—the new ones which were trying out, and the old ones which had hit the skids.

The Maidens decor was ornately Victorian; black tie and floor length evening gowns were required after 7 P.M. Most

*Maidens*

of my gowns were waltz length, except for a Jacques Fath original I had purchased in Paris on the way over. In time, pulling on the heavy black satin sheath became as routine as putting on blue jeans, and so far as trained dog acts go, I don't care if I never see another.

I had no sooner checked into the Maidens than I became the darling of Manoel and Iqbal, who were First Secretaries of the Portuguese and the Turkish embassies, and who shared the kind of friendship that can only blossom from the compost heap of long historical enmity. One might say that these two had buried the Battle of Lepanto. Or sunk it. Old residents of Delhi and of the Maidens, they were connoisseurs of food and wine, topazes and star sapphires, carpets, currency regulations, and—since they were no longer young—new women. It was their custom to move in on newly-arrived females while they were still befuddled by the time change, and provide them with a mind-blowing introduction to Delhi life, beginning with Châteauneuf-du-Pape and ending with (when they hit it lucky) star sapphires. Each accepted graciously whatever favors the girls, many of them away from home for the first time, might care to bestow upon them, under the impression that this was *living*. Ultimately, they would watch with resignation as the girls moved on to younger, if less sophisticated men. But as embassy and business staffs were then growing in accord with Parkinson's Law, the airlines continually off-loaded new crops of girls to replace those who were graduating from Manoel and Iqbal's tutelage. It was a satisfactory arrangement for everyone, and good for business at the Maidens.

Physically, Manoel and Iqbal were quite different types, and this enhanced the symbiotic nature of their relationship: for what the one wanted, the other didn't. So they hunted comfortably in tandem. Manoel was slim and adorable. He danced an insinuating pasa doble in which he would twitch his little hips just slightly but with unmistakable intent, never abandoning the aristocratic sneer which adorned his pretty features under the thick thatch of grey hair. He was perfumed, one suspected, all over.

## Krishna Smiled

Iqbal had the build of a rugby player who has stayed too long on the field; and the mind of a customs collector. His chief weapon was a tango which can only be described as menacing. Since I had wasted my college years studying, I had never learned to dance. Now I took up the art on Iqbal's arm, there beside the Yamuna.

Both Manoel and Iqbal lived in terror of being called home for reassignment. Manoel because his womanizing would not have been tolerated in the repressive atmosphere of Lisbon; Iqbal because he would no longer be able to postpone marriage to the woman his parents had set aside for him in Ankara long ago, and who would soon be beyond childbearing age.

In addition, like most diplomats, they lived far better abroad than they could at home. Most of our currencies went so far against the rupee that we were incomparably better off than either our homebound colleagues or our Indian counterparts. We were not subject to local taxation or local law. Delhi, for instance, was moving over to Prohibition, but we had no difficulty in buying liquor, at prices far lower than stateside.

Traditionally, diplomats are outside the jurisdiction of the government to which they are accredited, and for good reason. It wouldn't do, after all, if one's government should send the message "We surrender!" only to have the emissary who carried it beheaded before he could deliver it. So the diplomat is immune to domestic law and cannot be tried in the courts of any nation but his own. Indeed, in the famous case of *V. vs. D.*, heard by the Tribunal of 1st Instance of Geneva, 10 June 1926, the court held that a diplomat could not even be sued to establish paternity of a child.

Occasionally, a diplomat does something which is privileged but embarrassing. A Latin American ambassador who pinched a lady cabinet secretary was called home the next day. A diplomat is unreachable by his host government, but totally vulnerable to his own.

As necessary as diplomatic immunity may be for the conduct of international negotiation, it had for us, and at that

## Maidens

time and that place, the effect of freeing us from the bonds of civilized society. We were aristocrats in a country with a long, hallowed tradition of debauched aristocracy. It was easy to slip into a pleasure-seeking pattern, because the pattern was there waiting. Perhaps, for some, the pleasure was heightened by knowledge that all around us, people were starving. At least, the existence of a huge and hungry populace made it urgent to join the Jet Set, and cheap to stay there.

My new friends Manoel and Iqbal gave parties several times weekly which began downstairs at the Maidens and adjourned at midnight to the Brazilian Embassy compound. Such was their adaptibility that they never objected when, having been invited to join them, I brought a date along. They lived in hopes of a later rendezvous. From their point of view, the more attractive young people who clustered round them, the better. For the young girls would attract young men, and the young men would attract new young girls, and new young girls have been known to flip their wigs by moonlight when they have quarreled with their young men, and gone to seek comfort in the arms of an understanding, older man.

On this particular evening, Iqbal invited me and I invited Simon Birdsall, who was Second Secretary of the Australian High Commission and my best source of publications on Burma. Simon had been a civil servant in Rangoon after the departure of the British, and retained the custom of wearing a sarong when at leisure. After all, a sarong is not so different from the kilt Simon's ancestors wore. Whether attired in a sarong with his knobby knees jutting out, or in a tuxedo that showed his knobby wrists, Simon looked somehow accidental, which was the way he felt. He had brilliant red hair and that white skin which is either sensuous or repulsive, depending on how its wearer feels about it. In this case, Simon loathed it, for it had failed him completely under the tropic sun. He had survived the fall of Singapore by floating away from it on a raft on which he lay exposed for two weeks before being picked up by a Chinese junk and taken ashore where he was wrapped in Tiger Balm and banana leaves until his skin grew back.

## Krishna Smiled

He had a well-founded hatred for the English, who had pigheadedly kept Singapore's guns pointed the wrong way, convinced the fort would be attacked only from the sea; and he despised Indians pretending to be English.

I myself was deeply surprised to find how many Indians admired their former masters and sought to imitate them. I should have thought they would hate them, since they were but five years out from under the yoke. But many looked back upon the days of Empire with nostalgia, and for an Indian to tell a foreigner that he was "almost British" was a compliment.

It took me a while to realize that Asians suffered tremendous feelings of ambivalence toward the West. They could not help but admire our superior technology; at the same time, they felt keenly that this technology had been used to exploit and humiliate them. Often, a refuge from this humiliation is found in an appeal to Asia's greater spiritualism. The Beatles and various maharishis have kindly introduced some of this spiritualism to the western world; but I confess its impact upon me was at all times negligible. I was unspeakably repelled by naked gurus smeared with the ashes of corpses, and by a pantheon of gods so jumbled that its devotees differ on their names and functions. My own experience was that the comparative wealth which we foreigners exhibited was not so much rejected as envied.

Many middle class Asians, of course, refuse to ape western styles and strive to retain their own cultures. Unfortunately, diplomatic life brought us into touch mostly with sycophants, the Kept Indians, or as Simon called them, the running dogs of the capitalist-imperialist warmongers. Whenever Simon felt himself surrounded by them, as tonight at the Maidens, he tended to become ferocious. That was when he danced best.

"What a charming fellow," the maharajah whispered to me, his watery eyes focused on a point just above my left shoulder. "Such a charming blend of British intelligence and American vitality."

For me, Simon was the only live person on the dance floor. The Indians danced jerkily, like puppets. It was not

## Maidens

their dance, not their music. What on earth are they trying to do? I asked myself on first seeing Indian couples dancing. They certainly were not enjoying it. Nor were they being artsy-craftsy. They were dancing because dancing suited their image of what they would be doing if they were English. And so they wandered over dance floors looking for a home. This night at the Maidens they had all they could do to keep out of Simon's way, for he liked to show off his restless energy among these peaceful, herbivorous creatures.

I watched as he clasped to his starched and studded chest the skinny maharani, who was wrapped in a black sari as in a shroud and wore a diamond stud nestled in the cleft of her nostril. She held a long jet cigarette holder clenched between her pointy teeth, dangerously close to Simon's ear. If she burned him, I'd smack her.

There was something wrong with Simon this evening, I thought. His smile hung slightly askew, though he didn't seem to know it. He was dancing even more ferociously than usual. But I didn't have time to observe him, for I had to rise to the challenge of Jagbir Singh.

Jagbir was a displaced Rajput with a heart of gall, a clever businessman who had bought his way into the capital's diplomatic circle. He had two wives, the second being his English nanny, but he used to bring the Indian one along on these romps, for she was more readily disposable.

Jagbir reached almost to my bosom, and sometimes I was afraid he would. His purple turban tickled my chin, and the silver sparkles he liked to scatter through the turban's folds made me sneeze. He had learned his English at dance halls on Piccadilly Circus, his dancing at George Raft movies, and he loved, not dancing, but to be seen dancing. He trod the floor like a rooster on a pile of manure. "Look at me, look at me, everybody," his eyes were crowing, and I am afraid many people did look at us, for I could not bear to follow his lead and we were constantly tripping one another up.

While I fended off Jagbir, Simon returned the maharani to our table and checked out the boyish Third Secretary of the German Embassy. She was wearing leather, but had left her whip at home. She was moderately successful in leading Simon, who didn't look as though he cared. The band played "La Vie en Rose" but it might as well have been the Toccata of Galuppi:

> Dear, dead women, with such hair, too,
> —what's become of all the gold
> Used to hang and brush their bosoms?
> I feel chilly and grown old."

From across the dance floor, a strident voice shouted at the cook in French, berating him for the poor quality of the lamb chops. It was the Dean of the Diplomatic Corps presiding over his nightly banquet. Judging from the size of his parties and the amount of food and liquor consumed, the Ambassador must have been the chief source of income for the Maidens.

The little cook nearly fainted while visions of his livelihood vanishing danced in the air. Trembling, the Annamese bowed nearly to the floor and made to remove the offending lamb chops. "Wait, you fool," cried the Ambassador. "Leave these. I will eat them while you prepare the others."

It was said that His Excellency had never set foot in his chancery. Instead, he held court every day but Friday in the swimming pool of the Delhi Gymkhana Club, mooring his vast bulk, of 350 pounds displacement, in a corner at the shallow end. There, resting his elbows on pillows which his servants placed on the tiled floor behind him, he allowed himself to float at anchor in the harbor, as it were, while the lesser tenders and pilot boats of his staff hovered round the shore to service him.

Despite appearances, he was a wily pro. He served many years in New Delhi. Then his rotten old king was deposed, and he was naturally called home. We were all certain that the hot young colonels' clique would stand him up against the wall. Not a bit of it. Within a month he was back in the Gymkhana pool, and once again the water level had to be lowered to take his bulk into account. Either he had something on the

## Maidens

colonels, or they figured it was worth keeping him on because of his position as dean of the corps at New Delhi, which he held by virtue of his seniority in residence. A new man would have gone to the bottom of the diplomatic totem pole. It was a pivotal position to hold, and one which he utilized to form a relationship between his country and India which was to prove enduring.

One by one or in pairs, Delhi diplomats came to have audience with His Excellency, most of them wearing pin-stripe cutaways for the occasion. They lent a sombre aspect to the pool. Some of us, after all, went there for healthy outdoor exercise, which we badly needed in that climate, and we did not enjoy being appraised by these gentlemen, all of them buttoned up to the gills, a large number of whom continued to seclude their own wives and daughters in purdah, and for whom a woman in a bathing suit was no better than a whore.

Apparently, Moslems never take their clothes off except for immoral purposes. A girl in a bathing suit is as good as nude; therefore, she must be immoral. Q.E.D. It is therefore permissible to stare at her in lewd fashion, whereupon the girl, who is ordinarily quite at ease in a bathing suit, suddenly feels nude and immoral.

Even Hashmi, over in Karachi, having driven us all to the Arabian seashore in one of his taxis, refused to join Charles, Raoul, and myself when we went surfing. He just sat up there on a dune with Tewfiq, the tortured Jordanian who had a dreadful case on me, but was ashamed of it (they'd string him up to a lamp post back home in Amman if he brought back a Jewish wife, he told Raoul, which is nothing compared to what my mother would have done to him), and the two of them kept their Korans dry while we decadent Europeans frolicked innocently by moonlight.

The well-known Dancing General now entered Maidens dining room in company with the Iraqi Ambassador and his party. The Ambassador's wife was wearing a spectacular gown cut from a purple and gold sari. Her dressmaker was a little crippled Polish refugee whom she kept sequestered in the embassy compound so that no one else could make use of her talents. There was some question as to whether the little seamstress had been crippled before she arrived under Madame's protection. The party was seated across the dance floor from us. The General bowed in my direction and arranged his expression in what may have been a smile. Undoubtedly, we both recalled that on the first day of summer he had invited me to his home for dinner. Delighted to be noticed by so august a personage, and wondering who the other guests would be, I arrived at his home to find myself alone with the General and a cozy dinner set for two. His wife had gone up to Ootacamund for the season. Exit one Third Secretary chased by a General.

I had not had time to finish my tournedo when Simon asked me to dance. A joyous shout went up from the band and they broke pell-mell for "Jalousie." A fortnight back, Simon had leaned me into the final dip of this tango and busted my placket. Now it was apparent that "Jalousie" was to be our theme song.

Tonight, however, Simon responded poorly to the goading of the band. Something obviously was on his mind. As we danced, he clutched me to him with the desperation of a mayfly who knows his end is near, but who would not trade this May for all the Junes and Januaries. His face was flushed from exercise and wine, and I wondered just how good he would look to me if I had more to choose from.

"I've been transferred," he muttered in my ear. "To London."

Now I knew just how good he looked to me. My heart sank. The whole thing was done and gone. Goodbye, Simon. There weren't many people in New Delhi I could talk to, and Simon had been one. Not that we'd really understood one another, for he was as reserved as the English he hated so heartily. But he was civilized. He knew Brahms from Bartók and El Bosco from El Greco; he read things he didn't have to read, and he played a heroic game of tennis. "Richard the Lion Hearted," he dubbed me the first time we played doubles, and we became cobbers. Additionally, Simon was extremely knowledgeable about Burma, and I had been counting on his

## Maidens

help when I went there on an acquisitioning trip. I leaned my head momentarily on his shoulder. There wasn't an ounce of comfort on that knobby frame.

"Well," I said, "you could do worse than London," thinking how all his provincial innocence would go unadmired there, until some sophisticated Englishwoman who understood his weakness intuitively would move in bloodlessly and make hash of him. "Damn!" he exclaimed. "'I've been asking them for years to assign me to Burma or Malaya. You'd think they could use someone there with some knowledge of the area. Anyway, my regular tour here wasn't supposed to be up for another year."

I figured it would have taken him about another year to open any meaningful conversation with me. Nothing lost there. "They must have needed someone for the Colombo Plan," I said. He had the lightest blue eyes I had ever seen. You almost wondered at first if he could see.

"They need someone, all right, but they're putting me into emigration. Just stuffing a body in a slot, as usual." To that, there could be no reply. It was every diplomat's nightmare, to get put into a passport or visa post where there were lots of headaches, but no honor to be won. "Anyway, that's that, and I'm leaving next month."

We jalousied back to our table. Jagbir gave Simon a wicked leer, meant to elicit from the Australian whether or not I had agreed to go on to the swimming pool with the rest of the crowd. He had already sent his silent wife home with the chauffeur, and was organizing a démarche on the Brazilians.

Simon and I thanked Iqbal for his hospitality and left. I knew the Turk would be cut, but it didn't matter. Iqbal never thought of women as actual human beings, not in the same sense as he regarded himself as a human being, so anything I did could be chalked up to feminine caprice and would only lead him to redouble his efforts with more wine, more parties, and more displays of jewels. There was no way on earth my behavior or my words could affect him, unless I gave him what he wanted. So I left with Simon.

Coming out of the hotel, we were mobbed by beggars

who clustered at the restaurant door. They were all there: the shoeshine boys, the tiny abandoned girls, the man nursing an infant at his breast, the silent shrouded women. A Sikh rushed up to tell our fortunes, and the amount of private information he shouted after us made it plain he was either clairvoyant or a transom snooper. It was worth a rupee to shut him up. He glided off with his painted eyes glistening.

Beggar children besieged us, and the half-eaten tournedo turned over in my stomach. "Jao! jao!" Simon shouted at them in time-honored Indian fashion. "Scram!" but he threw them money at the same time, so it did no good. No Indian gives alms. If people are wretched, it is because of sins committed in a previous existence, which they must expiate before they can be reborn into a better life. One cannot change the decree of fate with a few pennies, so Indians curse the beggars and cuff them away. Only the crazy, guilt-ridden foreigners try to buy off their consciences by giving alms.

Simon eased his little Hillman-Minx through the crowd of beggers. We were quiet a few moments, while our dinners did battle with the sights and sounds of beggary. Finally, since we were young and healthy, our digestive tracts won out. But this sort of thing played havoc with the soul. Perhaps it would be better to imitate the Indians and become callous toward the poor. Then it wouldn't hurt so much to see them. But speaking for myself, when the day came that I got mad at the beggars because they had ruined my dinner, I knew it was time to go home.

The Hillman-Minx tooled along Alipur Road toward New Delhi, a green and pleasant city where the beggars hardly ever came, and where one could believe that India was a wonderful place to live.

"How about a swim at Rashtrapathi Bhavan?" I asked Simon.

"How do you plan to get in?" Simon answered a question with a question.

"Oh, can't everyone?" A question inside a question inside a question.

My first night ever in Delhi, the man I was replacing (he

## Maidens

told me he was humiliated; it was like a frontline soldier being replaced by a WAC) took me to a cocktail party. There I experienced real culture shock, for I met all the types I thought I had left behind me in Washington. The intrusive, personable journalist; the world renowned statesman who was not above goosing a girl behind the grand piano; the doctor hoping to land a contract to examine embassy employees; the beautiful, beautiful girls who could hold their liquor—any amount of liquor—and who were aging right before your very eyes.

One type I was unprepared for, however, was the handsome young Indian pilot in gorgeous white uniform and gold braid, who invited me to a party the next evening over at his place. His wife smiled silently beside him. Had I ever worn a sari? No, I had not. The next morning, he appeared in an equally gorgeous blue uniform at my hotel room door with a suitcase full of his wife's saris, and his wife's maid. He left all with me so that I might become familiar with Indian dress. I spent a few hours trying them on, then sent them all back by tonga to the lieutenant's wife.

For casual dinner at my new friend's house, and my first essay at representing the United States, which after all is a diplomat's primary function, I thought I ought to wear American clothes. Envisioning a barbeque on some suburban verandah, I put on a cute peasant blouse, dirndl skirt, and sandals. Outside the Maidens, I handed the lieutenant's card to a taxi driver. The card said simply (or unsimply) "Rashtrapathi Bhavan." "Do you know where that is?" I asked the driver. "Oh, yes, Missahib," was the reply, with a military salute.

I should have suspected something was wrong because the driver drove straight across the city without detour, into a large estate bounded by thick red stone walls surmounted by pudgy elephants. By the time we reached the house, or I should say palace, my little peasant blouse and skirt were burning holes through my skin. But as a round trip to the hotel and back would take forty-five minutes, and I had been warned to be punctual, I pressed on to the front gate, where I was admitted by an armed guard.

## Krishna Smiled

It was the home of the President of India, and Lieutenant Jha was his aide-de-camp for Air. The company dined on bone china with sterling silver flatware, and were served by a battalion of servants in blindingly white uniforms with red and gold embroidered vests, and bare feet. There were several English women present whom I never met elsewhere in Delhi society, and with whom I found it absolutely impossible to talk, shielded as they were by startling floral print gowns of some impermeable material that fell from the neck straight down to the floor, without pause for bosom, waist, or hips. It was inconceivable that they possessed any of those things. Everyone, including the soup and fish, was dressed in formal attire.

Whether out of compassion or because he was genuinely taken by my American informality, about which so much may be read in books, Lieutenant Jha welcomed me to New Delhi with a marvellous present: he gave my name to the palace guard. Henceforth I could go and come on the palace grounds at will.

The chief attraction here was the lovely, secluded swimming pool embedded in roistering clouds of brilliant red-blossomed vines. The pool had not been used since President Rajendra Prasad, an elderly and a religious man, had been persuaded to occupy the palace. It had not been well riled since Partition days, when Pandit Nehru used to come to cool off with Lady Mountbatten. In fact, I was told that if the two of them ever showed up, I should scoot. But here I came every day I was in Delhi, and never met a soul till Krishna materialized.

As Simon and I entered the hidden doorway into the pool enclosure, the moon rode high overhead and the jasmine breathed a heady perfume. We swam lazily in the tepid water, stirring little ripples that broke up the reflection of the pillared colonade which ringed the pool.

Later, we went for a stroll in the formal gardens and plucked tiny oranges from dwarf trees, which we ate peel and all. The garden was so precisely laid out, the trees standing so modestly in their Buster Brown haircuts, that I half ex-

*Maidens*

pected a deck of playing-card gardeners to come rushing out with their ladders to paint the white roses red. But there was only the cooing of doves and the gurgling of water that crisscrossed the garden in miniature canals.

The flowers were deep and deeper shades of grey and black under the moonlight, but by day they were a melange of red, purple, pink and orange such as I had never seen elsewhere. The Moghul gardens were the scene of frequent immense diplomatic receptions, and then the flowers had to vie for attention with brilliant saris, obis, and dashikis. Orange punch was served and Pandit Nehru circulated argumentatively among the guests, who included the diplomatic colony, cabinet members, writers, artists, members of Parliament, and visiting dignitaries. Tito was a favorite guest of the time, running second only to Adlai Stevenson in charm. Every conceivable language was to be heard in the garden, but only one topic: the weather.

Now here was Simon and here was I, walking hand in hand through the Red Queen's garden. The crowds had fissiparated; Nehru and his eternal bumbershoot gone to bed; and for all the hours I had spent in that garden I could remember just one conversation that was not as insipid as the punch.

Sarevapellai Radhakrishnan, India's great philosopher and at that time her Vice President, had offered me a brief disquisition on the status of women in India. Although woman's scope has traditionally been limited, he pointed out, still, within her sphere of family and the home, she is supreme.

"My own name," he said, "signifies the esteem in which woman is held, for Radha's name is placed before that of Krishna." And he smiled that beneficent smile that always seemed to flit before me.

It perched now in little trees, that disembodied smile that Alice saw, and watched events take their course toward romantic self-destruction. The executioners were approaching, and I could feel my exequator slipping right off my wall.

Simon felt it too. So he asked what I thought about going to London with him. I said "Not much," and the smile extinguished itself.

I liked Simon well enough. But was *liking* a substitute for *being*? I was far too involved in unravelling my own life to consider giving it up for someone else's version of life. God knew who Simon really was; for that matter, who was I? Could I accept him, before I had accepted myself?

And there were corners of Asia I hadn't entered, languages I hadn't heard uttered, foods I hadn't tasted, dictionaries I hadn't caught up with, and lots of telephone directories still to be acquisitioned. I hadn't even approached Angkor Wat. How could I give up this great scavenger hunt and become a found object?

And of course, marrying a foreign diplomat was an embarrassing proposition, for the American Government is a jealous Government, and suffers no other Governments to come before it, or even with it.

So I said, "Not much."

"Well, in that case," said life's escapee, "how about a brief encounter?"

This was a more viable proposition, and all there was time for. No commitment, no regrets. Just a little Australian comfort.

There are advantages to slicing up your life in two-year segments: you can experiment with impunity. You can try everything. Why not? The rule book is back home, and its precepts don't apply here.

But what if a person existentially becomes what he does? In that case, there is danger of turning into someone other than you thought you were.

Well, if you don't like the person you become, you have only to sweep the character under the rug as you go out . . .

And I liked Simon well enough.

But liking was the last thing I would need once he was gone. The least dependence would penetrate my self-control, and I could no longer accept the isolation of my life, which was the only way that I could live it. Liking was the last thing I would need when Simon was gone. Better to leave him with moonlight and jasmine. Let *him* fret over *me*.

In driving me home, we passed the Brazilian Embassy

*Maidens*

where there was a sizable convention of mayflies. They might burn for a day only, but what a day they would make of it! At the rear of the embassy grounds, a graceful brick building housed a swimming pool where, in accordance with ancient lusitanian tradition, swimsuits were not worn. One might say the Brazilians had dispensed with the convention that so disturbed those orthodox gentlemen around the Gymkhana Club pool. I shuddered to imagine the scene within. Iqbal and Jagbir appearing simultaneously in the altogether was as upsetting to my digestion as the beggars had been; and I could scarcely have endured the unveiling of the flat fräulein, who probably was even now giving her all for the Vaterland. But to whom? And for what?

As for the skinny maharani, she would be in her element. All Delhi knew, because she told them, about the peephole and mirrors her husband rigged in her bedroom in order to watch her cavort with her lovers. The maharajah was impotent as the result of excesses made available to him by his household staff when he was a boy. But he had the legal limit of four wives and still managed to get his jollies.

After Simon dropped me off, I lay in bed and thought a long time, while dance music continued to drift upstairs through the open courtyard. In the morning, I would be awakened by doves.

Living like a mayfly is all right for a man. You burn your candle to the stub, and when the pace catches up with you, you marry someone congenial who is willing to pack your bags for you every two years, and from then on you carry your home and your heart with you when you are transferred. Your private life stays intact, wherever in the world you may happen to be.

But consider a woman. One day she looks in the mirror, the pace has caught up with her and it is too late. That little bitch Snow White is alive and well in the forest. Our lady of the world, still handsome and full of spunk, may not relish a lifetime of meeting airplanes to pick off the new arrivals. In any event, they are bound to run into Snow White sooner or later. As for marriage, the market was always limited, and a woman's valuation does not rise with the years. If lucky, she finds someone congenial and (in my day) has to quit the service. Although the Civil Rights Act of 1964 purports to rectify this situation, no legislation can alter biology. A woman stays with her husband, or there is no point in marrying. And she can hardly expect him to abandon his work in New Delhi because she is transferred to Oslo.

The career woman Foreign Service Officer is on her own, single, transient. That would mean a parade of Simons and Iqbals and Dancing Generals reeling in and out of my life. I could not, as Simon would one day, choose one companion to take along with me. Mine would be a life of permanent impermanence. At each post I would have to work out a whole new web of personal relationships as well as professional ones; only to see it destroyed two years later. At least, a man could maintain continuity in his emotional life.

The obvious conclusion was that I should limit my foreign service career. Perhaps one more assignment . . .

Or did they all say that, all those women who were preserving themselves in alcohol and exotic objets d'art?

Well, as long as I was here, I was going to do a good job of it. I got out of bed and started getting my papers in order. Maps, passport, carnet, insurance, check book, book lists, journal . . . Funny, I could have married Simon without effort, but it took some doing to get to Sikkim.

# 12

*I climb a Himalaya and miss a coup d'etat*

The stream, ripped from the belly of some Tibetan glacier, was boisterous and frigid where I bathed in it. Ignorant of the wild life of Kashmir, I kept an eye out for leeches, lobsters, and piranha, but what I felt were a million tiny electric shocks as the icy water dashed over me. Five minutes of scrabbling for foothold on the slippery rocks was enough for me. I could imagine myself tumbling downstream to be chewed up by jagged rocks and digested leisurely in the fields below.

Awkwardly—I came to being a nature sprite late in life—I slogged over to a boulder in midstream and hauled myself out.

At that moment, three men came trotting out of the woods, propelled downhill by the loads they carried. The first two bore a massive tree trunk on their shoulders. The third was bent double under a basketful of logs. He was using his arms as a stirrup under the load and, since the basket was

## Krishna Smiled

lashed to his forehead as well as to his back, he could not toss his head to shoo away the flies that clustered on his face.

If they saw, or thought they saw, a naked white and pink woman on a rock, they gave no sign. I imagine it would have been too hard to check the momentum of their loads.

Pulling on my clothes, I was ashamed. Not at being caught naked, for these mountain folk might have thought I was a gopi waiting for my divine lover, Krishna. But because here were men loaded like mules, running doubled through the wood; and here was I, who had climbed their mountain for pleasure.

Drying my skin roughly, I jumped to the bank, and entered the greenly fragrant wood. Here the gothic trees contained the air in upright shafts, still and warm. Through stained glass leaves the sun broke in quick, sharp blows from which sprang purple flowers. The breeze cozened me under light cotton. My skin, sensitized by the icy bath, felt each blade of grass growing.

From a precipice I looked down on the valley below. Three thousand feet down, the mountain stream had been domesticated, so that it flowed tamely in canals, flooded obediently into pools of paddy, drooled over rocks, and eddied greenly around the stilted houses. The green was marvellous, as though I had uncurled a single lettuce leaf and now looked into its secret convolutions, hidden, mysterious, and unknown to anyone but myself. Across this valley, a dike was flung. Atop it, poplars feathered a road.

Farmers, shin deep in mud and anonymous as insects, transplanted paddy, sparely, stem by stem beneath the water. Ahead of them, the rice was poisonously green, dotted, when the wind passed, with poppies. Where the farmers had already worked, the rice plants were mere brushstrokes on a Japanese screen.

Lying flat on my back, I could see a complete 360° range of mountains hemming the horizon. The snow which they stored on their crenelated peaks traced them whitely against the clear blue sky. Thus, the morning. By afternoon, there would be showers. At sunset the sky would clear, the peaks

## I climb a Himalaya

turn briefly incandescent, apink with light as banal as a picture postcard.

I was visiting Kashmir despite some unencouraging correspondence on the subject of publications which had passed between the U.S. Embassy and the government of Jammu & Kashmir State some months previously. An Economics Attaché had written to J & K for books, and received back three slim pamphlets comprising, said the accompanying note, the "entire stock" of the government book depot, and requesting a goodly list of titles from the United States.

After that it was hard for me to get the go-ahead for a personal reconnaissance of the area. But I knew that correspondence of this sort was an unreliable guide to the realities of the situation, and one of my Washington libraries had a penchant for forestry reports. I figured there must be some available somewhere in Kashmir, and ultimately I wrangled permission from the embassy, which was never quite certain what I was up to on these trips anyway.

Once having actually gotten to Kashmir, I should not have been lying around mountains and bathing in glacial streams. The fun part of my trip was due to the whim of the charmingly obdurate Chief Secretary of Kashmir. He was the man without whom nothing got done, and I wasn't going to get my forestry reports or anything else until I had his permission. Sophisticated and handsome, he served me coffee in his office, ascertained that I was not bright enough for espionage and was therefore engaged strictly in overt intelligence collection, and then authorized me to procure whatever books I might want from the government printing office, but . . .

Here, as so often, I was up against the pun on my name: *but* is rendered *laikin* in Hindi. A communist newspaper editor over in Bombay used to call me the prime minister's favorite word. "The country is progressing along all fronts," he would mimic Panditji. "But . . ."

"Laikin, Laikinji, you must see our hill stations. I cannot possibly allow you to leave Kashmir having seen Srinagar only! No, no, my dear Laikinji, it is quite impossible. I won't hear of such a thing.

## Krishna Smiled

"Look here, today is Friday, everything will be closed soon, and you can't possibly get your books from the press at Jammu over the weekend. So you just run along and enjoy yourself. I have made reservations for you at our new hotel at Pahalgam. I am most interested in your opinion of it."

To make certain that I would in fact spend the weekend at Pahalgam, Mr. Kidwai took the precaution of withholding my exit permit. I was, whichever way you looked at it, his prisoner. But as it was a weekend, and Kashmir is beautiful, and Mr. Kidwai so very, very nice, I drove compliantly up to Pahalgam and never regretted it.

In Srinagar, I had come to hate Kashmir and the Kashmiris. The town defaces the landscape it sits on. The despicability of men in their struggle to survive at the expense of other men shows up in peculiarly Brechtian terms there against the majesty of the mountains.

Srinagar is built on a chain of glassy waterways. Few sights are as soothing as a shikara flitting over Dal Lake, or moored beside the gardens of Nishat Bagh. The little boats bear such names as *Blue Jay* or *Humming Bird* or *Inner Springs*, and they are paddled by small grey men in coarse grey nightshirts. Occasionally, a girl sits in the bow, plucking water lilies while her father guides the boat.

The tourist is gulled by false idylls. For the shikari is not drifting, he is gunning his motor and scanning the horizon for prey. He may spy a covey of American being wafted across the lake toward the floating gardens. Or he may startle a flock of Angrezi diving from the roof of an anchored houseboat named *Honolulu* or *Beau Rivage* or *Severn Side*, into the weedy waters. Or, far up on Shankaracharya Hill, he may descry through squinted eyes a party of Frenchmen, determined on pilgrimage to the temple of Shiva, erected, says our guidebook, in 200 BCE.

The shikari now takes off after the tourist, his cockleshell loaded with fresh fruit and vegetables, scarves of flowery crewel embroidery, cunning all-of-one-piece wood carvings that are timed to spring apart during the next rainy season, and the calling cards of merchants in town who might be will-

## I climb a Himalaya

ing to part with star sapphires, karakuli lamb skins, elephant-print prayer rugs and ivory furniture. The shikari himself is loaded for bear.

It is uncertain whether the tourist is at a greater disadvantage on the mountainside, where he is bound to be winded; or in the water, in which case he can be prevented from getting a grip on the side of his boat; or in the water taxi, where he is at the mercy of another shikari, the brother of the man who is chasing him. But as a matter of historical record, no tourist has ever won a skirmish with a shikari, including the American I saw who pushed his tormentor over the gunwhales of his houseboat. In that instance, the American's wife was so upset over her husband's boorish lack of culture that she bought half the peddler's stock.

What the summer tourist, fighting to rid himself of this perpetual nuisance, cannot know, is that he is up against desperate men. Tourists in vacation mood are no match for Kashmiris, whose wits are sharpened by generations of preying on that canniest of prey, other men.

For the Kashmiri knows that the short summer will end and the wild flowers die. The tourists will retreat southward through the airfields and mountain passes, to their homes in Delhi and Buffalo and Leeds and Munich. The Himalayan wind will come spiralling down out of the mountains and freeze the lakes. The shikaris, who have no home but their boats, will pull these up on the bank and hibernate in them. There is nothing to roof them with, so they grip their shins with their arms and pull a poncho-like garment over their heads. At the pit of their bellies they place a small earthern jar, which is filled with live coals. If they don't move too much, it keeps them from freezing to death.

Shikaris are tanned — literally tanned — a crackly black from chest to groin.

There is a lot of literature available in Kashmir concerning the atrocities perpetrated by one side or the other in the fighting which has gone on intermittently since 1947 over the question of sovereignty of this wretched state. But the greatest atrocities are committed in Kashmir not by marauding tribesmen, nor by disciplined armies, but by the ordinary good citizens of the town who make a living out of one another's flesh. So far, the problem of Kashmir's pulverizing poverty has received rather less attention from either India or Pakistan than has the "nobler" problem of sovereignty.

I had my relaxing weekend at Pahalgam and, on my way down through Srinagar, attempted to call Mr. Kidwai to thank him. He was not, however, in his office, and I continued to Jammu. There, at the government press, I found my books waiting for me as Mr. Kidwai had promised — over 300 pounds of them, including several generations of forestry reports. I also incidentally cleaned out all reports concerning the administration of the area during the nineteenth century, and these should provide someone with material for a very interesting doctoral thesis.

The tail of my Vauxhall dragged considerably under the weight, but even so I made good time going down. I was eager to get back to Delhi and unload my cargo on the desk of the Economics Attaché. As I drove, I wondered about the ponderous convoys of Indian army trucks, all driven by stone-deaf Sikhs, which had so impeded me on the way up the week before. Where were the trucks of yesterweek?

The question was not impertinent. Kashmir was under what amounted to a military occupation, and the Indian government had built this road expressly for the purpose of fielding its troops there. For the Kashmir that is beloved by poets for its beauty, by women for its wool, by men for its women, and by travel bureaus for its tourist appeal, is also a festering sore in the severed bodies of India and Pakistan.

This quarrel, like so much else, has its roots in Partition. Pakistan was split into two wings with a thousand miles of India between, because the densest concentrations of Moslems were in Bengal on the east, and Sind, Punjab, and North-West Frontier Province on the west. Two other areas, by virtue of their large Moslem populations, might well have gone to Pakistan: Hyderabad and Kashmir.

These were the largest and richest of the princely states, and possessed distinct "national" cultures. Hyderabad actu-

## I climb a Himalaya

ally had a Hindu majority, but a Moslem ruling class. India feared the possibility that the Nizam might try to take Hyderabad into Pakistan: not so much because of the potential loss of a large Hindu population, but because Hyderabad is situated right in the middle of India. A three-piece Pakistan, triangulating in on New Delhi from the east, west, and south seemed a menace the new government could not tolerate. In a cynical "police action," India engulfed Hyderabad and ended any possibility of a link-up with Pakistan. A decade later, during the reorganization of Indian states, Hyderabad was divided into its linguistic components, divvied up among neighboring states, and lost whatever historical identity remained to it.

Kashmir proved more intractable. Contiguous to both India and Pakistan, it might logically have gone to either, had logic had anything to do with it. Kashmir is also next door to China and the USSR (across the panhandle of Afghanistan), and this does nothing to desensitize the issue.

So far as a decision on communal grounds goes, 80 percent of the population are Moslems. Aha! cries the observer. Let them join Pakistan. But to accept religion as the sole basis for national affiliation would be to decree the end of India: for India at Partition retained more Moslems than there were in Pakistan. Many stayed because they could not leave; but many others favored a secular state over the theocracy which Pakistan became. Within Kashmir itself, Sheikh Mohammed Abdullah, the great charismatic leader, never pronounced in favor of Pakistan.

Furthermore, the ruling family of Kashmir were Hindus. Both sides had agreed that, in the princely states, the decision to adhere to one country or the other was to be left up to the ruling prince. Possibly, had the maharajah acceded to one side or the other without tergiversation, Kashmir might not have become the running sore it did become.

From all accounts, the lapse of British rule found the maharajah paralyzed by indecision. Perhaps he hoped that by playing a waiting game and refusing to accede to one side or the other, he could make a successful bid for independence.

## Krishna Smiled

Whatever may have been going on in his mind, he hadn't made it up yet when Pathans of Pakistan's North-West Frontier Province began pouring in over the border to help him decide.

He did. The maharajah acceded to India. By that time, the road had been cut and the Indian government had to airlift its soldiers into Kashmir. Battle was joined.

A United Nations ukase halted the fighting at a line which left the Paks in occupation of the northern, wooded part of the state and India in control of the south and east, including the fabulous Vale with the capital city of Srinagar and the storied gardens of Shalimar: the tourists' Kashmir. An international team of truce observers was sent up to patrol the line. The road which India built into Kashmir became the focus of Pakistani attacks in the war of 1965, and again in 1971. Cutting it would render the Vale of Kashmir vulnerable to Pakistani absorption.

The stakes in Kashmir are doubled by the fact that the Indus River rises here, before forking its five arms across Punjab. The food supply of millions of people in both India and Pakistan depends on Indus water. This may not have been uppermost in the minds of the seminomadic tribesmen who charged into Kashmir to aid their co-religionists; but it was certainly the motivation of the government of Pakistan when they dug into the "liberated" areas and refused to leave. Control of "Azad" (Free) Kashmir assures Pak control of two Indus tributaries.

When the smoke of Partition cleared and the blood stopped running, the economy of the entire area was in shambles. Much depended upon the willingness of India and Pakistan to share the waters of the Indus between them—to stop cutting off one another's water to spite their own fields, as it were. Eventually this was accomplished, through the mediation of the World Bank. But the sovereignty of Kashmir remains at hazard.

Probably no one knows what the Kashmiris themselves would prefer. There may once have been a nationalist sentiment holding together all Kashmiris regardless of religion,

## I climb a Himalaya

but it is likely that tribal butchery and civil war dissipated all that. Holding a referendum on the matter, following so many years of off-and-on warfare and inflammatory propaganda, would be all too likely to end up in another Partition, on a smaller but equally bloody scale. On each side of the border, large minority groups are hostages for their co-religionists in Kashmir, and any communal rioting that erupted there could spread all too easily to the rest of the continent. It was discovered in 1947 that the easiest way to win an election was to murder your neighbor or burn him out, so that he could not vote, and I had seen the wreckage of Lahore. So India, in particular, is reluctant to redeem its pledge to hold a plebescite in Kashmir, for a resumption of religious warfare could destroy its nature as a secular, multireligious state.

Meanwhile, both India and Pakistan have integrated their zones of Kashmir into their respective countries. And both continue to fear a Kashmiri bid for independence, each believing that such a move would benefit its opponent.

When I arrived in Delhi I learned of the coup d'etat which took place in Srinagar while I was up in the hills. No wonder Mr. Kidwai hadn't answered his phone. Sheikh Mohammed Abdullah, the Lion of Kashmir, had been deposed and incarcerated by his old friend and fellow freedom-fighter, Jawarharlal Nehru.

The charge against the Sheikh was that he was plotting to end the partition of Kashmir by declaring its independence. In this venture, he was alleged to have the support of the United States, which was to get some air bases out of the deal. It was pointed out in the popular press that we had historical precedent for this move, having split Panama off from Colombia when we wanted to build the Canal.

Every American who had been in Kashmir that weekend was implicated in the plot, with the exception of myself, oblivious in Pahalgam. The highly pregnant wife of an American Embassy official, whose doctor had recommended the cool air of Kashmir, was touted as the Mata Hari of the manouevre. An American diplomat, returning from a mushroom-picking expedition along the Jammu road that Saturday

## Krishna Smiled

(the road Mr. Kidwai kept me off of) was charged with having subverted the Sheikh to the American scheme. Missionaries, anthropologists, and a rather kooky lady journalist were all pressed into service as spies and provocateurs, with Adlai Stevenson, Chester Bowles, and Moral Rearmament cast as the heavies.

The only way in which I was affected was that I never again saw a good friend of mine. He was an American naval officer who was stationed on the armistice line with the U.N. truce observation team. It got pretty lonely up there in the Himalayas with only Abominable Snowmen for company, and Tom used to call me up when he got down to Delhi on leave. Now, with an American plot afoot, it was too risky for him to contact anyone from the embassy lest he compromise his position on the team. So goodbye, Tom, wherever you are.

Had anyone asked me for my solution to the tangled Kashmir question, I would have said: turn the place upside down and shake out the political and religious leaders of all denominations. Then return the country to the raving black-eyed girls with their hair done up in a hundred pigtails, wearing coin-sewn skullcaps. And to the farmers, patiently transplanting rice knee-deep in muck. And to the little boys who go blind doing crewel embroidery. And to the shikaris, who die of skin cancer.

# 13

*Through Kerala with coir and cashew*

The panty raids which were pulled off at the University of Michigan in 1953 were a propaganda windfall for Asian communists. Widely distributed photographs in *Life* and other magazines showed coeds welcoming the men students aboard through dormitory windows, in what was obviously the first stage of mass rape, while the rest of America, including the girls' maternal uncles whose duty it should be to protect their nieces' virtue, stood by and laughed. Nothing could show more clearly the decadence of American society. Or, as the communists put it, the irreconcilable contradictions which would lead inevitably to the collapse of the capitalist system.

Nothing that we Americans did during the two years I was in Asia—not the alleged attempt to take Kashmir, not arms aid to Pakistan, not the refusal to repatriate Korean prisoners of war—caused as much furor as these innocent collegiate games.

## Krishna Smiled

In vain did I try to describe to friends and communists the jolly atmosphere of a large coed campus, the easy fraternization between sexes, the freedom of girls to accept or reject what men would thrust upon them. Even sober friends of the United States found in the panty raids an argument against the American custom of coeducation. You see what happens when boys and girls are allowed to mix. It is far more civilized to seclude your women and marry them off at the onset of menstruation.

I spent a lot of time talking to communists (Harry Truman once scribbled a note in the margin of a document written for his signature, to the effect that he saw no reason to capitalize the sons of bitches) because commie propaganda was a staple in the diet of some of my libraries. The stuff was widely available all over India. At any bookstall or bus stop one could buy the *Life* of Stalin, or Lenin's *Complete Works*, or the latest Stalin Prize Novel, or other hardbound classics for the equivalent of thirty-five cents. Topical pamphlets sold for a penny or two, used ones for a farthing. Most of this literature was published by the Foreign Languages Press, Moscow, or its up-and-coming competitor, the Foreign Languages Press, Peking, the foreign language in question being English.

All this was sent into the country free, courtesy of the Soviet and Chinese diplomatic pouches. It was then consigned without payment to the large communist book depots spotted about the country. The personnel of the depots were thus subsidized by, and acted as agents for, the Russians and Chinese.

The depots in turn consigned the books to local retailers, allowing them a one-third cut, which was more than they could make on any other type of publication. Communist literature thus was a good source of income for the bookdealers, so most kept it in stock whether they were sympathizers or not. They were rewarded by brisker business than was done by those few holdouts who declined to handle communist publications.

The Soviet pamphlets were a taxidermist's dream. Stalin

was shown stuffed and painted a healthy pink, looking quite pleased with himself and with the toiling Soviet masses. The pamphlets were immediately identifiable by their covers: if it wasn't Stalin, it was an earnest young man gazing hard at the horizon as though in imminent expectation of the arrival of Socialist realism; or a muscular young girl with a kerchief on her head and no makeup, reaping sheaves in communal fields. They were identical with the pamphlets currently available in Hong Kong, Copenhagen and Marseilles. We also got the current editions of *For a Lasting Peace, For a People's Democracy*, which tied us in to the party line that girdled the globe. It gave some country boys quite a cosmopolitan varnish, to be able to read the same literature that the bigwigs in Paris and Moscow were reading.

The Chinese output tended toward the pragmatic. In addition to the authorized biography of Mao Tse Tung (the *Little Red Book* had not put in its appearance as yet) there were various pamphlets of the "how to" variety, advising peasants how to wrest control of the land from their landlords, and women how to gain freedom from their men. A runaway best seller was the novel, *The Girl with White Hair*, which combined both these themes against the background of the Chinese revolution. This is the same story which was performed as a ballet for President and Mrs. Nixon on their visit to China in 1972, attesting to the vigor of the theme of sexual revolution within communist revolution.

Indian communists were also hard at work translating such documents as *Fundamentals of Marxism*, the Soviet *Constitution*, and the *Directives* of the XIX Party Congress for the Fifth Five Year Plan of Development of the USSR. Additionally, one could choose from among a fistful of languages in which to read about the agony of Indochina under the French, Malaya under the British, or the Negro under the Americans. Paradoxically, there was no communist literature available on India. It seemed that the hardest thing for an Indian to get to read was a Marxist analysis of his own situation.

This information gap may have been due to lack of funds

among the local party cadres to support research and publication (although there was apparently plenty of money around to do translations of Russian and Chinese documents into the vernaculars), or it may have been due to lack of originality among Indian communists. With unbelievable docility, they flocked to their bookshops to buy and study the various party directives, or the latest report on progress of construction of a hydroelectric dam in Bulgaria. The titles alone were enough to put one to sleep.

Meanwhile, their noncommunist buddies were flocking to college classrooms to study such timely works as *Wuthering Heights* and the *Mill on the Floss*. While all about them, the country was crying out for engineers, entreprenuers, surveyors, agronomists, accountants, and even intellectuals with the ability to criticize constructively, the bulk of the young intellectual class was burying its head in Victorian sands. It made one think their slogan should be, "Backward into the future," or perhaps, "Forward into the past."

Once, while travelling in the countryside of Uttar Pradesh, I picked up a young man who was walking beside the road. He had just graduated from the university and was going home to his village to visit his parents. Then he would take up a position teaching. Teaching what? Victorian literature. He was the counterpart of the young communist clerk in the bookstore near Lukri Bridge in Poona, whom I asked for a copy of Bukharin's works. (Bukharin was read out of the party and destroyed in the great Soviet purge). Oh yes, he had heard of Bukharin. Oh no, unfortunately he had none of his works in stock at the present time. Certainly he would be glad to place an order for me. Ours not to reason why.

The largest infestations of communist bookshops were around the colleges. It was physically impossible for an Indian student to get to class without running a red zone of bookstalls set up to waylay him. On my visit to Allahabad University, a century-old institution in the north, I was asked by one of my libraries to photograph all the buildings, which I did, but I could only feel that someone was missing the point. Not only because all the buildings look alike, but be-

## Through Kerala with coir and cashew

cause stone walls do not a college make. The libraries and bookstores do. No one ever asked me to photograph a bookstall, but this was where the students were to be found, and the students were the next governing generation.

Of course, not everyone is rich enough to go to college. Some people are so poor they would even feel uncomfortable venturing into a store. So the communists picked up little boys (one of the cheapest commodities in India) and trained them to hawk the party line on street corners, bus stops, and boat jetties. They permitted the boys to keep the entire proceeds of their sales, and thus bound them to the party with ties of income and loyalty, presumably in readiness for future use when they were grown. It is fair to say that every communist publication sold at that time served a dual purpose: it was, in itself, a vehicle of propaganda; and it was a livelihood, often the only source of livelihood, for the vendor.

At one point I thought I would give my libraries a thrill by providing some Marxism à la Malayalam. In order to procure this rare treat, I travelled by motorboat through the canals of what used to be called the Malabar Coast, was at that time called Travancore-Cochin, and is now called Kerala. Sometimes, in India, the toughest thing is just finding out where you are.

Kerala is what professional travellers call a tropical paradise. I coasted southward through cerulean lagoons bathed by waves of color. The water is incredibly blue, the land and all its little islands sensuously green and skirted by blindingly white sand, the sky nearly white with the tropical sun that has no counterpart in temperate climates. To our right, the combers of the Arabian Sea susurrated gently; to our left, palm trees dipped and bent over the inland lagoons, which naturally cause the area to be known as the "Venice of the East." This is misleading. Malabar is much cleaner than Venice.

I boarded the little boat at Alleppey at nine in the morning. Though I did not know it at the time, I would not reach Quilon, fifty-seven miles down the line, until seven that night. I was in no hurry. Never did twelve cents stretch so far.

## Krishna Smiled

Passengers, including myself, travel in motor launches, in the absence of roads. Freight is carried in long narrow canoes with thatched roofs, called vellums, which are poled by a man at either end. These men always seemed blacker than anybody else, as though natural selection had been at work. As I sat in the rear of the line boat, islands seemed to float past us, laden with families, huts, cows, and naked children. As it was a school holiday, canoes shot past loaded with brown-skinned youngsters vigorously paddling, red flags flying, chanting "Inqilab zindabad!" ("Long live revolution!")

Most adults seemed to be sitting slumped against trees, unpleasant caricatures of the lazy southerner. Put large straw hats on their heads, and they would look like the Mexicans of the cartoon strips. Closer inspection revealed that they were anchored to the ground by prodigious legs which had swollen and decayed with elephantiasis, forcing their owners to lie around watching the disease spread to their arms. There was no known cure. Other people were bathing in the lagoons, which is probably where the disease incubates, bathing with their clothes on and washing these clothes while they wore them, for they had nothing to change into. Children under the age of puberty ran naked because their parents could not afford to clothe them.

At noon I bought a coconut to go with my can of tuna. Usually I ate off the countryside, but in Kerala I was put off by the smell. Coconut oil is favored for cooking, rather than the ghee (clarified butter) of the north; and for me the effect was of biting into a bar of Palmolive. Had I been travelling by train, a three-course meal would have shown up at one station or another. But then I would not have had the pleasure of this leisurely trip; nor would I have acquisitioned any communist literature in the railway stations, because the government of India banned their sale there.

Not so the jetties, which are the bus stops of rural Kerala. At each one, there stood a lad with a stack of fascinating and incomprehensible publications spread out for sale on tarpaulin. I would jump out each time the boat stopped, but always with trepidation that the boat would leave without me, since

*Through Kerala with coir and cashew*

I couldn't communicate with the pilot. I had no idea when another boat would come through. But the little sons of communists who were selling the pamphlets didn't want anything to do with me, and for the first time in my book-buying career I was thwarted. I could not speak or read Malayalam. I had no wish to burden myself with a pony for the *Merchant of Venice* or even a novel by C. P. Snow, who was very big just then. I wanted communist propaganda, but without pictures on the front covers I couldn't tell the sheep from the goats.

At one jetty, a boy came aboard and sat down next to me with a great deal of self-possession. "Good morning, Madam" he saluted me. "My name is Joseph. May I be of assistance to you?"

As these were the first English words I had heard all day, naturally I was curious about the youngster. He was twelve, an orphan, and was being raised in a Catholic mission in Alleppey. He had heard of the United States; his school received books and clothing from America. When he asked me who I had come to India with (again, the assumption that a woman does not act autonomously) I told him, in the simplest way I knew how, "I am with the American Ambassador."

"Mr. Chester Bowles!" Joseph exclaimed, and wrung my hand. What was I doing here for Mr. Bowles? Was there any way in which Joseph could serve Mr. Bowles too? "Well, I'm buying books for him," I said. "Mr. Bowles wants to learn all there is to learn about India."

"He is such a wonderful man," replied Joseph. "He is so good. But he will not like the books you bring him back from Cochin. They are all communist."

"I suppose he wants to read even those books, Joseph," I said. "It's a good idea to know what other people are thinking."

From then on, Joseph hopped out at every stop and bought me an armload of pamphlets with the money I gave him. We spent the time between stops translating the titles. So we acquisitioned a variety of primitively printed pamphlets, distinguished by the vitality and originality of their texts.

## Krishna Smiled

Kerala was the only place in India where I found Marxist minds turning their dialectic upon their own lives.

My most interesting acquisition (interestingly, this was in English, for an Indian author who hopes to reach a nation-wide audience must write in English) was a booklet called *The National Question in Kerala,* presenting a case for creation of a Malayalam-speaking state. The communists learned through their Russian experience that the quickest way to arouse the peasants, dull and conservative as they are, to political action, was by appealing to their national loyalties. As Stalin said when he was Commissar of Nationalities: "the national question (is) virtually the peasant question."

The Indian National Congress did not organize in the princely states prior to independence, and so the communists had a relatively clear field in Travancore-Cochin. From the start, they espoused the cause of a separate Malayalam-speaking state, and succeeded in identifying themselves as defenders of local interests against the imperialism of the Hindi-speaking north.

In 1956, the communists won their point: the old princely state of Travancore-Cochin was joined with parts of Malabar, some Tamil-speaking areas to the south were shifted over to Madras, and the new state of Kerala came into being, with Malayalam as its official language. The communists rode to victory in the first state elections on a wave of communism, nationalism, and gerrymandered districts. At their head was the author of *National Question in Kerala.* To my knowledge, the people of Kerala were the first on the face of the earth to use free and secret balloting to elect themselves a communist government.

Several factors predispose any underdeveloped area to communism; they were all at work in India of the 1950s, and in Kerala they happened to find congenial conditions. Perhaps primary among these was reaction against the imperialist world of Britian, France, Belgium, the Netherlands, and Portugal (all United States allies). Any state which opposed them on the international scene automatically reaped the friendship of the former colonies. The Soviets, whose imperial

## Through Kerala with coir and cashew

gambits had never taken them into Southeast Asia, were able to pose in Asia as friends of the downtrodden. Naturally, there was great interest in the philosophy which seemed to motivate them. At this period in history, that philosophy happened to be communism.

The communists, of course, worked at developing this friendship, because of their belief that the western world can be brought to its knees through being severed from its colonies, its source of wealth. In the case of France battling to retain Algeria and Indochina, the theory came very close to the mark. In the case of Britain, which relinquished control of India, Pakistan, Burma, and Ceylon in a semi-voluntary manner, collapse was averted, at least for some decades, by rational provisions for continued trade relationships.

The experience of capitalism which the underdeveloped world has had, has been almost totally negative. It was the capitalist world which colonized the southern hemisphere, exploiting natural resources and labor, selling back manufactured goods at prices which constantly advanced as the western economies expanded. For over a century, the terms of trade went against the primary producers, for reasons they could not control, and in favor of the industrialized countries. So far as foreign trade is concerned, many Asians, Africans, and Latin Americans experience capitalism as a form of piracy, in which technologically superior industries move in and loot the national resources, then turn around and sell luxury goods to the elite.

So far as domestic trade is concerned, capitalism as practiced by local elites too often displays those features which Europe discarded after Dickens: child labor, debt bondage, maximum hours of work at minimum wages. I had seen the weavers chained to their looms by debt; I knew there were places in India where farmers who had tilled the same plot for generations had to pay 90 percent of their crop to the landlord as rent; I had seen the workers of Calcutta go from air-conditioned factories to homes you wouldn't keep a pig in. In Coimbatore, where the ordinary people stood in line for hours to get a jug of drinking water from the municipal

## Krishna Smiled

truck, the industrialist who invited me to his home for dinner boasted of his spacious green lawn, freshly watered.

Even those Asians who bear no grudge against capitalism aver that the developing nations have neither time nor wealth to allow themselves the costly detours inherent in a free enterprise system. How can they allow scarce investment funds to pour into a hula hoop factory, when there are hydroelectric stations to be built? The market may "demand" hula hoops, but the country needs electricity and water. How can a responsible government permit capital to be wasted in building competitive railroad lines which duplicate one another's services, when, with a little planning, rail networks might open up all sectors of the country for development? Developing nations are too hard pressed by accelerating population growth to waste time in competition.

But, asks the western liberal, if you permit government to plan the economy, won't you lose your personal freedom?

Of course, as American farmers have learned. But the issue of planning is not all black and white, as the rest of us know. You can plan certain aspects of the economy (in the developing countries today, this would include construction of the high-cost, long-term social overhead such as highways, schools, hospitals, harbors, railroads, etc.) while allowing the rest of the economy to remain competitive, operating on the profit motive.

To the degree that planning is involved, the citizen does become subject to the demands of his government. But here one may stop and ask: who formulated these demands? Elected representatives of the people who are responsible to the electorate for their actions? Or despots accountable only to themselves? There is a world of difference. The latter is the road to dictatorship; the former, one way for society to reach decisions for the common good.

It is apparent that a person living within a traditional society may be more willing than ourselves to accept paternalistic government. One who has always lived subject to the authority of father, village elders, caste, has simply never experienced personal liberty in the sense in which we enjoy it. Where tradition takes precedence over individual desire,

## Through Kerala with coir and cashew

people are subject to such strong social control that, even if they possess certain liberties by law, they are unable to exercise them. Thus, many persons in a traditional society experience, or believe they will experience, the shift from an authoritarian family to an authoritarian state as progress. To them, the shift of power to the state represents moving with the times.

One cannot speak of loss of freedoms to people who have never exercised any. For most Indians alive today, their occupation, marriage, social status, were dictated by birth, from the time of birth (and before). What is freedom?

If the state is to proceed along authoritarian, or at least paternal, lines, it might as well proceed intelligently. For this purpose, it is useful to study the experience of other societies which, beginning from an agricultural base, have succeeded in turning themselves into first-rate powers. So, the Soviet Union and China provide relevant patterns. The main thrust of communist propaganda in India was that the Soviet Union had not only organized substantial economic growth starting from an agricultural base, but that this had been accomplished in a multilingual state and had resulted in the resolution of all national tensions.

What kind of example can the United States provide, with our unimaginable wealth? Or European countries, which derived their wealth from plunder of the colonies? In the 1950s, communism was a most attractive alternative.

In Kerala, there were special forces urging toward a communist solution. Unbeknownst to the theatergoing public, Kerala is the cashew capital of the world. It is also big on coconuts, from which is manufactured coir, the stuff our doormats are made of. Speaking for myself, I can take coir or leave it; and sometimes I prefer walnuts to cashews. A lot of people feel the same way, and so Kerala is at the mercy of the consumer's whim. When we eat lots of cashew nuts and remember to wipe our feet, there are jobs for the people of Kerala. When our demand drops, prices slump and factories close. Employment rises and falls in a way which is not controllable by the people most concerned.

There are other social factors urging people toward radical restructuring of their society. Malayalees, like all the people of India, are divided by caste; but the inequality among these castes is far more acute here than anywhere else in the country. In this agricultural state, at the time of independence, 40 percent of the farmers owned no land, and another 37 percent owned a half-acre or less. Almost all of the landless belonged to specific depressed castes. At the same time, the high caste farmers tended to own land in larger acreages. Kerala as a whole produces only half enough rice to feed its people. The implications for low caste parents of little children are terrifying. It was upon them that the communists concentrated their efforts, and they succeeded in translating ancient grievances into substantial political clout.

Perhaps not irrelevantly, Kerala also has the highest percentage of Christians of any Indian state, accounting for 35 percent of the population. Christians are queer fish. They believe in the Fatherhood of God and the Brotherhood of Man—a subversive notion, as the Romans found. If Christians go around propagating their theories, a lot of people may get the idea that they are just as good as anybody else. Although Kerala's two million Syrian Christians generally stayed within the ranks of Congress, the communists were able to take advantage of spreading notions of equality to get Hindu outcastes to go to the polls and vote against domination by higher castes.

Over half the population of Kerala can read and write. This introduces a volatility which does not exist elsewhere in India. Ignorant peasants starve to death quietly. If they rise in desperation, it is easy to shoot them down. They are, after all, savages.

But the man who has learned to read and write is a human being and must be reckoned with. He knows some of the causes of his misery; and he can learn techniques for ridding himself of these causes. Educated men expect more from life than a sentence of hard labor on short rations. Educated men demand jobs, and in a pre-industrial society, these may simply not exist.

With more than half the population able to read and

## Through Kerala with coir and cashew

write, they longed for a meaningful text. There had been a message long before: a message of brotherly love. It offered infinite hope, but no means of implementing that hope. A promise of life eternal for those meek enough to sit under their palm trees waiting to die of hunger and bilharzia may fail to satisfy some. Is it conceivable that a religion which inspires hope, but which makes no change in the objective conditions of life, may actually pave the way for a new religion?

The new, like the old, came from out of the west. Like the old, it too promised justice and equity. In *this* life. "Expropriate the expropriators!" is not a cant phrase in India. It is an anguished cry for justice.

In 1910, the first translation of a life of Karl Marx into any Indian language was published in Malayalam. By the time I arrived, communist publications were rampant.

Ernakulam boasted one of the large bookhouses which the communists located around the country in the major linguistic areas (in Madras, Kerala, Bombay, Bengal, and Andhra). Uniformly clean, neat and efficient, they were obviously closely supervised. The party workers employed there were young, serious, and dedicated to Truth. Very polite, and very belligerent.

At the book depot named Truth (Prabhat), I was challenged: "You are an American lady, isn't it? Please, tell me why your government melted down the Statue of Liberty to make munitions?"

"What about the Scottsboro boys?" a bystander asked.

"And the panty raids?" demanded another.

I was exasperated; yet it all seemed unreal. These were wealthy young men who were challenging me, judging by their clothing and their language. What were *they* doing for their country? As for me, I had never heard of the Scottsboro boys (although I read about them that evening in a pamphlet I picked up that day). And I had taken on protective coloration to the degree that I was as horrified about the panty raids as they were.

About the only charge I was equipped to fight was the

one about the Statue of Liberty, since I had seen her recently. But who was prepared to reason? I began picking out my books.

The crowd was mollified by that action. It appeared that I was an American who was willing to learn. So they scrambled about bringing me all sorts of titles and translating their contents for me in brief. In no time at all, I had a pretty good selection and may State have joy of them.

In a friendly mood now, the crowd insisted that I come along with them to the street of the ivory carvers, and I did. Personally, ivory interested me a good deal more than ill-printed communist pamphlets, but I was going to have to watch my spending because I had only about ten dollars of my own money along.

This posed another problem. How do you explain limited funds to these young men who think all Americans are millionaires? Or, if you succeed, how do you avoid cultivating the opposite idea, implanted so cunningly by the communists, that American affluence is a myth, and ordinary people do not share in it? There never seemed to be any middle ground: either Americans were fabulously wealthy (as indeed we appeared to be, by comparison with Indians) or the whole thing was a lie.

Eventually I found the perfect piece: a little dancer of Bharatanatyam trailing scarfs of ivory, her delectable derrière cunningly worked from a slight defect in the material. Having liberated her, I lingered in the shop over some jewelry which I also coveted but could not afford.

Among the jewelry under the counter were certain small triangles of silver, no more than an inch along each side, with holes bored at two corners and a string run through the holes. I asked the proprietor to show me one, which he did. I asked him what it was; and, though he probably told me, I could not understand him. No one in the crowd offered an explanation. It certainly seemed to be jewelry, but it didn't fit any portion of my anatomy.

Thinking it might be a tiqa, I took it up by the string and tied it around my forehead, the triangle just over the

## Through Kerala with coir and cashew

bridge of my nose. The crowd, which had by now grown so as to fill every corner of the shop, went into hysterics. Good-natured, but hysterical. I removed the dingle-dangle from my forehead and tied it around my ankle. More laughter. At last, an earnest young man came forward and said, "Madam, that is a modesty, to be worn by very small girl children." As I say, the children go naked.

At Quilon, at night, a deputation of Englishmen arrived at my traveller's bungalow to invite me to the Planters' Club for dinner and dancing. I accepted, although, usually, I avoided the English. I didn't want to be tarred with the imperialist brush and spoil my welcome by Indians. But I was lonely, and though it may be true that the English and ourselves are separated by a common language, the gap is nowhere near as wide as the one which separates us both from Malayalam. That good language is so mellifluous that it quavers in the air sans consonants, melting away without leaving behind a single consonant for the listener to grapple and imitate.

In a pleasant palm-fringed bungalow, I found a bachelor colony of British planters, as isolated as though they had been living beside the Mare Imbrium among little green men, rather than beside the Arabian Sea among little brown ones. They wore black tie for dinner, summoned the servants with a peremptory "Boy!", and referred to local citizens as "natives," a word that had long since gone out of the language up north. The servants in turn addressed the white men as "Master," a reasonable translation of the northern "Sahib" but a good deal more offensive.

They had a joke about an Englishman, newly arrived in India, who was invited to the Club. (It didn't have to be this Club, it could be any Club, they were all alike). Sitting around after dinner, one of the Old Hands called, "Boy!" A moustachioed old man appeared. "Cross my right leg over my left knee," the Master ordered. The bearer did so, saluted, and left.

The newcomer stared in astonishment at his host. "Oh, I beg your pardon," the Old Hand muttered, realizing he had committed a faux pas. Calling the bearer back, he ordered, "Boy, cross this Master's legs too."

It was gallows humor. As representatives of the old order, these men were doomed, and they knew they were doomed. Sooner or later they would have to go back home and live like other mortals. How much longer could they hang on here, now that the country was independent and the school children were paddling around the lagoons yelling "Inqilab zindabod?" The whole trouble was that the British should not have yielded power. Whatever happened, they should have stood firm. It was obvious the Indians were incapable of governing themselves; only the presence of the British had prevented the niggers from killing one another off. Now there was only chaos, and the communists would reap the whirlwind.

We danced to Noel Coward records, and for a while forgave one another our political sins and pretended. When Mr. Jones (a real Jones, a Welshman) placed his hand around my waist to dance, I pretended he was that boy back in college who had the great sense of humor; and I suppose he pretended I was that girl from Cardiff with frizzy hair and no sense of humor. At least, it never occurred to him that having his arm around my waist gave him a license to place it somewhere else. It seemed to me that Indians could never grasp this subtle distinction. If a woman allows a man to touch her at all, what then can she possibly forbid him? In a moment, she is prostrate across an easy chair.

There was a piano and I played some Chopin. Blue-grey-cool ballerinas in icy tutus glided across the frigid stages of my memory. The carnation-scented perfume which my mother gave me for my twelfth birthday and which I always and only wore to concerts, insinuated itself into my nostrils. The ballerinas' faces were aloof, their toes disdained to touch the floor, but shifting harmonies suspended them bodily over the stage in their subtle tights.

There is an awful lot of commotion in India.

We all went swimming the next day on a spectacular white beach that the waves soothed as gently as a sleep ma-

## Through Kerala with coir and cashew

chine. The palm trees were painted on the sky. The waves rolled gently in upon us, washing the waters of the Arabian Sea around the sweep of Comorin and into the Bay of Bengal. At the cape, I was told, there stands a castle whose walls are painted with a mixture of sugar and egg white so that the whole thing looks like a frosted wedding cake. The maharajahs at least don't worry about hunger.

It was all so lovely, the whole world so beautiful, except for the people in it: the starving, disease-ridden Indians, the boring, self-satisfied Englishmen.

Long after I had left India, and a scant two years after the communist government was voted into power in Kerala, the people threw the rascals out. By means of a passive resistance campaign, yet, the very technique used by the Congress coalition to evict the British. In power, the communists had behaved very much as their predecessors had, even ordering police to shoot at striking workers in order to protect the property of the factory owners. There was some land reform, but probably no more than there would have been under a Congress government; much corruption, probably no less than there would have been under a Congress government; and there was a divisive school reform, riddled with the same errors the Congress party might have made. In the end, the people threw them out: not because they were communists, but because they could not do the things that needed doing.

Communism was no more a panacea for the area's ills than capitalism had been, or feudalism or monarchy or a republic or Christianity or Islam or the matriarchal family, all of which have had their turn in Kerala. It is just possible that conditions there are past mending by any ideology.

I headed inland by train for Madurai and Tirruchchirapolli, two fabled temple cities where I saw nothing, heard nothing, smelt nothing, and certainly ate nothing. Away from the moderating winds of the coast, the heat was unendurable. I slept in railway dormitories, all the women and babies piled in there on their bedrolls and locked in for the night with barbed wire strung across the doors, and no one speaking to

## Krishna Smiled

me nor I to them. By day, like an ox harnessed to a water wheel I plodded through bazaars, desperately in search of enough books to justify my having made the trip, buying all I could carry, feeling like a nail being hammered into the ground by blows of the terrible, terrible sun. My only thought was to buy my books and get out of here, if I could, alive. The fabled temples would have to find another explorer.

In Madurai the temples have roofs like cake wedges standing on end, intricately carved, garishly painted, more alive than the streets below them for the gods don't mind the heat, and I did not stop to look. I passed a temple on whose terrace horses of white stone plunged and reared, while under their pawing hoofs tailors sat oblivious and cross-legged, turning the wheels of their Singers with their toes, and I did not stop to look. To spend one unnecessary moment in that heat was unthinkable, though I might go ten thousand miles, ten thousand years, and never come again to such a sight. I wondered how human beings could think or dream or plan in heat of that intensity. Of what importance is dialectical materialism or the categorical imperative, the duality of matter or free will, when one cannot breathe? The body wants to survive, so one must drag it up and down streets, exposed to the sun like a chop upon a grill. There had been no rain in five years, and nobody knew of a philsophy which would change that.

The Colombo plane touches at Trichy, and I got on it hot, dusty, my toes caked in dirt within worn sandals, loaded with books packed into haphazard packages. Decently dressed tourists enroute to Tokyo draped in cameras stared at me coolly. I hadn't had the decency to dress.

The plane rose from off the baking, drought-stricken land. Ventilators poured cool air into the cabin. A good fairy appeared, bearing lemonade. My gills twitched. I wanted to jump right into the glass. For the first time in days, I breathed.

Looking out the porthole, I could see India narrowing, narrowing, till it slipped into the sea. The water was fawn-colored, then tan, then light blue, dark blue and *the* blue of Ocean. A breath of a moment, then Ceylon appeared dangling from a chain of islands that drops from Dhanushkodi.

*Through Kerala with coir and cashew*

An embassy car, complete with Singhalese chauffeur and American girl, awaited me at Colombo airport. The embassy had reserved a room at the Galle Face Hotel, with a hot bath and a window looking out over the harbor, through which blew delicious sea breezes, containing moisture enough to sustain mammalian life. I believe, I believe, I believe, Man is descended from aquatic creatures! I showered South India off me, shampooed, breathed, showered, shampooed again, and breathed. The airplane had wrought a miraculous deliverance.

That night when I looked out my window while dressing for dinner, there was this absolutely improbable four-masted frigate riding in the harbor among the much larger passenger liners and freighters. She was a-glowing like a jewel, her masts and sails outlined in strings of electric pearls. *Der Flugender Hollander*, perhaps? Darwin's *Beagle*? Captain Kidd? It certainly was a four-master, but what time was it?

Over dinner in the elegant dining room, a naval officer approached me, not in pantaloons but in a natty blue uniform. Dark, well-built and handsome, his eyes glistered and danced, but his tongue was curiously slurred. I could not understand a word he said. Verbally, that is.

Then he asked, "Castellano?" Si, I could speak Spanish. He beckoned the waiter and ordered champagne. "Drink a few copas," he said in horrible Spanish. "Then you will speak Portuguese like me."

Aristotle—an improbable Greek name went with the improbable Brazilian frigate—suggested in pantomime that I change into an evening gown (oh, evening gown with the crumpled crinoline that sailed the Malabar coast rolled into my bedroll, and slept on the floor of Madurai railway station with me, Arise! Awake! And sing a new song!)

At nine, Aristotle appeared at my hotel room door. We laughed all the way to the harbor, laughed at the Old World which is too old, laughed at the New World, which was us, we two Americans who could not understand each other but who understood each other very well, and took a cycle rickshaw to the quay. I suppose the sun still shone hot in Madurai, and the communists continued to march in Ernakulum, but we were picked up by a little boat that took us out to sea. The wind ruffled his jacket as he straddled quay and boat to hand me down, and I could see a luger packed in close to his groin; ruffled my hair, which Aristotle, his hands deep rooted in it, declared to be like a goat's; ruffled the sails of the jewelled ship as it lay pinned to the dark waters of the harbor.

We climbed the Jacob's ladder and were piped aboard this toy ship, which was rocking like a live thing as five-hundred Brazilians, maddened by the rhythm of a Dionysian band, sallied her from side to side. Champagne was the only cargo she carried, and handsome men who lined up to dance, but always Aristotle waited, glass in hand, to cut back in. He was first mate of the *Almirante Saldanha,* on a goodwill cruise around the world. It would take them two years to circumnavigate the globe, a little less than it took Magellan, and just in time they reached Colombo. I needed all the goodwill I could get.

# 14

*The good servant, Jesus Christ*

When Emmanuel came to work for me, he asked whether I could help him not have any more children. I made an appointment for his wife to see the doctor at Lady Hardinge Hospital, and gave him ten rupees to pay the fee.

A year later I paid for Salome's confinement, and after some discussion, for the baby's baptism as well.

Although Emmanuel explained to me it was not a baby —"Just girl, Missahibji,"—he nevertheless insisted on giving a party in her honor. I pointed out all the other good uses to which he could put his money, but to no avail. He would feed all his relatives and neighbors, and it would cost him— or me—a month's salary.

I am not suited by nature to the role of fairy godmother. When I first realized that, like other foreigners, I would need to hire a bearer to mediate between me and India, I had looked for a woman. Impossible, I was told. No woman works outside her own home (except for college graduates, and they are all physicians or Members of Parliament). It had to be a man. Well, a bachelor then. But where are the bachelors of India? Gone to marry, everyone. There are in fact no bachelors, nor spinsters either, save for the pathetic virgin widows who were engaged in infancy but whose husbands died before coming to maturity, condemning them to a life of isolation and taboo. So I ended up hiring Emmanuel although he had a wife, six children, two nieces, and a mother to support.

Emmanuel turned out to be a good servant. He kept my various dwellings clean and guarded my belongings while I was on the road. He hired, as needed, laundrymen, carpenters, gardeners, taxi drivers, guides, tailors, water carriers, and once even dancing *boys*. He was a great cook, having learned the art from a thugi, one of the caste of murderous highway robbers whom the British weaned from their ancestral vocation and resettled in kitchens throughout the land. He translated back and forth between English and Hindi (or Urdu or Hindustani, whichever it was that he spoke) with a fine sense of impartiality and a heavy reliance on the literal. When I hired him, I asked him what his name meant. He replied: "Jesus Christ."

Considering Emmanuel's many virtues, I donned my fairy godmother outfit and accepted an invitation to the naming party. On the appointed night I headed for the pink gingerbread spires of Lakshminarayan Temple, turned down Panchkuin Road, and sought out the barracks in which my bearer's family occupied a room.

If I expected the string of parti-colored lights which adorn Hindu festivals, I had to be content with one bare electric bulb which, hanging from the limb of a tree, illumined half the barracks and obliterated the rest. In the bright half of the compound stood our host, a bantam black Methodist with a crucifix tattooed on his right forearm, a bleeding heart on his left, and no front teeth, the result of a bet one of his sahibs had made that his bearer could beat the next-door sahib's bearer.

By the time I arrived, the compound was already filled with men in white ducks or dhotis, squatting over bowls of

## The good servant, Jesus Christ

curried mutton which they scooped up with wheat chapatis. They were being served by little boys. The poorest Indian family never lacks servants, because children wait on their elders and are in turn waited on by toddlers.

Among these I recognized Emmanuel's, for they mostly wore fragments of my clothing. A particularly favorite skirt, which had seen the pine forests of Maine, the sands of Jones Beach, and the Arboretum at Ann Arbor, was now running in several directions around the compound, covering tiny brown bits with bare bottoms for whom U.S.A. would always be a clutch of half-understood stories brought home by their father.

Against a wall the women sat, obscure in a muddle of saris and tumbling infants. I scrutinized them for one who might be Salome. In vain. I should have thought that, as Emmanuel's employer and sole sustainer of eleven Christian souls, I would have had some consideration in this matter. But though I visited the household several times, Salome remained for me an unembodied biblical reference.

My dinner was served to me by Salome's father, the blackguard who had conned the family into arranging this marriage many years ago, thus withering Emmanuel's ambition on the vine.

"I never want to marry," Emmanuel told me toward the end of my stay when we were driving down from Simla. "Woman be big trouble. My father, he work always for other people, he be bearer too, Missahib. But I want to be for myself, and woman, she be big trouble."

He looked at me to see whether he had offended me. Emmanuel did not consider me a woman, since I was a boss.

"I live then by Amritsar and work very hard with my big brother. My brother not smart, Missahib. Is something wrong with head, he cannot think. But we be working hard and soon we be having one cow, three buffalo, many chickens. We sell butter, ghee, milk, eggs make some money.

"One day my big brother he take my jacket and my tie and is say is going to town. I say, 'Why you dress up to go to town?' He say, 'Our Daddy he write go take my picture.' I

## Krishna Smiled

say, 'I take my picture too. Why you pay three rupees, I pay three rupees? We brothers, we take one picture together.'

"We take picture, send to Daddy, I be getting letter, come home. I come Delhi, Daddy he say to me, you make marriage, I be having nice girl."

Emmanuel's daddy had made a match with a "very big man, a kabardi, and a good Christian." A kabardi sells old bottles and rags. They made the deal for Emmanuel's older brother, but that lasted only until the kabardi saw the photograph. Then he rejected the weak-minded son in favor of Emmanuel. "Daddy say, 'I take a thing which is freely given'," and the bargain was sealed.

Emmanuel protested briefly. But "I always do what Daddy say."

"Day after I be married, Missahib, I go Nucklow ('Lucknow'). I never be taking my wife to me." There he got a job as bearer to a red-headed Scotsman who promised to apprentice him as a mechanic if he stayed two years. Emmanuel passed a year of happy servitude. "He be fierce, Missahib, one time he come home from barracks, Memsahib not there. When she come home, he take all her clothes off and lock her out of house." Thus, life in the cantonment.

One day a telegram arrived. Emmanuel's mother was dying. His master gave him leave grudgingly, paid his return fare but withheld his salary.

On arrival at the Delhi railway station, Emmanuel was met by the wedding party. Naturally, it included his mother. Again Daddy won out; Emmanuel wrote his Scotsman, who cursed him and sent two months' pay.

"And now I be having six kids."

"But she's a good wife, isn't she?"

"Oh, Missahib, she be talking very much."

Now the paterfamilias welcomed his guests to his front yard. People moved into blackness and reappeared outlined by the single electric light bulb. Time passed slowly for me as I sought but could not find a pattern to their movements. Silently, girls sat shrouded in their saris. Old women hissed to one another, young men giggled, infants sucked with little choking noises.

### The good servant, Jesus Christ

It was midnight before the religious service began, the sermon and the hymns in Hindi. It was two in the morning before the infant had been named after the Hindu goddess of the dance.

As the congregation broke up and the minister departed, I staggered onto feet numbed by hours of sitting tailor fashion, my senses equally deadened by the assault of liturgical Hindi.

Emmanuel forestalled me. "Wait, Missahibji. Is Bengali dancer. Is come all the way from *Cal*cutta. Is very good."

"Where?" I asked. "I don't see any dancer." Emmanuel shifted feet. The Bengali couldn't dance without a drink. Liquor couldn't be allowed at a prayer meeting. So the Bengali had been sent out in the care of a neighbor's son to tie one on discreetly.

I was sceptical of the Bengali's artistry, drunk or sober; but Emmanuel had a roguish look to him. He knew something he wasn't telling me. From behind him came an artlessly tricky arpeggio chased by a double entendre on a drum. I sat down.

A young man with clipped moustache had taken over the harmonium that had been used to accompany the service. Gone were the four-square phrases of the hymns. In their place I could hear the casual fall and languid rise of Indian music. The tabla player, as though ignoring his companion, yet mysteriously in tune with him, beat his spatulate fingers on the two resonant tubs he clasped between his legs.

I had already learned to enjoy Indian music by suppressing what I took to be the melody and following the beat. Percussion is the essence, melody only an accompaniment. Listening to the repetitive scales of Indian music leaves a westerner as bored as an Indian is when he listens to western music, for he finds our rhythms unbearably monotonous, and the melodies go right by him.

A man began to hum and then to sing, weaving between the syncopated tablas and the seemingly casual harmonium. He did not strain his voice as the academicists do, and he avoided the tawdry quavers of the film singers. This was the voice of the folk without foreign improvement. This was the rhythm children beat out on curbstones with sticks—but I could not. This was the rhythm the garbage collectors bang out on lids as they ride into Delhi on the backs of trucks at five in the morning and I never minded when they wakened me (cousins of the Italian garbage collectors of New York, who wakened me with *La Traviata* on Mondays and Thursdays). This was the music I had heard before on hot nights from across the garden, but always when I crept up on it, it had disappeared.

But now the Bengali was here! Excitement stirred the people apart, clearing a space some ten feet by ten. I wondered how a man could dance in so small an area. A jingle of bells sounded inexplicably from Emmanuel's doorway, the sort of bells that are fastened to a horse's harness. The harmonium player ran his fingers up an erratic scale. Shhh! A bare foot slapped the ground. I wheeled around. The Bengali stood in the doorway.

He was dressed as a woman. Her sari was orange, the color of happiness. Her face was powdered white, and sprinkled with glistening bits of silver dust. On her arms were bracelets, on her ankles leather straps sewn with dozens of little bells. Her face was haughty as a camel's.

She stamped once more. The twittering of the guests fell away. Once in command, she took her time, adjusting the folds of her sari as a queen might adjust the order across her breast. With one arm, strangely thin and muscular, she signalled the musicians.

A sinuous rhythm began on the tablas, the harmonium pattering aimlessly behind. The Bengali walked proudly into the cleared space, her ankle bells becoming the third instrument of the orchestra, and slowly began the dance. The extraordinary ugliness of the man cried out through the glittering ornaments of the woman. A proud sneer filled the large painted lips.

I had seen popular dancing in India before, as it is done by the sluts who are all that remain of a splendid courtesan tradition. They are clumsy and indifferent; they tug at their underwear and clean their ears with their fingernails, and roll their vulgar mechanical eyes at the men who lounge

## The good servant, Jesus Christ

about on canvas pillows trying to copy the sly remarks heard at the movies.

This man was more girl-like than the nautch girls, with the grace of a woman and the hauteur of a princess. He swayed and writhed, stamping his belled feet, flirting the tail of his sari. He was female, not effeminate; artful, not arty. And somehow, despite his appalling vulgarity, he was not vulgar.

Apparently the slow dance ended. The artists seemed to have failed to agree when to stop, one finishing and then the other, and then the Bengali melted into the doorway.

Some discussion brought him out again. He had drawn the sari between his legs and hooked it at the waist to make a dhoti of it, that bulky loincloth made known to us by Gandhi.

Unexpectedly, to a hesitant rhythm, the Bengali was making his way through jungle. The mime of the dancer evoked heat and tangled brush, thorns, and immediate danger. A tiger was spied, a spear flung, a fight fought to the death, the beast's neck broken. The hunter bathed in a clear running river, flinging himself into its cooling waters; and triumphantly dragged the carcass home.

Howls of delight demanded another performance. The Bengali was reluctant, as though distasteful of further contact with us. He leaned against the wall and lit a cigarette, holding it upright between his knuckles in order to draw the smoke through his fist more deeply into his lungs.

By this time, the dark around us was rimmed with passersby who had stopped to watch. From the darkness of the street, two policemen came, leaned on their long sticks angularly, the whites of their eyes gleaming from dark brown faces. Emmanuel served them cups of tea and they drank, patterned against the black sky.

Now the harmonium player swished his fingers down the keys, enticing the dancer, who seemed reluctant. The tabla player hammered the pegs that held the skins taut on the little drums, dropping their pitch two full steps. I realized for the first time that they are tuned, like tympani. As though he couldn't care less, the Bengali jingled into the center of the square. Taking a handkerchief, he hung it by a corner from between his clenched teeth. A shout of recognition went up from the crowd, and then we were still.

As the musicians organized themselves, I recognized the snake charmer's rhythm. The Bengali, manipulating the handkerchief, seemed to be playing a pipe. His entire body played, rising and falling with the notes soothingly, enticingly. His eyes focused on a spot of bare earth at his feet.

Across from me, a man got up, removed his turban, and placed it, still bound, under the snake charmer's stare. He took his own handkerchief, knotted it so that one point stood up, and placed it inside the turban. The cobra was in his basket.

The coaxing cadences of the music changed, tightened up, put more pressure on the senses of every living being present. The Bengali was kneeling beside the turban, supplicating. Whatever was inside the turban rose inquiringly. The Bengali rose with it.

And now they danced together, the charmer on his forked legs, the cobra like some hideous flower that had its blossom in the menacingly spread hood.

The music was spiralling faster and faster, and the snake was visibly agitated. But it calmed as the charmer slowly sank to his knees again, his eyes always focused on the deadly spot. The cobra sank too, withdrawing almost from sight beneath the folds of the turban.

At the height of the cobra's fascination, the charmer took his pipe from his mouth and extended a hand over the reptile's hood. The cobra braced itself to withstand the loathsome approach of a human being.

The charmer breathed deeply and resumed his playing. Then again he passed his hand over the hypnotized snake, and again the cobra remained transfixed by remembered rhythms.

On the third pass, the spell broke. So swiftly my eye could not see it, the cobra lunged. The charmer, fatally bitten, flung away his pipe, thrusting his hand upward to heaven in a gesture of terror and betrayal. He danced a wild dance of fury and writhing. And then he died.

*The good servant, Jesus Christ*

We sat stunned. I wondered what Emmanuel would do with this dead snake charmer in his front yard. But even as we sat silent, the melody which the charmer had played crept back to life slowly, slowly. The Bengali stirred, and slowly rose. Dazedly he footed the old rhythm again until faster, faster he whirled with joy to live again. With a tremendous jingling of bells, he leaped over our heads and disappeared.

I was sweating. Across the circle a matter-of-fact young man unknotted the cobra and returned it to his pocket. He rewound the turban on his head and, chattering, went his way.

It was full morning. The bells of Lakshminarayan were clanging, barefoot worshippers climbed the temple steps with offerings of marigold and pice. In the yard next to Emmanuel's, a woman was building a fire and mixing the day's chapatis. Children were running and crying in the streets, and on Panchkuin Road the nighttime train of bullock carts had yielded to the day's stream of bicycles. New Delhi was coming awake. Was I?

Emmanuel thanked me. The neighbors were satisfied by his generosity that he was in fact the father of the new baby, a point which I now learned had been shrouded in doubt so long as he held off giving the party. I was out a month's salary, but he and Salome could hold up their heads again.

As a last favor, would I drop the Bengali off at Connaught Circus? I agreed with surprise—surely he had already left, for he was nowhere in sight.

But at Emmanuel's nod, a man detached himself from a nearby group. He was sallow and pockmarked, his teeth rotted, his eyes lack-luster. He walked with one shoulder slightly forward of the other. Hangdog. Bengali.

We got into my car. I asked him his name.

"I have no job Missahib," he said in the small voice of shame. "I very good cook, Missahib. Do you know anyone needs cook, I work for him for very little money. I read, write English, Missahib."

"Cook?!" I said, "why don't you dance?"

He looked at me, flattered but unbelieving. "Dance? Missahib, this first time dance in four, five month. Nobody ask now. Is no good time for dance, Missahib. But I very good cook." He looked at me hopefully.

I stared back at him. The haughty curve of his lip had never existed. His head had never sat on his neck like a camel's. Face powder would be an obscenity here. He was hungry. He had never been a queen; he was only just alive.

The Bengali had no bundle with him. I suppose he had borrowed the sari from Salome. I gave him ten rupees when I let him off, then sped back to my apartment. Emmanuel was already there, waiting to cook me breakfast.

I was surprised at the calibre of the musicians who performed at Emmanuel's party. He really knew music, as I learned one day soon after. I was reading in my living room, the winter sun streaming through the window lighting up the embroidered Kashmiri shawl which Captain Kitu had given me. Suddenly, it seemed that the crewel flowers were quivering in a breeze such as comes before the rain. I even smelled freshly watered earth, though winter is dry in Delhi. Gooseflesh sprouted along my arms. Through these bumps I became aware that All India Radio, to which I had been only dimly listening, was broadcasting a song which descended upon me like rain upon parched earth. It took an effort to raise my voice in order to call Emmanuel into the room. With one finger I bade him listen.

"What was that?" I gasped when it ended. I thought he would listen to the announcer and then translate, but he answered right away.

"Ah, Missahib, that very fine tune," he began, then lapsed into Hindi (or Urdu or else it was some pretty high-class Hindustani). I rushed him to the car before he should have time to forget the name of the very fine tune, and headed for a record shop in Chandni Chowk, where he picked it out for me. It was a setting of a poem by Tan Sen, court musician to the Emperor Akbar; a prayer by a maiden for water to descend from heaven to quench the flames that parch her lover.

("I want no woman, woman be big trouble," Emmanuel told me on the way down from Simla.)

## The good servant, Jesus Christ

Generally I preferred to travel alone. That way I attracted a good deal of attention and never wanted for help. In fact, I had come to depend upon ad hoc acquaintances to locate my books, particularly in non-Hindi areas. The presence of my bearer, on the other hand, would indicate to strangers that I had the situation well in hand, and no help would be offered.

But Emmanuel always badgered me to take him along, possibly because of the intolerable overcrowding in his home. So when I went up to Simla to negotiate a book exchange with the state press there, I took Emmanuel along since we were staying within the Hindustani linguistic area anyway (ignoring Pahari, a variant of West Hindi). It worked out all right, and between us we managed to buy a racy collection of government reports as well as some ancient phonograph records and hand-copied folksongs of the Himalayas.

Who knows? We may be partly responsible for the invasion of American pop music by Indian modes.

Heading back to Delhi, later on the road than I had planned, Emmanuel began to reminisce about his life before coming to work for me. He was at that time thirty-eight years old, old enough in Indian terms to be my father.

The land he had farmed with his brother fell out on the wrong side of the border and had to be abandoned. The animals went the way of all flesh when some Sikhs ran them off. Partition presented him instead with two children, when his sister and her husband were killed.

His capital gone, and with no trade—he lost out on the chance to be a mechanic when he quit his job at Nucklow because of having to stay with his wife—Emmanuel did what the depressed classes do everywhere: he turned to housework. He became bearer to a succession of Americans. But he vowed his sons would have a trade.

For a while, it was quiet in the Vauxhall. The road was long and late, and though I disliked the smell of Indian tobacco, I told Emmanuel he might light up. He had eaten nothing that day; he never did until he boiled some tea down to tannic acid at 4 P.M. and drank that. But we hadn't stopped for tea. With a sigh of relief, the unknown black man stuck a bidri upright between his third and fourth fingers, lighted it beneath his cantonment moustachioes, and sucked the smoke deep into his lungs. In Hindustani, we drink cigarettes.

The first two children born were boys. This was a good thing. Since he never could earn enough money to save any, and since there was no such thing as Social Security, the boys would provide for him and Salome in their old age. He thought one might be the mechanic he never was; the other a carpenter.

He enrolled them in the same mission school where he himself was educated. They did so well that the school reduced their tuition. He transferred to his sons all the hopes he had once had for himself. They would not be servants.

Of course, he wanted to educate the girls too. But there was not the same urgency about it. He would have to furnish dowries for them, and then when they got married they would take their earning capacity to their husband's families. Nevertheless, it would be good, he felt, if at least two of them could become nurses. That trade was open to Christians because Hindus and Moslems refused to let their daughters into it. "They t'ink, Missahibji, that nurses be same as Hindu widows (prostitutes)."

One night when the boys were eight and nine years old, they died. In the evening they were running through the streets of Panchkuin in the shadow of Lakshminarayan Temple; in the morning they were dead on Emmanuel's floor. He did not know what they died of. "Maybe they go eat some-t'ing."

They died, and I suspect, all the moxie went out of Emmanuel. From then on it was just a matter of feeding his family one day to the next. With everyone piled into one room, without electricity or money to spend on entertainment, their numbers increased each year. Separation was the only form of birth control, and there was no room to separate. One time, when he took to sleeping outdoors to escape the marital embrace, the neighbors so taunted his wife that he had to move back inside.

*The good servant, Jesus Christ*

And now Indira ("not child, Missahib, just girl"). All the others had Christian names, but he called this one Indira. He was going under. Smiling, honest, courteous, loyal, intelligent, christian, desperate, going under.

Life had made Emmanuel a good servant.

# 15

*After two years, I finally acquire some intelligence*

Newspapers provide the foreign observer with a sense of touch. No one is better equipped than local journalists to put their fingers on the native pulse. Reading, the diplomat can get a feel for the local scene, and possibly even make it.

It is a truism of the intelligence community that you can learn more about a country through its newspapers than you can from all the top secret intelligence operations ever mounted. A controlled press, on the other hand, shuts the diplomats out, leaving them to grope around in the dark with the aid of ouija boards.

Since factual information has got to be at the base of any workable foreign policy, embassies consume newsprint voraciously. It was part of my responsibility as publications procurement officer to purvey the necessary newspapers for use in the embassy as well as for shipment to my client libraries in Washington. The business part of this was handled commercially by a newsdealer whom I taught the trick my

*I acquire some intelligence*

home office taught me: all around his warehouse walls we posted mastheads and calendars, beneath which his employees stacked the matching newspapers for labelling and dispatch. Although between them they knew eight or nine Indian languages, they couldn't really be expected to read all 845.

From my office I handled the accounting, and seldom had to soil my hands with newsprint except on such occasions as my visit to Kabul, where I found an embassy interpreter almost buried under a two-year accumulation of "news." He had been told to subscribe to the papers, but not where to send them. So I dug him out from behind his desk, and taught him the trick too.

Occasionally, newspapers would swim past my ken which had never entered regular commercial channels and which the newsdealer, consequently, never called to my attention. These were always of special interest since they reflected new political views just beginning to appear over the horizon. With a change in the political situation, minority voices could achieve importance, and I regarded it as a coup when I could pass such a newspaper along to Washington for inspection, together with information on who was publishing it and why.

One such arrived at the embassy one day, and was kicked to my desk by the mailroom because they didn't know what else to do with it. It was printed on a single sheet of handmade paper folded over once so as to produce four pages. The print appeared to have been set by hand with wooden type. Somewhere out there, Johannes Gutenberg was at work.

The language was something else. Research at the embassy library and among our small staff of interpreters revealed it to be Tibetan. In the upper right hand corner there appeared in English the date (several weeks in the future) and the name Kalimpong. That sent me back to the library, and the atlas.

I had never acquisitioned anything in the Tibetan language. The Library of Congress was always pestering me about some Tibetan palm-leaf manuscripts they wanted, but they seemed unable, or unwilling, to provide me any clues as to where these might be found. The palm leaves were apparently inscribed with religious verses, or tantras, and I considered them secondary to my main effort, which was directed toward political reporting. In that context, Tibetan was a very interesting language, and my blood tingled as I located Kalimpong within spittin' distance of the Tibetan border. If I could locate this newspaper and throw a tantra towards the Library at the same time, the trip would pay off.

The next time I was in Calcutta, I took a plane to Bagdogra, a way station distinguished only by the passage through it weekly of the late king of Nepal, bound for fun weekends in Calcutta. En passant, I flew the plane over Mount Everest, which from that height is a mountain like any mountain. From Bagdogra I travelled by jitney to Darjeeling, then by Land Rover to Kalimpong, driving through a remarkable rain forest of giant trees hung with moss and bedight with orchids. Incredible butterflies floated in the air, as though entire flower beds had become airborne. At 3,500 feet, the Himalayan foothills were smothered in poinsettas, azaleas, rhododendron, and cherry. One could weep to think what the twentieth century will do to this place when it arrives.

But the twentieth century was arriving already, hard on the heels of the army of the People's Republic of China. China had just reconquered her old vassal state Tibet, an action which won the acclamation of the Chinese not only on the mainland, but on Taiwan as well. And the Indian Prime Minister, in a fit of absent-minded generosity, had acknowledged its right to do so. The troops now stationed on the roof of the world were badly in need of consumer goods which the conquered countryside could not produce. Coincidentally, Nehru and Mao agreed upon Panch Sheila, Five Principles of Peace, one of which was free trade between their countries.

As a result, the border was wide open along the Kalimpong-Gangtok-Gyantze road. The entire area was booming, and more Tibetans were at large than had ever been seen before.

They were marching their yak trains up and down the

*I acquire some intelligence*

mountain trails, bringing up supplies for tl
son: mill cloth, boots, and kerosene from In
rice, which had to be shipped by rail from
Peking, by sea to Calcutta, then forwarded o
pong whence it went up the Himalayas by animal or human
pack, because there was no railroad or even highway across
mainland Asia to Lhasa. The yak trains returned southward
with that ages-old export of Central Asia, raw wool. Of late,
the southbound caravans were also bringing down brass pots,
mountain horns, jewelry, the lootings of Tibetan households
for sale to the gewgaw hungry Americans in New Delhi.

Kalimpong itself had the bustling air of a frontier boomtown, like Peshawar in its time, or Carson City in its. The Tibetans, larger than life, loped through the bazaar buying bars of Cadbury chocolate and cans of Yardley talcum powder which they stuffed into their wide leather belts, whether for themselves or for their yaks, I could not know. Treading softly in soft leather boots, they let their full-skirted coats hang down behind them in the soft November air. High brocaded caps with fur earflaps covered their braided hair. In every right ear, a turquoise stud; in every left, a golden hoop from which a lump of coral or turquoise was slung. (Where do you get coral, as far inland as anyone can get inland?)

Their resemblance to American Indians was startling. But our Indians lived in a hospitable land compared with the one Tibetans call home. According to some royal anthropologists who were living in the hills above the town and who were making a study of the matter, these lusty men usually shared one wife among a family of brothers. Life is expensive in Tibet, and polyandry is one way to keep the birth rate down.

Pandit Nehru had recently observed that Kalimpong was a hotbed of spies. The name of the hotbed was Himalaya Hotel, where I stayed. The air of the little inn was thick with the smoke of intrigue, some of it produced by enigmatic Tibetans meditating in rocking chairs, some by equally opaque Englishmen striking their national posture in front of the fireplace. The proprietress was the daughter of the former

British trade agent at Gyantze and a Tibetan. She arranged nightly games of cards and dice among her guests, who included not only Indians of every style but some Europeans of a kind I hadn't met yet: a frowsy, blowsy White Russian who sculpted outlandish busts in the garden and was rumored to have been an enchantress under, literally, the Czar; a really smashing British army captain who was recruiting Gurkha soldiers to fight communist Chinese in Malaya; and the daughter-in-law of the King of Bhutan who had just then departed on a six-week funerary expedition, his own. The shadowy world of espionage lurked ready to pounce, and for a moment I regretted not belonging to it. If you're going to be a lady spy, Kalimpong is a lovely place to practice your profession.

A little discreet inquiry enabled me to locate the press of the Tibetan newspaper. Walking over to the print shop, I introduced myself to the editor, an ascetic looking gentleman in conservative grey kimono and braids. I gave my full identity since he seemed to want recognition from us; besides, I suspected that in Kalimpong there were no secrets.

This Tibetan Gutenberg considered himself a refugee from his homeland, a ludicrous idea on the face of it since everyone in India knew the Tibetans were grateful to the Chinese for having liberated them from an oppressive theocracy. But the editor saw things differently, and told me of Chinese massacres of civilian populations, the starving out of monastaries by siege, and the building of military highways and airports, which he thought should be of especial interest to the Americans.

I thought so too. Our sources on Tibet were preternaturally thin. Of course, I was in no position to verify either his information or his pedigree. But he looked interesting. I placed three subscriptions to his newspaper, not because I expected it to be published regularly, but as a token of interest. It was a way of keeping him on the phone until the regular intelligence types could talk with him.

That was an error on my part, because nobody in Washington was interested in him, and he may be on the line yet.

*I acquire some intelligence*

I found this out a few weeks later while being debriefed by some intelligence types back home. During our session I mentioned the Tibetan newspaper and its editor, and was met by a deep freeze. In fact, each time I tried to discuss any possible source of intelligence on the communist side of the bamboo curtain, my interlocutors changed the subject.

What kind of intelligence, I wondered, were they interested in? Only news which had already appeared in the New York Times? Only news from our side? Only good news? The answer, I realize in retrospect, to all these questions, was Yes.

Back in Intelligence Acquisition and Distribution, I mentioned this peculiarity to members of my own office, all of whom were now strangers to me. My old boss had died; my immediate superior had gone on to his reward in Stockholm; everyone was new, due to mandatory shifts in assignments every two years. I was now the old hand, the one who knew what it was really like in the field.

But I was innocent as to the ways of Washington. When I brought up the matter of the so-called intelligence debriefing, I was met by warning hand signals and crossed eyes, urgent messages telegraphed to me nonverbally. It became clear they assumed the bug in the office wall was not friendly.

"My God, where have you been?" a colleague mumbled thickly over lunch. Talking with his mouth full and his lips shielded from possible lip readers, he spluttered, "You can't talk about that kind of thing. Aren't you aware of what's going on?"

"Of course I'm aware," I said impatiently, "if you mean aware of the communist menace. Don't we want to know more about the people who are menacing us?"

My colleague gave a derisive snort. "Keep your mouth shut."

In Washington in 1954, a State Department officer who expressed an interest in communism acquired a pink tinge which made friends desert him as abruptly as the onset of the plague. The anti-communist crusade of Senator Joe McCarthy was in full cry and, though from the perspective of India it had seemed unreal, here in Washington it was the only reality. I had thought that no one could take seriously the vague charges of treason in high places, unsupported by evidence and laced with inconsistencies. Despite two years in Asia, I still did not recognize the power of irrational thinking. McCarthy's assistants, characterized by the press as junketeering gumshoes, appeared on the world stage as latterday manifestations of Laurel and Hardy; impossible to take them seriously.

Except that, here at home, everybody did. Heads were rolling down the hallways of New State which, not unsymbolically, was really the cast off shell of the War Department. Foreign Service Officers who reported on communist activity were being accused of being communists themselves.

One political officer who correctly predicted the coming to power of the communist party in Kerala was summarily fired, without being advised of the charges nor being given an opportunity to defend himself. We FSOs had believed it to be our job to keep the government informed on developments abroad: to be the eyes, ears, sense of touch of the American people. Instead, FSOs who filed reports concerning communist activity were accused of being sympathetic to the events they described. Anyone who reported the growth of communist strength, must be a commie himself.

I looked this man up and had lunch with him in the State Department cafeteria, at some risk, I suppose, to my own career. His advice to me was to watch my step, since I was Jewish.

It is not difficult to believe there was a loss of accuracy in reporting under such conditions. No one dared report bad news. Intelligence sources dried up for lack of tending. Suspicion flared among colleagues. Even those who were not attacked directly lost their effectiveness, as it became apparent to foreign diplomats that Americans could be accused of disloyalty and destroyed overnight by their own government. Our status was thus diminished within the diplomatic colony, and this loss of confidence undermined our ability to work and brought on a pervasive sense of futility.

*I acquire some intelligence*

Demoralization decimated the ranks of the service. Fully one-third of the members of my entering class had left the service at the end of four years. Recruitment could not make up the difference: the elite would never join again. Men and women of spirit will not compete for service in a corps which offers its members up like lambs of sacrifice to any demagog with sufficient gall to mention their name.

The harm which McCarthyism wrought on our foreign service was doubled by the pusillanimity of the State Department, which either could not or would not defend its officers. We had all been investigated before being commissioned, and were subject to frequent security rechecks. If any spies had been found among us, it was the FBI which needed looking into, not State.

For those FSOs who were accused of disloyalty, it might be thought that the innocent could be vindicated by scrutiny of their record of service. However, these officers were amazed to learn that their personnel files had never been asked for by the senators who brought the charges. A senator had only to name an officer to damn him. Once named, he became expendable in the eyes of the department, the press, and the public.

An FSO is peculiarly incapacitated for the Washington battlefield, because he spends his career in the political boondocks. Unlike other federal officials who are domiciled in the capital, and for whom mending fences is a continual—in some cases the only—preoccupation, the FSO cannot form links with the people who count. Passing through Washington briefly every two years, he may never even meet the men who dominate his life.

Outside the State Department, the men who dominate the FSO's career are congressmen. These fall into two categories: those who sit on committees which are charged with legislative oversight of the State Department; and those who represent the home district of the particular Foreign Service Officer.

The chairman of the subcommittee which allocates funds to State is and has been, off and on for a quarter century,

## Krishna Smiled

Congressman John Rooney of Brooklyn. Far from having received any commission from a president to engage in the conduct of foreign affairs, he has been known to decline invitations from presidents to discuss such matters. When the Democrats control the House, he is the most powerful man in the State Department, and disposes of more influence over American foreign policy than any FSO, or for that matter, than any senator whose foreign policy views are a matter of public record. No State Department official has developed a power base to rival that of the congressman's, who has won reelection thirteen times by showing his constituents that he really knows how to keep the foreign service in line by trimming its budget.

Two examples of congressional parsimony will suffice. At the time of the increase in communist activity in Kerala, budget cuts required our Dravidian language interpreters to be laid off. From an intelligence point of view, the effect would have been the same if the government of India had closed down all the southern newspapers. We would have deplored such an act of censorship; but our own action was just as effective in screening our embassy from learning what was going on.

Within the service, it is well known that some ambassadorial posts are closed to career officers because pay and allowances are not adequate for upkeep of the post. Down at the Third Secretary level, my entertainment allowance the first year was zilch, the second year, twenty-five dollars. Since Congress grants tax breaks to businessmen for entertainment expenses, the message is clear: it is more important to know what's up with the Revlon account than it is to know what's going on in India's parliament.

Accustomed to governmental parsimony, to which as a taxpayer I could not object, I was startled when, on my first run to the airport to meet a clutch of visiting congressmen, I was handed envelopes of cash to present to them. I had supposed they were submitting expense accounts to the General Accounting Office. Possibly they were. In that event, how

*I acquire some intelligence*

did they enter the cases of tax-free liquor which I, in my capacity as embassy duty officer, was told to deposit in their hotel rooms?

Every congressman must serve his constituency if he wants to stay in office. This constituency is domestic, rooted in local politics. The congressman who is beholden to the county courthouse or dairy farmers or aircraft manufacturers or urban blacks is in no danger of losing votes when he underbudgets the State Department, all of whose constituents are foreigners who cannot vote, and most of whose employees are overseas where they cannot defend themselves. State has no domestic constituency, no group which can be counted on to vote in its support; therefore there is no congressman who can be counted upon to stand up and speak for it.

The position not only of the department but of the individual officer is precarious. Typically, the last refuge of the wronged citizen is his congressman, and that goes for federal employees too. The lady who was assaulted in the file room of the Central Intelligence Agency was quite correct in catching a train and crossing the country in order to hide out in her senator's home. Only from this bastion could she defend herself against the rapist's charge that he had caught her redhanded in the top secret safe.

Plenty of foreigners have had congressmen go to bat for them too. Italian prostitutes, Chinese ship-jumpers, Basque sheepherders, and convicted felons of every and no nationality, have all benefited from congressional interest and generosity, provided someone in the congressman's district took an interest in them. There are a lot of votes to be quarried in the process of digging some unfortunate alien out from under the legislation which Congress itself has passed.

But FSOs historically have found congressmen slow to rise to their defense. Perhaps there is built-in antipathy between diplomats who make the world their home, and representatives who must base themselves on local issues in order to win election. The multilingual diplomat in cutaway and top hat makes a strange buddy for the congressman who must assume a drawl and a coonskin cap in order to persuade his constituents that he is an American even if he was educated overseas.

Consequently, although the diplomat may have a good working relationship with foreign cabinet ministers and play golf with the editors of powerful foreign newspapers, he is apt to find, when the hot irrational glare of publicity is turned upon him by his own government, that he is friendless and alone.

Orphaned by a weak department, starved by misguided congressmen, buffeted by political winds, the foreign service never grew strong enough to dominate foreign policy making. The State Department never became influential enough to counterbalance the weight of other federal departments. State became only one among many sources of advice to the president, and by no means the strongest.

George F. Kennan, who rose as high in government circles as any FSO has, states in his memoirs that the State Department was often pushed aside during the making of momentous decisions, while President and senators conferred with the military. During the height of crises in Korea, Japan and Germany, he continues, it was often difficult for State to learn what was going on.

The influence gap which State could not fill was filled by the Defense Department. Garlanded in its death-dealing trinkets whose production is so important to the economy, the Defense Department is infinitely more attractive to vote-counting congressmen than the State Department could ever be. How many jobs does State generate, after all? A vote for the State Department budget is just a vote. State has behind it no identifiable body of people whose support a congressman must woo. But a vote for Defense Department budget means jobs, factories, prosperity, and campaign contributions which can be parlayed into reelection by those senators and representatives who are canny enough to get themselves placed on the right committees. Defense has the strongest clientele of any federal department—industry: and Congress responds to that clientele.

*I acquire some intelligence*

It is very fashionable these days to criticize industry for its malevolent effect upon American foreign policy. But industry was never dedicated to anything but profit-making. What is Congress dedicated to?

If, looking beyond the aggrandizement of their own districts, congressmen had allowed the State Department to attain a reasonable strength, we might today have civilian control over foreign policy instead of our present situation, where much policy originates in the Defense Department, with State providing apologies after the fact.

Electronic gadgetry would no doubt continue to exude a certain glamour, and congressmen will never be totally impervious to free flights on supersonic jets. But ideas are not without their attractive powers, and leadership generated within a strong State Department might have kept our foreign relations under civilian control, where the Constitution says they belong. Americans have known from the beginning that war is too important a matter to be left to soldiers, but who is brave enough to tell that to the Pentagon now?

It is certainly paradoxical that we Americans, so persuaded of our peaceful mission in the world, have entrusted the conduct of our foreign affairs to soldiers trained to search and destroy, rather than to diplomats trained to reconcile differences peacefully.

In its first destructive half-life, McCarthyism poisoned the atmosphere of free debate and destroyed reputations. In its equally poisonous second half-life, McCarthyism reduced the State Department to the status of a despised and mistrusted servant. This was immediately apparent to a returnee to the Washington of 1954. When I told acquaintances that I was with the State Department, the standard comeback was: "Are you a commie or a fairy?"

The necessary adjustments were far-ranging, and began my first night in Washington. I called up my former chief of mission, lost now in the anonymity of an apartment house on Dupont Circle. In India he had been a big man.

"Ah, Judy," he said, "come along to a party I'm giving tonight for the Chinese mission."

## Krishna Smiled

I was stunned. I couldn't believe the Old Man was making contact with the Chinese in the very shadow of the White House. I dared not reply. Fyfe sensed my embarrassment. He must have gone through the same process of re-think some months earlier. "The Nationalist Chinese," he said drily. I had forgotten about them.

In the real world of power politics, the Nationalists had ceased to exist. It was not Nationalist China that had invaded Tibet. There were no Kuomintang agents in Kalimpong. Chiang Kai Shek was not breeding insurrection in Malaya and Indonesia. Taiwan was not developing atomic weapons. But in Washington Wonderland, the Nationalists were the only Chinese we would deal with for the next eighteen years.

It was scant comfort to know that the Indians were suffering delusions too. They were living a different fairy tale than ours: that of the benevolent new government which had come to power by the will of the Chinese people and therefore could do only good, not evil.

The Indians befriended the Chinese revolution early in the game, which was their prerogative, even if it had fatal consequences for Tibet. But then they allowed their enthusiasm for communist reforms to distort their assessment of what was good for India. This was not their prerogative, since their fundamental obligation was the defense of India.

So in the 1950s, India welcomed all sorts of Chinese cultural missions to the country bearing an astounding message: "Hindi Chini-ki bhai-bhai" ("Indians and Chinese are brothers"). The communists actually managed to persuade thousands of Indians, including many who should have known better, that the two nations had enjoyed a long and fruitful cultural association.

The basis for this extraordinary statement was found in the journals of two travellers: Fa Hsien, writing about 400 A.D. and Hsuan Tsang, who wrote in 629, and who appear to have been the *only* Chinese to venture into India during the course of that millennium. They were on pilgrimages to the birthplace of the Buddha, which is reputed to be near Banaras. More than a thousand years later, they were put to

*I acquire some intelligence*

use in an intensive friendship campaign conducted by the Chinese communists in what we can now see, with hindsight, was a softening-up process for the attack on India.

Both the United States and India suffered the consequences of their delusions. We thought that by ignoring China we could weaken her, while she grew stronger in fact and came to dominate the better part of Asia. Indians believed they could get along with China by befriending her blindly, and found themselves instead the object of Chinese aggression. Both the United States and India suffered reverses because of a failure to assess realistically the China that *is*. Both of us were blinded by preconceptions of what China *should be*.

Having been employed for two years in providing the raw material of which such assessments are made, I came back to find Washington in the grip of a perverse know-nothingism. I wondered whether my acquisitions had been worth the money the government paid for them. I might have made a more lasting contribution to American scholarship by ignoring politics and pursuing the matter of the tantras. But in this I was forestalled.

From Kalimpong I had gone up to Sikkim, a tiny mountain kingdom as tall as it is wide, tucked into the Himalayas between Tibet and India. From the jewelled gorge of the Tista to the snowy spine of Kanchenjunga is a distance of five miles—up. Sikkim used to be a dependency of Tibet, was liberated by the British, passed under Indian protection in 1947 and now, in an inexorable process of westernization, has an American queen.

I was the houseguest of the Dewan, New Delhi's man in Gangtok. He and his wife gave a state dinner for me, the state at that time comprising himself and Rajkumar Palden Thondup Namgyal and his wife.

We dined off a wild boar the Prince had shot that morning on the higher slopes of the mountain, where snow already lay. In Gangtok, the air was just getting nippy. A few miles below, on my way up, I had seen oranges still ripening on the trees. Sikkim's climate is vertical.

## Krishna Smiled

The conversation and the wine sparkled, the humor and the cigars were dry, and all in all we had around the table the most elegant little government in the world. The life of Sikkim swirled past the Dewan's picture window; from the door, he dispensed paternal justice to complainants who stopped by. The Princess, who was a Tibetan noblewoman, sat wrapped in her unknown language, smiling and whispering with her husband. The Prince complimented me on my dress, recognizing it to be handspun.

He was trying to revive Sikkimese handicrafts, and had moved some village weavers into the royal compound where they could teach their craft to young apprentices who might in their time hold back the tide of Japanese and German textiles which were flooding the market. It may already have been too late: the people of Gangtok were wearing European milled cloth rather than their peasant weaves.

With all my heart, I wished him well. Once factory products come to Sikkim, the place will crumble and disappear, like the contents of those melancholy pyramids the archeologists unwisely opened. Brocade flowers cannot compete with mill cloth. Scarlet lacquered temples and golden dragons crumble on contact with factory smoke. The benign expression on peasant faces is no match for the televised grimaces of Lucille Ball. The next step is Kanchenjunga-Disneyland, and then the gods will truly have no more home.

Of all the places I ever visited, Sikkim was the one where religion, nature, and the life of the people blended most harmoniously. Was this a foretaste of the mystery of Central Asia?

I steered the conversation round to Tibetan tantras, and the Princess, through her husband, let me know that my British colleague, Thackeray, had made off with them. The little gems which the Library of Congress was seeking were even now on their way to the British Museum. I wasn't surprised. Thackeray was closer in temperament to twelfth century tantras than to twentieth century newspapers, especially those printed with movable type.

By way of consolation, the Dewan presented me with

*I acquire some intelligence*

the first issue of the *Darbar Gazette*, published that afternoon. He was trying to get a representative assembly going. This was the first document ever printed in Sikkim, and the only document of all I collected which I kept for myself.

The reason for this was the enchantment which Sikkim had cast over me. It began with prayer flags planted round the rugged hillsides, tattered banners inscribed with supplicants' prayers, repeated ceaselessly as the cloth flapped in the wind. And was repeated in the ragged white clouds drifting in sky of flawless Meissen blue like prayer flags torn loose from pine tree staffs. Sikkim is the Kingdom that Time Forgot, the beautiful Shangri-La.

When I went to bed, I could hear winter scratching its back against the Dewan's little cottage. Fires were banked in each room; a guard huddled in his blanket on the verandah. From my bed I could hear bells, the same harness bells of those caravans I had first encountered on the Kalimpong road that winds through the enchanted forest hung with orchids.

Across the Dewan's front lawn, as neat and well-tended as the cricket fields of his native Lahore, a mule train was making its way up the mountain, heading north to meet the hardier yaks who would complete the journey to Tibet. The giant muleteers strode beside, whistling through their teeth, indifferent to the fantastic march ahead of them which would take them across the toughest topography in the world. They whistled, the bells clanged to a trot, and the caravan passed beyond the flower bed and into Tibet.

I don't know what kind of publications I would have found there, but I wished to God I could go find out.

# 16

*I become the first American girl to ride the Afghan Mail to Mazar-i-Sharif—and return*

All my life I have liked men; yet it never occurred to me until I got to Afghanistan that I might become one.

My change of life took place in a hotel in Doab, and it had a profound effect on me even though, unlike more widely publicized transformations, mine was not permanent.

At the time I am writing about, I had been scavenging books in India for about a year. I had my Hindustani down pat and was beginning to run out of itineraries when my libraries discovered that their Afghan collections were wearing thin.

So I made my way to Kabul, which is the capital of Afghanistan and the home of the most exciting men in creation. The Pathans or Pukhtoons or Pushtuns (you use your dictionary, and I'll use mine) claim to be the ten lost tribes of Israel. However, they have been Moslems ever since they stopped being Buddhists, which was some time in the eighth century.

*Riding the Afghan mail*

During my first week in Kabul, which I spent walking the streets, I learned a lot about Afghanistan. The comment that I heard from every Pathan I met was: "You look just like my sister." This I couldn't verify for myself, because at the time all Pathan women were still kept in strict seclusion. When allowed out of the house to shop or visit, they wore an eyeless and airless canvas sack known as a *chaudri*. Women have since been liberated by law, but only the young can take advantage of freedom.

I once asked a Pathan lad whether, when faced by a bazaar full of chaudris, he could recognize his mother. When he grasped the question he started laughing so hard that he fell down. I never did find out how a man recognizes his female relatives in Afghanistan.

Kabul homes are encysted in mud walls which provide privacy within each courtyard so that the women of the household can breathe. It used to be a capital offense to climb your roof.

Although you scarcely see anyone in the mud corridors which wind among Kabul homes, the bazaar is as vibrant as the rest of the town is dead. The busiest sector is along the curving Kabul River, where the townsmen sit on the dike sunning themselves, gossiping, and polishing their rifles. Most of the traffic is made up of tribesmen in from the hills, doing their shopping in consultation with the tents who churn along behind them.

Pathans are tall, fair-skinned, ruddy and muscular, with black hair as coarse as goats', and eyes that are traditionally compared with the eagles'. They are addicted to pyjamas that run to about twelve feet in circumference, cinched in at the waist by a cord. Shirts are worn loose, and topped by a sheepskin bolero. Pathans always keep their heads covered—first with a skull cap that may be either boxy or conical; then with a turban that gets wound in a manner characteristic of the wearer's place of birth.

Afghans say that the history of their country is written on the faces of her people, and I spent a lot of time studying history in the bazaars—something that was to get me in trouble later. Did you know that a shocking percentage of Pathans are blue-eyed blondes? A souvenir of Alexander the Great.

Genghis Khan slept here too, and left the Hazaras to prove it. These Mongolian people live on the mountainous central spine of Afghanistan, the Hindu Kush (Killer of Hindus). They are distinguished from Pathans by their olive skin, flat noses and stocky build. The two races mingle in the bazaars, but not in homes. Hazara women skip the chaudri, wrapping themselves to the gills in brilliant shawls.

One day as I was walking through the grape bazaar, where merchants were standing knee-deep in the gutter washing their wares and cursing the goats that splashed through with little boys in hot pursuit, I came up against a camel caravan. It looked so real that I half expected it to lead me to a movie studio lot. Instead, and more sensibly, it led me to the Kabul bus station.

This is a converted caravanserai, and all the other camels had already been converted into trucks. The open square is walled by an adobe barracks, in whose dark cells grain and camel gear have been replaced by spare parts and jerry cans. The old camel drivers have become mechanics, and at that moment there were numbers of them clinging batlike to their front fenders, turban-side down inside their engines. They have the local reputation of being able to fix anything with a bicycle pump and a length of baling wire; and with the fever of the open road rising in me, I hoped so.

As I stood in the arched entrance to the serai, most of the men downed tools and looked back at me. Although I was never stoned for going around with my bare face hanging out, other women had been.

Deep in thought, I wandered back to the home where I had been billeted by an unexpectedly solicitous American Embassy, and broached my idea to my American host, Blucher. He hesitated a moment, belched, did a passable imitation of a raven, and croaked a word which I took to be "Nevermore."

What I wanted to do was to travel by bus to the northern border of Afghanistan, cutting across the trail Marco Polo

## Riding the Afghan mail

took between Venice and Peking. My announced purpose was to procure more publications; my real purpose was to get out among those handsome men.

Apparently no unaccompanied foreign woman had made the trip before. Blucher prophesied death or dishonor. Then, on the assumption that I would choose the latter, he predicted that I would be stuffed inside a chaudri and carted off to Tashkurghan or Herat or even Aq Chah, from which I would emerge only as a legend to plague future female adventurers.

After all, even the British had failed to subdue these people. The most they had ever been able to do about it was to produce Kipling.

The next morning I went back to the bus station and bought a ticket for the end of the line: to Mazar-i-Sharif, where the Amu Darya marks the border between Afghanistan and the Uzbeg Soviet Socialist Republic.

It was a keen December morning. Blucher took me by jeep to catch the bus. At the last moment, he had contributed his arctic bedroll which he prized second only to his psychopathic dog. It was very nice of him since he never expected to see me or the bedroll again. Into it I stuffed a change of clothes, some souvenirs I had bought in the southwest of Afghanistan, a comb, and a whopping big sandwich of roast beef, for I had been assured that Afghan food was poisonous.

The Afghan government provided me with a safe-conduct, written in several languages with an equal degree of illegibility (for me; I do not know either Farsi or Pukhto, the two languages of Afghanistan). Somewhat fatuously, perhaps, in a land more enthralled by marksmanship than by literacy, I slipped it into the lining of my jacket, just over my heart. An Italian switchblade knife completed my equipment.

Back at the caravanserai, a retired muleteer got me to the right bus and bawled out Blucher for letting his "wife" travel alone. Then he weighed my bedroll against a boulder that hung from the limb of a dead tree which stood in a corner of the serai. My baggage was then hoisted—together with tin trunks, knapsacks, livestock, and rolled-up carpets such as Cleopatra visited Caesar in—onto the roof of the bus, which

I now saw with horror was a sort of tin casket welded without benefit of springs to a truck chassis. After that, the steerage passengers climbed up. At times during the trip there were more people on the bus than in it.

The bus was fitted inside with planks about eight inches wide and scarcely two feet apart. A barrier separated first class (next to the driver) from second (the next three or four benches). I was in third class, where there were two rows of tandem seats with space for livestock in between. The fare to the end of the line and back (a week's journey) was four dollars first class and two dollars and fifty cents by the time you worked your way to the rear. Fifty cents topside.

The driver, a solid citizen in cotton pyjamas, white nylon turban and U.S. army jacket, came back to where I was trying to fit myself into a space not meant for the American femur. He was a stocky chap with a happy, wide-open expression, and pointing to his chest he bellowed "Khalifa" ten or twelve times.

Khalifa wanted to say something to me; he wanted to be friendly. But he soon saw that I was too stupid to understand, so he laughed instead. That laugh revealed one of the sweetest natures that ever drove a bus, and I laughed back with as much confidence as I could, considering that the benches had by now filled up with men who might in childhood have resembled my brother but who, let's face it, had grown into one hell of a rowdy crew.

Probably Khalifa decided things would work themselves out; because he got out the coach door, climbed in again at the front, and established his authority with a lengthy honk on the klaxon. Not for nothing was he called Chief. Then he shouted to the wiper. This lad, who rode postillion with his turban wrapped around his entire head as if it were a bandaged thumb, shouted to the stationmaster, who shouted back to Khalifa. The passengers murmured a prayer, touching their hands to their beards in graceful circular motion, and the bus started.

Rather, it was let loose. Bellowing like a crazed animal, the bus roared down the narrow mud-walled streets of Kabul.

### Riding the Afghan mail

Stampeded pedestrians fled down side lanes or jumped into gutters. I soon discovered what a tenderfoot I was, as I bashed and dashed against the bench, the window, and the floor. Even the toughest old travellers were pitched into the aisle or, on occasion, ricochetted off the ceiling. All at once I saw turbans in their true light—as shock absorbers.

I looked furtively at my fellow travellers, and they looked furtively at me. It was likely that many of them had never seen a woman's face before, with the exception of their own mothers', sisters', daughters' and wives.' Certainly, they had never seen an unaccompanied woman. In Afghanistan, a woman is an appendage of the man. An American would be rather surprised to see an unaccompanied leg or collarbone get on the bus and occupy a seat.

For my part, none of my well-wishers in Kabul expected me to survive the trip intact. I knew nothing about Afghanistan, and not a word of the language. I was setting out for a city whose existence I had learned of for the first time the day before. Until I got back to Kabul, I would be completely out of touch with anyone I knew, dependent on the mercy of men who have an international reputation for acting like Errol Flynn, but for keeps.

Looking at my fellow travellers in their voluminous pyjamas, their turbans like unmade beds, moustachioed, unshaven, and earringed, I wondered if they would like me.

What if they didn't?

What if they did?

While I was searching for a key to the situation, the bus lurched into a crossroads to pick up an old man. Since Khalifa considered it beneath his dignity to stop for just one passenger, he only shifted gears. The old man couldn't get his balance and pitched into the aisle, fetching his skull a nasty crack against the bench. Everybody laughed fit to bust. It made one think.

Evidently what I needed in order to get along in Afghanistan was a sense of humor. Waiting for the next big bump in the road, I bounced high on the bench and gave out with what I hoped was a carefree whoop, while shooting off imaginary six-guns. The passengers got the idea right away, and whooping and howling and shooting we roared along the road in what must have been the noisiest passage since the Third Afghan War. Khalifa gave us a rhythmic tattoo on the klaxon, and I was in.

For the first time, I relaxed and looked out the window. Leaving Kabul for the north, we had entered a great plain, its edges stained by the distant mountains of the Hindu Kush. The country markets were glutted with grapes, apples, pomegranates, gourds, melons and nuts of all kinds. All the kids we passed had sticky red faces. Pomegranate juice. They eat them like apples.

Pressing north, we came to the sudden foothills: rock in a variety of savage forms—boulder piled on boulder, red-streaked buttes, lopsided pillar formations, smooth cliff faces cleft as by a titanic blow. The bright unmisted sunlight varnished the mineral veins in them, clothing the rugged mountains in unlikely pink, purple and red.

My first lunch was unpleasant. All the passengers debarked and entered a dark, cavelike building from which came a concatenation of smells that started my salivary glands working. Unfortunately, all they were going to have to work on was the roast beef sandwich; my friends in Kabul had primed me well with stories of typhus, undulant fever, and amoebic dysentery.

A tall heavy-set man in western clothes came out of the cavern once and waved a steaming dish in front of my nose. I waved my desiccated sandwich back at him, and declined with a smile. But I wondered what I would eat the next day.

Our comfort stops were anywhere along the highway. Each time we came to a halt, the men would clamber down and stretch, relieve themselves and smoke. Shepherds would come tumbling down from the grassless cliffs where they grazed their sheep and goats, keeping a weekly rendezvous which was their only contact with the world. The passengers were very nice to the young boys, ruffling their hair fondly, and asking them questions to which the boys responded politely.

*Riding the Afghan mail*

As we climbed, the air chilled and the mountains coming into focus had their first light cover of snow. By midnight, a blizzard was blowing. I did not know if we would stop for the night, or ever. The bus grew dank and miserably cold. No matter where I put my head, it banged against something hard. I eyed the large, padded Tartar shoulder next to me, and then decided against it. I closed my eyes and prepared to die of multiple contusions and uremic poisoning.

We stopped at the Sheiber Pass, and under cover of night I did what the men had been doing all day long.

Black and blue and frozen, I returned reluctantly to the torment of my wooden bench. It seemed preferable, but just barely, to dying of exposure on the mountainside. On the bench, I found a chappan, one of those quilted robes the Uzbegs wear. I looked around. The nearest Uzbeg was a slight, austere man on the bench ahead of me, whom the others addressed respectfully as Hajji. He had earned the title, and the right to dye his beard red, by making the pilgrimage to Mecca.

I tapped the Hajji on the shoulder and smiled. He smiled back, not speaking. He was the only person I met on the trip who was sophisticated enough to realize that I could not understand his language even if he shouted.

Wrapping the chappan around my aching bones, I settled back and watched the full moon appear and disappear behind mountains. It was Halloween, but I didn't know whose party this was. The silhouettes of the passengers and their bundles appeared and disappeared with the moonlight. Talking and joking and singing died out. Only here and there, tired arms rewound an endless turban around a bruised head.

It was three in the morning when we reached Doab, which means "land between two rivers." By night, the adobe hotel is clothed in a sort of Egyptian grandeur which is foreign to it in the daylight. It seemed to loom forbiddingly and my first crisis loomed with it. Unknown hands grabbed my bedroll and sprinted into the night.

Since most of the passengers were sprinting too, I joined the rout. We headed pell-mell into the hotel, funnelling down the corridor like sheep into a dip. Suddenly a fearfully strong and unnecessarily handsome young man grabbed me by the wrist, flung me into a bedroom, and slammed the door.

"Lie down," he commanded me in English. "These are the only two beds in the hotel."

That was how I met Abdul Hakim Waziri, a fine broth of an Afghan lad. But before I could answer, there was a knock at the door and the rest of the passengers and crew came in. Lips curled as they saw Hakim and me reclining on our respective cots. It was the floor for them. I realized how lucky I was to have a bed for the night, but I did marvel over the speed with which the reservations had been made.

There was a Franklin stove in the center of the floor, and when it had been got going, we all had tea. For someone like myself, a recent escapee from caste-ridden India, the sight of everyone drinking out of the same two cups did my heart good. The wiper poured an extra cupful, fished the carburetor out of his trousers, and washed it in hot tea.

After some chitchat, the men moved off to other rooms and a night on the floor. A bit leery of the fellow on the other bed, I unrolled Blucher's arctic bedroll on my cot and lay down, pretending I had my magic chaudri on.

Suddenly I heard my roommate get out of bed. I pressed the button on my switchblade, and wondered if I would have the courage to press the cold steel home, and if so, on whom. Apologizing politely, Abdul Hakim made his way to the table and blew out the kerosene lamp. He sounded as anxious as I.

Sometime later I was roused by an argument, not at all to my surprise, and got set for the final chorus of "Sixteen Men On a Dead Man's Chest." Opening my eyes a crack, I saw Khalifa trying to pull Abdul Hakim out of bed. Since they were knocking some of the furniture over in the course of their discussion, I just lay still inside my magic chaudri.

Then they both approached my bed and suddenly I realized that the debate was running along chivalric lines. I ruled that Abdul Hakim should stay in his bed, and Khalifa should have my air mattress to sleep on beside the stove. So,

## Riding the Afghan mail

with one to watch me and the other to watch him, we all fell asleep happily.

It was, inevitably, the wiper who woke us, after watering and fueling the bus. This unfortunate, who was about eighteen, also had to keep the bus clean, inside and out and under. He loaded passengers and baggage onto the roof and handed them down as they left. After every hill he had to fetch water for the radiator, first chocking the wheels of the bus to prevent us rolling backwards to our destruction. He changed tires and checked the oil and ran errands for Khalifa. And he rode outside all the way, standing on a ladder that clanked along behind the bus.

Still, Khalifa shared his cigarettes with him and threw his arm around him when they walked. The passengers treated him as a friend, with that fine lack of class distinction that stamps the poorest Pathan a free man.

This, I thought first thing on waking, was just what I was missing. The men had shown themselves kind to me, but no one would talk to me—quite apart from the language difficulty, for even Abdul Hakim was silent. To speak or to be friendly to me would violate some other man's right in me. That my man was not present and not even known, was surely the ultimate test of their chivalry.

However, this created a number of other problems for me. I was afraid to enter a teahouse, where strangers might object to me. I didn't have a moment of privacy. Gradually, I could feel myself being pushed into that limbo which Afghan women ordinarily inhabit. This was a man's world, and I was on the outside looking in.

Not that there weren't others looking right back out at me. I drew capacity crowds at every stop. The stares were sometimes hostile, sometimes inoffensive—as open and curious as the glances which we might direct at any two-headed giraffe. But it was only with effort that I could move down a village street.

Something had to be done, and it was done in Doab. Waiting for the others to leave our bedroom, I hauled my souvenirs out of the bedroll. First I plunked a sequined skull cap on my head. Then I wrapped an orange and purple turban around it, in what I fancied to be the style of Kandahar, a district safely in the south. I let my shirt tails flap out over my trousers and covered the rest of the evidence with an embroidered sheepskin jacket that came from Ghazni. As a last touch, I jammed a cigarette in my face, and issued forth into the dusty square. Abdul Hakim walked right by me.

No one else greeted me either, and I was beginning to feel downright lonely when evidently someone spoke to me. Naturally, I could not respond and the next thing he did was punch me in the nose. I yelped and the other passengers, recognizing me, came to my rescue. Soon they were dropping to the ground helpless, in paroxysms of the purest, happiest, and most uninhibited laughter it has ever been my joy to witness.

There I was, arms and legs akimbo in the public square at Doab, Afghanistan, the proudest Pathan of them all, with my nose bleeding and forty adult males rolling at my feet. I had certainly been right about their having a sense of humor. As they struggled to their feet, each man readjusted my turban and said something encouraging. If clothes make the man, I was in business.

They do, and I was. From then on, the men talked ceaselessly and good-humoredly. Only a little bit of what they said got through to me—accompanied by pantomine and scatterings of Arabic, Urdu, and German—but the whole atmosphere had changed. Of course, anyone who took a second look at me knew I was a woman, but we simply conspired to suppress that knowledge, and this enabled us to talk with one another without breaking the code. So far as I could tell, they also kept my secret when we stopped, with the result that for the first time I was able to walk about freely without gathering a crowd.

That morning I learned that a teahouse is a *chai khanna*, and I had my first meal in one. We breakfasted on slabs of nan, a heavy tortilla that tastes like what passes in America for Russian rye. There were curds, as white as the whitewashed walls, and tea. We had our choice of green, which tastes fishy, or black, which is a solution of tannic acid. The

## Riding the Afghan mail

early morning sun shone through the narrow slits of windows, turning the nan to gold, and Sharif, the man who had tried to lure me into my first Afghan meal the day before, performed a mime to let me know that he was rich, and travelling third class to escape the attention of bandits, and owned thousands of karakul sheep, and would I like to visit his ranch? (It was all right, he assured me; he lived with his mother.)

Back aboard the bus, the tarantella began again, as Khalifa showed us no more mercy than he had the day before. But now I looked forward to the stops we made at villages for rest and refreshment. The bazaars were alive with activity; everything moved with a zing which was totally absent from the scene south of the Hindu Kush. My fellow travellers bought me nuts and fruits of every description, which they jammed in my pockets. I was never allowed to return the treat. That would not have been polite, and anyway Pathans don't have pockets. One object on the fruit stands puzzled me—a lump of mud the size of a football. When pantomine had been exhausted in trying to explain its use, Sharif bought one and split it open against a rock. Grapes. They keep all winter long when treated this way.

The larger towns have jewelry marts, displaying ear rings, nose rings, lip rings, finger rings and toe rings; silver chains and girdles, armlets, wristlets and anklets, and the large jewelled tiqas that Pathan ladies dangle right in the middle of their foreheads. Some of the nose rings are so heavy that they have to be suspended by a strand of hair or by a silver chain hooked over one ear.

Underfoot clomped always the ubiquitous fatty-tailed sheep. Their deceased brethren, flayed and impaled upside down, mark the entrances to butcher shops. Next to them, streaming in the wind, are turbans in every sort of plaid, and woolen afghans—made in Germany. Soap that looks like bricks, and cheese that looks like soap; woolen sacks that serve as gloves or socks; rock salt, coarsely refined sugar (jaggery) and snuff, all are common to every bazaar. I saw nary a book between Kabul and Mazar-i-Sharif.

Most men carry snuff in little tin or silver boxes, sneezing

## Krishna Smiled

happily in groups or with great melancholy all alone. I begged a pinch from one passenger and tried to savor it pasted to the roof of my mouth, but Sharif made me spit it out before I could get the hang of it.

Although my get-up as a Kandari baccha (a young man of Kandahar) seemed garish to me, it provided the means of getting about without being assaulted by fanatics or trampled by the curious. Only occasionally was I bothered by children who would follow me down the street singing the local version of "Georgie-porgie, puddin' an' pie," which apparently revolved around the fact that in this land of beards, I couldn't even cast a five o'clock shadow.

The teahouses were a delight and an enchantment. Generally these were small houses by the wayside, their interiors whitewashed and often covered by childlike drawings of flowers and muskets. A boy would pass among us pouring water from a Persian pitcher onto the the guests' hands. The water runs off into a brass bowl covered with an ornamental grill to prevent splashing. A rag is passed from hand to hand, and we are ready to begin.

Lunch is pilau, rice cooked with almonds, raisins, and chunks of mutton. It is served in large bowls, three or four diners to a bowl. You dig into the delicious mess, press a wad of it together, and toss it into your mouth without touching your lips.

Right hands only, please. Left hands are dirty. The Hajji, who had his right index finger in a splint, had to eat with his left hand. He did so elegantly, awkwardly, and from a separate bowl.

Tea manners are also important. You must never pour a second cupful into the first one's slops. To avoid this, when you finish drinking, you swing the cup gently in your hands and aim at the stove, where the tea leaves fizzle with a jolly sound.

A woman and two children boarded the bus one day. Khalifa tipped her off and seated her next to me. Looking at this typical Afghan woman was like looking at a tree. Behind the latticework of coarse embroidery that concealed a narrow eye-slit, hunted squirrel's eyes looked back out at me.

I coaxed her off the bus at one stop, and drawing her

## Riding the Afghan mail

into a corner, plucked at the cotton smock that started from a circlet around her head and enveloped her all the way to the ground. She drew it from over her face; I was astonished. Except for having a complexion like an unripe tomato, she was beautiful.

Still holding a fold of her chaudri, I clicked my tongue and hauled out one of my stock phrases: "Khub nai est"— roughly, "This stinks." She agreed. Then she pointed to the men nearby, rubbed her fingers together in a sign of shame, and covered herself over once more.

Abdul Hakim told me afterwards that all Afghan women are beautiful. I asked how he could know, when he had seen so few of them for himself. He thought a moment and replied: "I know that Allah is good, yet I have never seen Him."

Dinner that night in the chai khanna was cozy. There was shish kebab rolled in powdered grapes, an excellent substitute for wine sauce in a country where winemaking is prohibited. Outside, the wind was howling, but that only made the stove warmer, the food more satisfying, and the sound of the water pipe more comforting. However, I missed our woman passenger.

When I asked Abdul Hakim about her, he showed me what I had supposed to be a cupboard door. Opening it, I stepped through and tumbled down a ramp into a cave dug out of the hillside. The woman, her chaudri put aside, was sitting on the floor next to a bed mat. There was no heat, and only a candle for light. The place was airless and totally without cheer. She was eating her dinner, which had been brought in by her oldest child.

We tried to talk to one another, but could not. She offered me her red scarf, and I gave her my pocket mirror. Then I heard the bolt shoot on the heavy wooden door. I was caged! Enslaved, trapped, violated, insulted, humiliated, for thousands of years without end and on forever! Wildly I banged on the door, the woman sitting and staring at me without understanding, but I went on shrieking till Abdul Hakim let me out. I escaped, and left the Afghan woman to her fate. I never spoke to her again, and clung more tightly than ever to my male disguise.

No doubt what ensured the survival of the human race

## Krishna Smiled

in Afghanistan all these centuries was the fact that women needed children for their own survival. Nothing else would have prevented infanticide. But children are the women's only line of communication to the outside world, serving as waiters, messengers, errand boys, telephone, scouts, seeing-eye dogs, and newspapers. From the time they could talk, children were taught to report back to mother everything they saw and heard in the outside world—until the girls in their turn passed into solitary confinement, and the boys went out to the men.

On the afternoon of the third day, we arrived at Mazar-i-Sharif, which I now learned is named for the tomb of Ali, fourth Caliph and son-in-law of Mohammed the Prophet. We entered the town through the same bazaars that fester at every Asian crossroads from Ceylon to the Himalayas and from Sind to Bengal. But there is a difference here in the pace of the crowd and the electric clarity of the air. Burly Uzbegs and Tadjiks, pantalooned and booted, rode on wiry ponies out of the Central Asia that Marco Polo knew. They were wearing clothes and using tools that were not so different from those which the Venetian recorded seven centuries ago.

And then I saw the tomb of the Caliph Ali. Behind a wall at the end of the town's main street stands a confection of aquamarine tile glittering in the sun. To a barbarian like me, who always associated tile with plumbing fixtures, the building was a revelation.

"Ahhh," there was an audible intake of breath inside the bus, and men touched their beards. Some of them had lived all their lives within sight of the mosque, and still they gasped. Khalifa stopped the bus in the middle of the square. And suddenly a number of men got hold of me and pushed me out. I scanned their faces anxiously. But they weren't mad at me; they wanted me to photograph their mosque.

Arrived at the bus station, another converted caravanserai, the passengers quickly dispersed. It occurred to me that I should have learned the word for *hotel* before letting everybody get away. Sauntering through the portal of the **serai** with my bedroll on my shoulder, I expected at any mo-

## Riding the Afghan mail

ment to be denounced as an imposter. The trick was to look as though I belonged, and everything would be all right. But that way, how could I get any place, since I didn't know where I was or where I was going?

Abdul Hakim now materialized. "Do you," he asked, "wish to go to the hotel?"

I felt ambivalent toward this lad. It seemed to me that consequences were likely to flow from the fact that he spoke English and consequently always managed to get us two beds tête-a-tête. But I know when I'm hung up, so again I allowed him to take over. We got into a horse-drawn carriage. Abdul Hakim said "hotel" to the driver, which I could have said myself, and the driver said something to the horse which I could not have said, and we tore off through dusty streets until we reached an adobe barracks on the other side of town. Soon we were installed in a pleasant double room with southern exposure. We had our own bathroom, tiled like the mosque but not as stately.

I notice that Mr. Justice Douglas, in his book *West of the Indus*, does not think much of this hotel. Admitting that we start from different premises, I think it is one of the best on the subcontinent. What he said about bedbugs may be true, but the plumbing is superb, and all the rooms are equipped with walls, ceiling, and floor.

Abdul Hakim and I had not been long in the room when we fell to quarrelling. I was certain by now that he was a government spy. I knew that the Afghan government likes to keep tabs on foreign travellers. He, on the other hand, said he was an honorable man and that I needed protection. "Well, quit sharing my bedroom!" I said, heaving a pillow at him. "I am engaged to be married," he replied, heaving it back at me.

At this dramatic moment, the door opened and a man announced the Governor of Mazar-i-Sharif.

The Governor welcomed me and my "interpreter" to the province and invited us to stay at the State Guest House. If there was anything I wanted, I need only ask.

Now it was Abdul Hakim's turn to panic. He was sure

he would be arrested for this masquerade. But I signaled him to form a united front against authority and stick it out. So we packed up and moved to the State Guest House.

This turned out to be a country manor overhung by willow trees. In the salon, dusty satin curtains covered french doors of beveled glass, with a dozen panes missing. The wallpaper curled with mildew.

The steward welcomed us in German (I found that most foreigners are assumed to be Germans, though this may have changed by now, what with there being a few hundred Russian technicians in the country). Abdul Hakim immediately asked the steward if he could create a hot bath. In half an hour Ali was back, and with courtly gestures conducted me to a wooden lean-to. The tub of water which faced me had a thin skin of ice on it.

However, as I had a thick skin of Afghanistan on me, I ladled the water over my shivering, dirty body with a tin cup, scrubbed away, and told myself I was in Finland where this is healthy. I came down with the ague two days later.

Abdul had a nice hot bath because he knew that the water is heated in a container that fits into the pipe of the Franklin stove. One siphons it out through a samovar spigot, and mixes it with water from the frozen tub.

Everyday while we were in Mazar-i-Sharif, the Governor's man would appear at the Guest House to ask whether we wanted anything. Naturally, I asked for a copy of every book to be found in the bazaar. "That will be easy," he replied, "for there are none."

If I had had the wit, I would have asked the Governor's man whether old brass lamps were sold in the bazaar. As it was, Abdul Hakim, a practical man, asked for a jeep and it served us as well as the lamp served Aladdin, for it took us to Balkh.

Marco Polo described this town, which was ancient Bactria, as "a large and magnificent city," a center of learning, and an entrepôt on the silk route between China and India. One hundred years later, it was reduced by Tamerlane to a midden of pottery. We climbed a ruined wall and looked

### Riding the Afghan mail

down over acres of mounded houses studded with shards as brilliant as the day they came from the potter's oven. What a bull history let loose in this china shop!

At night, Abdul Hakim and I huddled late over the fire at the guest house, swapping stories, riddles and songs. We had three artifacts in common: the *Rubaiyat of Omar Khayyam*, the *Wise Men of Gotham*, and "MacNamara's Band," which his mother owned on a phonograph record—her only phonograph record. After we had exclaimed over the wealth of our mutual cultural heritage, we sang each other some folksongs, and I was not surprised to learn that love is as hopeless in the Khyber Pass as it is in the Cumberland Gap.

It was after lights out that Abdul Hakim and I always had our best conversations. He told me about his fiancée, and recited some poetry he had written to her in Persian. When I scoffed that he couldn't possibly love a girl he had never seen, he wept.

"You think I am not human, and that I do not feel the same passions as you do. But here in Afghanistan we love and we marry for love, just as in the West."

I was nonplussed, because this meant that some kind of personality emanates from beneath a chaudri. Here was the clue to why my question about recognizing your mother in a bazaar was so funny. But how?

"Anyway," Abdul Hakim continued, "I have seen her." He had swiped his sister's chaudri and gone to visit his girlfriend in her home. These men not only love and get married for love, they have great courage. He might have been shot.

The next morning, I went on the town while Abdul went about his own business. Mazar-i-Sharif is small and compact, with a bazaar that sells gorgeous carpets, indifferent pottery, and, as the man had said, no books. Most of the shops are meant for camels and horses, not people. The horses are smaller and more wiry than ours; the camels are understandably Bactrian.

When I had done the bazaar, I strolled into a crowded chai khanna, and squatting near the doorway, called for green tea in a loud voice, with a clap of my hands. The cup was

## Krishna Smiled

brought, together with a wet rag to clean up with, and I settled down to watch Afghanistan go by.

Anonymous in my brilliant turban and rumpled clothing, I experienced complete release from the relentless grip of femininity which immures all women, in all countries, within an invisible chaudri from the cradle to the grave. I knew I would return to Delhi, and even to Detroit, and I knew that I would never be anything but a woman. But for these few days, I was a free man.

I saw Abdul Hakim pass as I sat there—he never got so he could recognize me in a turban. After a cup of tea together, we walked over to the mosque and entered its courtyard unchallenged. The blue, green, and yellow tiles sparkled in the sun, lighting up the Arabic script that runs like embroidery around the arches of gates and windows. Doves flew in formation among the minarets, then settled like snow on the azure domes. Hand in hand, Abdul Hakim and I entered the mosque.

If I had been a girl, he couldn't have held my hand because that would have been immoral. If I had been a foreigner, I couldn't have entered the mosque, because that is illegal.

At dinnertime we shopped among the teahouses, and to Abdul Hakim's disgust, I chose the loudest honky-tonk in town. It got louder, as they brought up a three-piece combo: pottery drum, a large banjo-type instrument, and a horn that emitted a restricted but agonized range of sounds. An astonishing rhythm developed, accompanied by yodelling that would have curdled my blood if the singers hadn't maintained a perfectly docile appearance. As it was, I was glad to have the camouflage of my costume.

Abdul Hakim had been pouting for some time, and ruined my dinner by suggesting we leave. I demurred, but he repeated the suggestion in a way that got me to my feet, into my shoes, and out on the street in three seconds.

He joined me in the street after paying the bill, and trudged along at my side silently. At first he refused to say what had happened, but when he did, I knew that I had not only arrived, I had come full circle. It was time to go home.

*Riding the Afghan mail*

Within the chai khanna I had been studying a large and portly Hazara who installed himself among a covey of henchmen, diagonally across the room from us. I was anxious for any tidbit of history I might pick up from his face and clothes and bearing. Meanwhile, I forgot that my ignorance of the language rendered me dumb, not invisible.

It seems that he returned my gaze with interest, and leaning across his companions had exclaimed audibly: "In the name of Allah, has he dropped from the skies? I have never seen such a beautiful boy!"

Abdul Hakim then clammed up, and refused to tell me whether my admirer would have been disappointed to learn I was only a girl. So much for studying geography in people's faces!

I returned to the bus station next morning. Still black and bruised, and with a fit of ague chilling me to the liver, I was nevertheless sorry to turn my face southward. I was, however, cheered by the sight of Khalifa, whom a kindly station manager had held over in Mazar-i-Sharif so he could guide my return.

This is the way it was right through to the end. Where I had been told to expect barbarism, I met chivalry. Where I had expected anarchy, I met a sort of primitive democracy. The country was backward materially, and life was cruel—this much may be laid to geography and history, which opened Afghanistan to those vast series of invasions which left their mark upon the faces of her people.

But kindliness and hospitality are no accident. As a woman, I was treated with respect. As a man, I was met with friendship. Would I have met so much warmth, I wonder, on a bus from New York to Los Angeles?

And, as I say, my transformation had a profound effect on me. Once I got back to Delhi, I made an irrevocable decision to remain a woman.

# 17

*Holy, Holy, Holy*

A morose Dane I knew went hiking alone in the Himalayas and fell to his death. The news was sent to the Danish consul in New Delhi by a holy hermit of the mountains by way of a sherpa who was coming down to the plains on some business of his own.

In order legally to verify his countryman's death, the consul drove as far as he could up into the mountains, then hiked the rest of the way to the hermit's cave. Along the way, he told me later, he speculated on what had brought Halfdan here, halfway around the world, in order to die. Many of his acquaintances speculated; he had few friends. I wondered if I knew.

Halfdan had been tormented by a recurring nightmare in which he and his best friend, faceless in the dream, were marooned on a desert island with nothing to eat. The time comes when nature demands that one kill and eat the other, in order to enable himself to survive a few days longer. Which

## Holy, Holy, Holy

will Halfdan become: murderer or victim? On this point the nightmare teetered, fell, and shattered the dreamer awake.

"I don't think you have to be either," I told him while we were hiking one day in the tame hills around Mussoorie; thinking it a foolish conundrum. "I suppose you could die in one another's embrace, like Aida and what's-his-name."

I caught his green eyes looking inward, into himself, not seeing me at all. I wondered if we would have to enact his little psychodrama here and now, and looked around for a good heavy stone. I liked Halfdan very much, but there was no doubt in *my* mind whether I would prefer to be killed or to kill.

"My brother was in the SS," he said as though that explained everything, and later I decided it probably did. He himself had fought in the anti-Nazi underground.

Looking up at him as I picked my way downhill, I saw his eyes, like the flame on a kerosene stove, lick out again toward the external world, the one in which he was a totally rational agronomist employed by the U.N. Food and Agriculture Organization, and inheritor of European civilization, where people don't eat each other any more. He was in many ways the most civilized man I ever met.

"I think," he said in his light tenor voice that twanged as though a harp were being played inexpertly on his narrow rib cage, "I think I would rather be the victim."

When the consul arrived at the hermit's cave, the rishi received him naked except for a saffron-colored loincloth. His body was smeared with the ashes of the dead and marked in yellow swastikas. His hair was unkempt and matted with the refuse of years. He had trained himself to sit inside his clammy cave bolt upright, not moving, not speaking, not blinking, perhaps not breathing, one wondered about thinking, for hours at a time.

Nevertheless, he conversed quite amiably in English, the language in which he had talked with Halfdan up until the day of his accident. The rishi led the consul to a nearby valley, where he showed him a grave covered with rocks and topped by a cross.

*Krishna Smiled*

"I understand," he said, "that you do not burn your dead. I wanted to do what was right for his soul."

The place where Halfdan fell is sacred to Hindus as the source of the Ganges. Legend has it that the goddess Ganga Maya fell to earth here when Brahma, to fulfill the boon of a supplicant, caused her to leave her heavenly course. In pique, she flung herself down upon earth with such force that had it not been for Shiva catching and entangling her in his hair, she would have flooded all the world. Instead, she ran out of the god's coiled locks down either side of Mount Kailas, to form the rivers of Punjab which empty westward into the Arabian Sea, and the Ganges which debouches 3,000 miles to the east.

The epic is thousands of years old, yet it records accurately the fact that Indus and Ganges, apparently separated from one another by the width of the continent, actually rise within a hair of one another, on either side of Shiva's part, as it were.

When Ganges reaches Rishikesh, she disgorges icy and tumultuous from the Himalayas to begin her descent upon the plains of Uttar Pradesh. The upper reaches of the river are more sacred, but almost inaccessible, so it is to Rishikesh that the pilgrims come, by bus, cart, and on foot to keep a tryst with the river goddess. The terraced hills are striped in emerald and dotted with little temples studded upon banks which rise steeply away from the river. Here Ganges comes roaring like an express train through her narrow gorge, cold with the cold of mountain snows, and muddy with the mud of riverbanks she has torn out up the line. Approaching Rishikesh from the south, as I did, one has the feel of entering a Chinese landscape painting.

The pilgrims have been coming for centuries to this site, watched over by a fraternity of holy men in saffron robes. A caste of scribes has also come into existence whose function it is to keep track of the pilgrims in all their generations. The new arrival has only to circulate his name, his father's name and the village of his birth, and soon a man appears who is his family's record-keeper. The scribe can show the pilgrim

*Holy, Holy, Holy*

where his ancestors were inscribed in his book, which has been handed down to him from his father, and, for a fee, inscribes the newcomer's name in turn, for his son to show to *his* son.

For me, the first of my line to visit Rishikesh, the age of the place was irrevocably fixed in mind by a sign hand-lettered on cardboard and tacked to a wooden lean-to patched with flattened jerry cans:

LORD KRISHNA SLEPT HERE.

Right behind my own car, a tourist bus arrived, its occupants half dead of dust and heat. When its doors opened, a group of ladies in the sodden-hued saris of Madras disembarked and, as though in a trance, looking neither to the right nor to the left, walked straight into the river. I followed them down to the bathing ghat, but they could not have cared less about me. Along our path, holy contortionists performed, one with his head locked (permanently?) into his crotch; another scuttling forward and backward like a scorpion, on all fours, belly up. Under a banyan tree, a holy ash-smeared sadhu stared sightless into the sun, then turned to display his better profile when he saw me aim my camera. All Rishikesh shimmered in the sun, a painted ship upon a painted sea; or perhaps a stage set shimmering under klieg lights waiting for the performance to begin in a language no one knew, for an audience who will never arrive.

And Halfdan? Had he arrived? Whatever could have attracted him here? Whatever it was, was incomprehensible to me. I was totally a daughter of the scientific age, and wanted nothing to do with mystics.

Yet I knew that many practical people come to Rishikesh to live out their lives. Self-abnegation is a Hindu virtue, and many a man who has passed his youth in learning the ways of the world and his middle age in training his children to the ways of the world, renounces this same world when he grows old. At fifty he gives away his possessions and puts his family from him. Taking up a beggar's bowl he retires to a

## Krishna Smiled

holy place such as Rishikesh, joining the court of some guru (teacher) or rishi (wise man) who has spent his entire life in monastic contemplation of the divine. I saw in the practice only a wastage of India's brain power. Here, masquerading as beggars, were the men who should be running industry, sitting in Parliament, investing in growth stocks.

The gurus are held in high esteem by the masses, who cluster round them for audience. They are often attended likewise by foreigners, including many freaky ladies (in the fifties these were mostly German; in the sixties, Americans made the scene) who wish to learn the secret of eternal youth or to communicate with their deceased dogs. While westerners regard the gurus with respect, many Indians regard them as charlatans, and their medicinal distillations as quackery. They often drive the sadhus away from their doors when they come begging.

Yet these same sceptics may continue to visit one particular holy man who either comes from the same caste or has had some contact with the family.

There can be no doubt that some holy men capitalize on the faith of the people, taking their money and their prayers to perform feats which are impossible to perform. When commercialism adds its crushing weight, the phenomenon becomes even more distressing. In fact, my first encounter with holy men was through a movie which exploited mysticism, sex and patriotism in approximately equal parts, and which happenstantially I saw with Halfdan.

He was still under the spell of an experience the week before, when a travelling magician invited him up on stage as a hostile witness to his magic. Avoiding Gogia Pasha's eyes, so as not to be hypnotized by them, Halfdan watched the magician reach into his assistant's throat and cut his tongue out. The subject sat tranquilly, a doctor holding his wrist, where the pulse had ceased to make itself felt. Having given the audience a chance to view the severed tongue, while Halfdan looked deep into the assistant's mouth and saw none there, Gogia Pasha stuffed the organ back into the gaping aperture and made a pass in abracadabra fashion. Whereupon the man's pulse resumed and he wagged his tongue in greet-

## Holy, Holy, Holy

ing to the crowd. Halfdan was deeply puzzled by the incident, and I would have been too, had I believed Halfdan.

To get back to the movie. It was going around to great critical acclaim, reinvigorating the dormant patriotism of Indians like a good dose of salts. As it was in Bengali, of which neither Halfdan nor I could understand a word, the following synopsis may not be totally reliable. I am sure, however, that I have caught the spirit of the thing.

British soldiers occupying Bengal busy themselves beating up villagers and raping their wives. A rebellion begins to take shape. Men take a vow of brahmacharya (celibacy) until freedom is won. Rajahs run away from their palaces to join the People. While they are gone, their wives are abducted by worshippers of Kali (the black-faced, hydra-armed goddess of death, whose beak runs with human blood). In case you think that Kali is the villain of the piece, we then have a scene showing the guru, who is the leader of the revolt, taking a stranger on a tour of his temple and pausing to make obeisance to Kali, who is wearing her customary necklace of human skulls. He makes a pretty little speech about the goddess. The sound of his voice is so sweet that as he talks, the distressed widow of a revolutionary stops grieving, glazes over in a blissful smile, and draws herself snakelike on her belly along the ground to kiss the guru's feet. That old humbug ends his speech with the cry, "Vande Matram!" (Victory to the Motherland!), and then there is a scene of mass self-immolation as women kill themselves in throngs because their husbands have broken their oaths to remain celibate. C'est la guerre. Cut to a bunch of horses carrying men into battle, pawing their hooves in time to a syncopated version of the revolutionary anthem. The sight of so many Bengali actors on horseback convulsed me, until I remembered the demented smile on the face of the woman as she glided toward the guru on her belly. That troubled me: it was the smile on the face of Krishna, as it might be practiced by the Madwoman of Chaillot. And that was the glaze I saw on the women as they decanted from the tourist bus at Rishikesh and walked into the river.

Below Rishikesh, Ganges begins to spread herself out,

## Krishna Smiled

a woman of middle years, waxing broad and muddy and powerful as she sweeps across the Northern Province, joined by Yamuna at Allahabad, Gumti at Banaras, Gogra above Patna, till flooding through Bihar she joins Brahmaputra in the thousand deltas of Bengal.

By the time the river reaches Allahabad, she is moving slowly, her veins swollen with the refuse of cities along the way. Just outside the city, three sacred rivers converge. There are Ganges, still chockablock with people bathing; Yamuna which is India's gift to lovers who jump into it when the going gets rough; and Saraswati, which doesn't flow on earth at all, but comes pouring down from heaven out of a celestial pitcher.

Every twelve years, when the sun is in Aries and Jupiter is in Aquarius, a Kumbh Mela (Festival of the Pitcher) is held. In 1954 it was to be held at Allahabad, and a bookdealer brought me to the site, explaining the mystic symbolism of the once-in-twelve-years ceremony.

Viewing the riverbank in a nonfestive month, I saw nothing but rancid flats filled with desultory bathers. Try as I might, I could imagine no holy spirit hovering over this singularly dreary salt bund. It was another revelation such as I had experienced before: one sees just as much of India as one is willing to see. And I was totally unreceptive to mysticism. My only concern was that the rickshaw was a tight fit, and I could scarcely wait to get back to dry land.

As the time for the festival approached, fever ran high. The government did all it realistically could do to keep control: for example, proof of inoculation against cholera was required of anyone purchasing a railroad ticket to Allahabad, a restriction which was relaxed only on the high holiday itself, when it is estimated that an additional million souls entered the city.

During the course of the month, ten million people, including the President of India, arrived at the junction of the rivers to arrange for the release of their souls from the cycle of perpetual rebirth. The pilgrims camped on the riverbank, taking frequent ritual baths and eating even less than usual. From news reports, they seem to have spent much time rescu-

## Holy, Holy, Holy

ing their belongings from huts which set themselves on fire; suffering bridges to collapse beneath their combined weight; being trampled by sacred elephants run amok; and listening to proclamations by the Union of Sadhus supporting the government in any measures it might take to counter United States military aggression through the arming of Pakistan.

A little discomfort was not deemed too high a price to pay in order to escape living through another entire lifetime of India.

On the fateful morning at 10:30, when the planets approached their celestial cathexis, a parade of Naga Goswains, known in religious circles as the Unclothed Brigade, were proceeding to the riverbank for their baths when a group of pilgrims crept forward on their bellies to take a pinch of sand from beneath their feet. The holy men laid about them with their holy spears to prevent the people from touching their holy feet. Behind the crawlers, ten million people pressed forward to the river. When the riverbank was cleared, half a thousand people lay crushed to death in the slippery sand.

* * *

Of all the gods, the ugliest is Jagganath. He makes his home in the delta of the Mahanadi River on the east coast below Calcutta. Wooden, limbless, more mound than man, less man than lump, he reigns fiercely from his temple at Puri, whither he commands the faithful come each year to pull his image in procession. He is regarded by his devotees as one of the ten manifestations of Vishnu (five of which occurred in a world preceding ours, four in this world, and one of which has yet to come) although many a northern Vaishnavite in good standing has never heard of him.

Jagganath was aborted through the curiosity of the king who endowed him. Impatient with the slow work of manufacture, the king stole a forbidden look at the god in process of creation, and thus literally stunted his growth. Now, although happily endowed with a soul, Jagganath must be fitted with golden arms and legs before being wrapped in ceremonial robes for his annual run.

Perhaps because of this initial unhappy experience, the

curious are to this day barred from the Temple of Jagganath. One can get a good idea of what he looks like, however, from the souvenir portraits of him which are sold in the bazaar which runs fulsomely round the temple with its bulbous spires.

From a scarlet lacquered background, a rigid black face stares out through seashell eyes: blind, yet curiously seeing. He is flanked by his smaller sister and brother. All their eyes protrude with primitive force from what well might be the primeval Id.

When I visited Puri, three hulking gaadies still lurched in the courtyard of the temple, relics of the week before. *Gaadi* is a term which can mean, variously, car, throne, vehicle, or practically anything one sits upon, with overtones of majesty. In modern Hindi, gaadi came to be used for "train."

A mouse, for example, is the gaadi of Ganesh, the elephant-headed deity, and he travels everywhere upon it. Garuda the man-eagle is the gaadi of Vishnu (and incidentally the name of the Indonesian airline).

Jagganath's gaadis were handhewn massive wooden chariots thirty feet tall, not unlike medieval siege towers in appearance. Hung with tinsel, flags and portraits of the gods, and smoking incense, they had borne the idols of the Jagganath family in ceremonial procession to the sea the week before, while I, several hundred miles away in Calcutta, knew nothing of the matter because they have their own gods there. The massive lumbering vehicles, drawn by hundreds of men who lash themselves to the lead poles, smash blindly forward on their weighty handhewn wheels, jolt, surge, topple, crush the laggard underneath the wheels: the very juggernaut.

To worship that which crushes you; to desire to be crushed by that which you worship. To identify with that which humiliates you; to seek humiliation as an identity. Halfdan's sister went underground when the juggernaut reached Denmark; but his boyhood friend, about whom he dreamed, collaborated with the Nazis.

* * *

## Holy, Holy, Holy

I crossed three rivers to get to Khajuraho: Chambal, by pontoon bridge; Sindh, by causeway; Betwa, by ferry. After which the land greens up, becomes fresher and supports some forests. The people too are more prosperous than elsewhere: many of the farm women wear a hundred rupees worth of silver around their ankles as dowry.

The temples, what is left of them, are deserted save for tourists. Around their outer and inner walls runs a wild and stony parade of humans, gods and beasts. The complex, which used to include eighty-five temples but now has only twenty, is dominated by the sardula: a leogriff (half lion, half griffin, which is itself half horse, half bird) raping a woman. The sinuous curves of their locked forms are repeated endlessly throughout the temple sculptures, now emerging with clarity, now stylized into a geometric pattern, now dissolved into a curve which can be recognized only by reference to the original statement that stands elevated in front of one of the temple buildings.

All around, men disport stonily with their women, laying them horizontally and vertically, up against a wall or floating on a stream, right side up and upside down, actively and passively. Above, dancing girls swing their hips provocatively in the gloom of eaves and columns; over there, a girl with a delightful rump lifts her foot behind her to extract a thorn from her sole.

Sex had not been differentiated from religion when these temples were built, sometime between the ninth and eleventh centuries A.D. The stony bacchantes memorialize a time, if that ever existed, when ecstacy was one, whether its source was earthly or divine, and Lord Krishna sported with the dairymaids.

Poor Halfdan, I thought, remembering how this man, educated at Europe's finest universities, had told me his only happy experience had been with a cowlike farm girl. That had been Krishna's way, too, but Krishna enjoyed his girls, and loving them, smiled; while Halfdan's voice was sardonic when he told a woman he loved her, so that she knew he was only trying the words to see how they sounded. When he danced, his lithe body stiffened within the ridiculous tuxedo which Delhi nightclubs required men to wear, and showed none of the suppleness he really had, and which he revealed only to mountains. Ultimately, all to mountains.

Well, Halfdan was a monotheist, son of a Lutheran minister. And when that god died, there was no other to take his place. Hinduism provides the believer with a veritable supermarket of gods, and there is something to satisfy every conceivable taste. Would you care for Vishnu in the shape of a boar? Or the black bull Nandi, Shiva's gaadi, brooding over the city of Mysore? Hanuman the monkey god or Ganesh the elephant god or Thing the anything god? The Hindu consumer is not tantalized by a multiplicity of canned soups or motor cars; but he certainly has his pick of gods.

He may be small as the tiny lingam I came across at a village crossroads: so formless and indistinct as to suggest the clitoris of the town rather than its penis; and I would have missed it altogether were it not for the flood of orange paint and marigolds which had been heaped upon it. Or he may be fifty-seven feet tall and naked as a jaybird, like old Gomatesvara posted atop his hill. Grey granite vines climb his legs, grey granite curls adorn his head; the Buddha's contemplative smile transfigures his great granite face. Every twelve years, whether he needs it or not, they bathe him down with coconut milk, plantains, ghee, jaggery, gold, silver, and flowers mixed with nine varieties of gems, "etc." Whatever is left to be included in that "etc?"

Everything seems so hodgepodge, so undiscriminating, at times so vile and dirty, so seldom sublime, that a visitor is baffled. How can anyone worship such things? Could you pray in a public bath house? A zoo? Disneyland? Where is the ideal, the belief that takes a man by the heart and renders him more than he was? Must Hindus remain mired forever in the verdant excretory fantasies of the childhood of their race? One ought to be able to believe that all life is sacred without having to worship it in its lowest forms. Even a scorpion which invades a village hut may not be killed, but only thrown gently out into the path, presumably to sting the neighbors. Where everything is sacred, human life is less so.

## Holy, Holy, Holy

But after a time, the same visitor may feel he has missed the point. Is not life itself hodgepodge, undiscriminating, at times vile and dirty, seldom sublime? Is man necessarily the center of the universe? Does believing that he is, make western history any more humane than eastern? Are there more gentle souls among us, or more brave, or more wise? In my observation, the answer must be no.

Perhaps Hindus are not saying: these horrible things are worthy of being held sacred. Maybe they are saying: the entire universe is sacred, and that must necessarily include what is horrible as well as what is beautiful.

* * *

On my return to America, I met Kali. She had dyed her hair blonde and was having more fun. Smiling for the photographer, she steps down from her bloody dais to mount her new high-performance sports-model gaadi. With a screech like that of a predatory animal, she tears down the freeways of America, laying down rubber all the way, slaughtering innocent and guilty alike in such number that she cannot even drink all the blood.

The high priests of her cult vaunt Kali in her latest manifestation, broadcast the virtues of her gaadi, and keep count of her victims, comparing this year's Memorial Day toll with last year's. The announcer's voice is neutral, we do not expect him to break down and cry. We know that some will die, it is Kali's will, and we have no time to dedicate all those corpses.

While we scorn the tale of 60,000 princes turned to ash by an ascetic's glance, our widescreen Indians and cowboys send one another to blazes. Only bizarre forms of death divert us: a man killed by a car at his own breakfast table, a construction worker fallen into wet concrete, mother murders babe, a busload of Mexican migrants ... the door groans open, and the monster enters to read us the six o'clock news. Murder by car, murder by war, murder by peace, murder by the little boy next door who always seemed so nice—we are bathing in blood. But unlike Hindus, we deny death any significance.

We labor toward our ideal of objectivity in cold blood. While Moslem and Hindu hack each other to bits, we pay journalists to record the slaughter dispassionately. Having made the transition to a market economy, we pay the murderer cash to tell his story to the pulps. Pulps: now there's a word! Give me Kali any day, for her blood is hot, and her victims know why they must die.

Jagganath immigrated to the United States too. He has left Puri with its clean sea breeze and the horrifying undertow of its sea beach, and adopted television for his gaadi. Ensconced therein, he turns his eye upon us and bids us serve him. I, for one, cannot refuse. The hammer pounds my head to sell the pain-killer that will ease the headache brought on by the hammer's blows. The insistent drip of gastric acids eats through my entrails, which obligingly turn to plastic. The foaming beer mug drives me mad with thirst. All the complex technology of the space age is put to use in order to replicate the compulsion which Jagganath exercised for centuries with his vacant seashell eyes and ineffectual stick hands.

"At least," I tell myself, "at least we of the West are individuals. What were ten million people doing on the beach at Allahabad all at the same time?"

Worshipping the sun, the moon and the stars, of course, like the millions who crowd Jones Beach or the sewer's edge at Santa Monica. One cannot walk the summer shores without stepping on the naked and/or the dead, as well as on their sandwiches, umbrella poles, and trash. Is it really more meritorious to flock to the beach in search of a suntan, rather than in search of nirvana?

Imagine that the suffering crowds at August beaches should be uplifted by the Word that their immersion was going to wreak a spiritual change in them. "And ye shall be received into heaven as the result of a day at the beach." Well worth a sunburn and chiggers in the coke! How patient and docile we would be in homebound traffic, how oblivious to accident, knowing that our souls had been placed in perpetual trust. There would be no hurry to get home. Our home would be the ultimate universe. We need ask no longer, "Are you running with me, Jesus?" because the rat race would be ended.

Silently, gaunt grisly men stalk past us in bikinis, scuffing

## Holy, Holy, Holy

sand into our sandwiches. Or are those loincloths they are wearing, and are they Naga Goswains?

Americans are so often accused of being obsessed by sex that it was a relief to find the Indians are too. But Hindus accept sex as divine recompense for the miseries of life, while we persist in counting sex among our miseries. Hence they can display their lovers in temples, while we hide ours in darkened theaters. Their gods are participants; ours a voyeur.

Presumably, as western civilization makes further inroads into the Hindu psyche, neurosis will invade their erogenous zones too. Great lovers will be consigned to legend, the statuary will be banished from the temples and arrested for indecent exposure, the *Kamasutra* will be censored, and Hindus will begin to sublimate. India will build a growth economy, and forever look back in anguish at the erotic chaos of the past.

The guide who showed me Gomatesvara took me up to a balcony where giant granite genitalia confronted me. He thought I might want to take a picture. Accordingly, Gomatesvara flexed his grey granite muscles and advanced upon the west, where he was photographed for the cover of *Physical Culture*. The dancing girl of Khajuraho finally removed the stony thorn from out her upturned foot, and became Playmate of the Month. The sporting lovers came down from off the temple walls to be photographed in living color, and the resultant TV special became the subject of a decision by the Supreme Court which found the sculpture had redeeming social and artistic merit. But neither attackers nor defenders of Khajuraho cared to attribute divinity to those darling lovers, though, nevertheless, approval was given to viewers to have sex when the commercials came on.

I liked Khajuraho better than Banaras, possibly because there were no people there. And celebrating sex seemed like a marvellous idea. Remembering the parking-lot-marker-Shiva-lingam having his makeup applied in the courtyard of that Banarsi temple, I had to wonder: was Adonai wrong to take godhead away from that miserable stone, and leave him —a miserable stone?

The stone continues to exist whether or not you call him

## Krishna Smiled

Shiva and paint him orange with two blue eyes. So also do sex, violence, thrills, fairy tales, art, commercialism, patriotism, fun, terror, and—incidentally—religion. In America, we recognize and endure all these, but for us these experiences are fragmented and meaningless. In India, these elements are integrated and sanctified, rolled into a single ball of wax ready for the Hindu to pick up and throw at the unanswered question.

And what of our poor fragmented selves? Children of men whose faith was as a rock, we have seen that rock shattered by war, by fraternal treachery, by cannibalism, until our very souls fragment and we become, like Halfdan, both murderer and victim.

For us, traditional answers no longer suffice, and we no longer know what questions to ask or of whom.

* * *

Smiling, Krishna rose like Venus on the half-shell from the azure depths of the President's swimming pool, breaking the calmly reflected pillars with his sleek form as he boosted himself up to stand before me the figure of a Greek god, only I supposed he must be a Hindu one, though he had no more arms than necessary, and he was laughing at me.

"You mustn't jump into the water as if you were a frog, you know;" and Krishna taught me to dive, a feat which half a dozen gym teachers had pronounced impossible. "It is only a question of confidence;" and unexpectedly, I was confident.

Krishna himself had learned to swim in distant dawns in sacred pools atop a hill crowned by one of those temples so detested by Jehovah. He qualified for the Olympic team there.

"In a sacred pool? For God's sake!"

"Oh, yes, I snuck over there before the religion business opened for the day, and when the priests and pilgrims arrived, I would run home," he said. The water rippled smoothly off his muscles; he swam without a sound. "I could do a mile in 4:02, if traffic wasn't heavy."

Idol-of-Krishna was his full name, he had no other and didn't need more: just Krishnamurti.

*Holy, Holy, Holy*

Krishna was the eighth avatar of Vishnu, Protector and Sustainer of Life who rides a man-eagle for his gaadi and lies down to rest among the coils of a giant cobra. In babyhood he was the pet of dairymaids, whom he later mounted, becoming a combination Pan and Tyl Eulenspiegel, not above lifting up mountains to shelter his beloved cow girls from the rain. The two of us used to go picnicking alongside Okhla Canal where otters carry their sleek heads above the tops of the browning grass and oxcarts creak past loaded with hay. There under the mango trees, Krishna taught me his smile.

I imagine it was the same smile that adorned the face of Apollo when he played his flute and the birds stopped singing to listen. Krishna plays a flute too, but he paints his face allover blue and until you get used to that sort of thing it can stop you cold.

"I never thought that I would love an American girl," said Krishna, who had 1,363 wives and loved each one of them each night. They were all Indian, of course. It is well known that western women are too demanding. They have not been taught to regard their husbands as incarnations of God.

Krishna was surprised at how he grew in stature when he saw himself reflected in my eyes, the eyes of an autonomous human like himself, rather than in the god-crazed eyes of some supine cowherd. It woke him from the habit of centuries. He took a new interest in the world around him, and walked to the office instead of taking his gaadi. Leaving behind the security of temples, he strode out into the contemporary world. He'd had one foot in it when I met him; all he'd needed was a shove.

He turned out to be an excellent manager, a hangover from the days when he advised King Arjuna and drove his chariot in the great battle which provides the setting for the *Bhagavad-gītā*. Later, he was an officer in the British Army. Now, he took an interest in computers, and conducted some highly efficient military operations. As he began to pay attention to business and leave the dairymaids alone, gross national productivity rose, schools were built in rural areas, some

## Krishna Smiled

villagers agreed to separate their sewage from their drinking water, some college graduates forsook the fleshpot cities for the benighted villages, the flamboyant eccentricities of outlying provinces were reduced in importance until they became no more than colorful elements in the Republic Day parade, Indian civil servants took over the United Nations Secretariat, some intercaste marriages took place: in short, an ancient civilization cracked and, animated by the dybbuk of Henry Ford, India staggered out to greet the twentieth century.

But we who were so concerned about our impact on Asia never anticipated Asia's impact upon us. We brought efficiency; she touched us with mysticism. We preached utility; she taught us elaboration. We planted industry; she reaped population. We taught her how to manipulate the external world, abjuring prayer; she taught us that the internal world is not beyond manipulation. We brought our vision in black and white, for or against, with or without; she opened our eyes to subtle gradations of life's spectrum, things which are at one and the same time right and wrong, yes and no, and smiles that are, of all things, blue.

For me, that smile dissolved the harsh dichotomies of life in the northern hemisphere. Western categories fade in the light of Krishna's smile, dissolve into the shimmering colors of secret gardens that lie enclosed by palaces where Kitu used to wait for me beside the swimming pool.

Nor was mine the only mind expanded by that radiance. Gasping beds of pink and orange and purple flowers, plucked by the hands of itinerant flower children from the gardens of Rashtrapathi Bhavan rose into the air and, blown across oceans of time, reassembled themselves with psychedelic gaiety on posters and movie screens upon the walls of America, their amplified voices breaking down the walled cities of our minds. Soon Krishna himself, in his avatar as a hippie, arrived in America, riding the Garuda label at 33 1/3 rpm. I recognized his gear: it all came from a cunning Jain temple in Ajmer, bedizened in mirrored hippogryphs and purple elephants. All he lacked were strobe lights, and the Americans supplied those.

## Holy, Holy, Holy

Behind Krishna came Yehudi Menuhin holding Ravi Shankar by the hand, and they were followed by hordes of beatles, mothers, and freaked-out dionysian creatures half divine, half mad, couldn't care less. The exuberance of the Hindu pantheon burst through the worn facade of the Protestant ethic.

Temple bells were rung, not by saffron-robed monks, but by long-haired lads in cast-off clothes of foreign cultures who had fallen under the spell of Khajuraho and would make love indefinitely but not war. Astrology storms the bastion of reason and drama enters the House of Aquarius, the very sign which presided over the stampede at the Kumbh Mela.

I felt warmly superior over the Kumbh Mela until the advent of rock festivals. It is true we do not mob our holy men, nor stampede in and out of churches like they do in Delhi. We treat religion with respect, wearing our nicest clothes. But that is because we have lowered our sights.

Celestial stars don't determine our lives so much as human ones do. It is the singing stars who set the tone for our society, decree what we shall wear and be, the shapes our fantasies and our shirts will take. So it is they whom we stampede to adore. They are the gurus of our culture, and the chief difference between the riverbank at Allahabad and the pastures of Woodstock is that people came to Allahabad to redeem their immortal souls, while we went to Woodstock to pleasure ourselves.

# 18

*It's a long way to Khajuraho,
we'd better get started*

**I**, Marco Polo, launched into fabulous adventure strapped into an upholstered chair, waterproof paper bag in hand. I had saddled no camels, climbed no mountains, endured no sandstorms, but I reached India anyhow. Someone else attended to the details, leaving me no role to play. No role? There was no drama—one hoped for no drama, it could end only in oblivion. Captive in the aircraft's cocktail lounge, the adventurer could not advent. Anxiety, the disease of passivity, replaced courage, the disease of action.

Aloft. The vistas of this hugely revolving world constricted themselves into an 8 mm reel. The endlessly varied faces of mankind were replaced by the xeroxed countenances of airline employees. And those egg crates, those wastelands, those airports, resounded with the noise of my own language. Someone had forbidden airline personnel to speak their mother tongues, on pain of life. English pursued me like a surface-to-air missile, sucked in by the very accent I emitted.

*It's a long way to Khajuraho*

And that stewardess! I had gone to high school with her, but they had tied a sari round her as she went about her business of eliminating wonder. Wander?

Imagine fabled lands which Tamerlane and Genghis Khan labored to achieve, dragged forward for my delectation, without any exertion whatever on my part. A cosmic conveyor belt took me to India, of which I saw only the cogs: Orly (grey), Bonn (brown), Beirut (blue), Iran (apparently, since the Shah's picture was on the wall). Now, because I had drunk black tea in the middle of the night at a bare trestle table under a picture of the shah, had I *been* to Iran? Perhaps it was Montana. It was too dark out to tell.

I saw Kilroy on a bathroom wall in Bonn, his peculiarly American phiz peering out to see what those foreigners were going to do next. A familiar face at last. I may never have been east of New York before, but he had been. So had all the mass media. With lens, cartoon, and poster, they have uncovered the subtle mysteries of the world to millions who associate "mystery" with murder, and "world" with problems. Proxy travel has wafted us in carefree, permapress documentaries from Hong Kong to Kathmandu and back via Paris ("Vous est Americaine?" inquired the waitress. "Ham and eggs!" she shouted to the cook). Why travel?

In short, the passage to India was boring. The irksome interior of the plane raised for me a philosophical question: Was I in fact travelling? What did it mean to travel? Was it only the passive consumption of miracles? Delhi's pellucid air may be as intoxicating today as when Shah Jahan sat his peacock throne; but could I enjoy it as fully, who had not labored through choking sands to breathe it? The winking campfire below spelled life or death to the earthling; but it was meaningless to me at 30,000 feet. History was below, I was among the mindless clouds. Where was Marco Polo now?

Somewhere between Abadan and Karachi, I decided that if I could not actively relate to the world I was passing through, then I would just go back home and frequent the movies, where I could see the same marvels from a more comfortable seat. I knew very well that the homebound traveller, his feet not quite damped by the Cinerama tide, is soon surfeited with the appearance of reality: the rest of the world is apparently very much like us, but the natives wear these funny costumes. With such comforting thoughts, we leave the travelog yawning, we already know more about India than we care to know, actually to go there would be redundant.

Most of us feel alienated when we travel, which is why we buy souvenirs. We think that through them we can annex reality. The truth is, acquisitiveness is a cop-out. It prevents one from noticing that he hasn't been there. Brass urns, star sapphires, embroidered handbags, fake antiquities, and all the other bric-a-brac of the tourist trade merely symbolize one's failure to make contact with the outside world.

Airlines and steamship companies were just then uncovering the Far East for hordes of Far Westerners who had already done Europe and were looking for something new. It made quite an impression on Indians to have a boat dock in Bombay with seven hundred of the elderly infirm, some actually confined to wheelchairs, but festooned with their all-seeing cameras and armed with American Express checks, descending upon the chawls and chowks of the city in pursuit of ivory elephants and embroidered teacozies. No one could believe they had come so far, expending so much effort and money, in order to purchase these worthless objects.

But shopping is a substitute for experiencing reality, much of which is too repellant to enjoy anyhow. So a sequined cap becomes a stand-in for incomprehensible Bhopal; a fur jacket substitutes for ruined Ghazni; and a star sapphire is some recompense for Srinagar, which stinks, you know, really stinks.

What meaning do these objects have once they have been severed from their origins and become an item of barter among the In people? Anyone who actually buys a brass bell while in India might as well be in Times Square, and deserves to be. Travel must be more than a spectator sport, or it is an affront to the world one travels through.

Souvenirs seemed to me an insult to my life in Asia. What souvenir of blind tap-tap-tapping in the dark, what souvenir

## It's a long way to Khajuraho

of exhausted children, what souvenir of hunger in a loom-festooned cottage? Besides, I had no money. Star sapphires were beyond me, wooden bookends beneath me. And I took my job seriously: I didn't need to collect brass bowls and Nepalese battle horns, my job was obsession enough.

Photography is another way to cope with the alienation of travel. Trying to capture reality, we photograph the alien swoop of a sari as a woman bends to the well; an old man singing by a fountain; temples marching with determination into the sea. Each moment is an apocalypse, each picture worth a thousand words. Then, viewing the pictures which have made words unnecessary, we find their sense has gone. Devout Moslems fear we shall capture their souls when we take their pictures. They can relax. Photography is barely skin-deep; souls elude us. The camera has made us observers rather than participants.

Landing in India, I got rid of my movie camera. It seemed to me to proclaim my otherness, my outsideness, the fact that I would be there for the moment only. Then I would take my film back to the United States and exhibit Asia as a curiosity to my friends—my real friends, the American ones. After coffee, they would show me their slides of Acapulco.

In such pictures, the world becomes a set piece against which we arrange our preconceptions. We think we are photographing the Taj Mahal, but we project reels of ourselves grinning foolishly in front of what might as well be a painted backdrop in a photographer's studio.

I wanted to record my impressions in greater depth, using a longer time exposure. I therefore chose the most sensitive and durable instrument I possessed: myself. And if my travel into inner space has not always been commensurate with my travel into outer, that is to be expected: it is a long way to Khajuraho, but even farther to my Self.

# Index

Acheson, Dean, 11
Afghanistan: Kabul to Kandahar, 108-22; Kabul to Mazar-i-Sharif, 206-25
Anti-Americanism. See Culture, Indian

Banaras, 21-29
Bangladesh, 79-81. See also Linguistic nationalism
Bathing: in Ganges, 23; at Delhi Gymkhana Club, 136-37; in Arabian Sea, 137; at Rashtrapathi Bhavan, 142; at Brazilian Embassy, 145; at Malabar, 172-73; at Mazar-i-Sharif, 222; at Rishikesh, 231; at the Kumbh Mela, 232-33; in America, 238
Beggars, 24-25, 139-40
Bhilsa, 41-42
Bowles, Chester, 163
British Raj: origins of, 51; British provinces, 51-52; princely states, 52-53; hill stations, 104-5; castaways of, 171-73

Capitalism. See Culture, Indian
Caste: and conversion to Islam, 25; untouchables, 98-99; lack of literature on, 99; description of, 99-100; and representative government, 100; and race, 101; and the foreigner, 103-7; contrast with Afghanistan, 214
Cattle, 41

Censorship. See Publications procurement
Ceylon, 174-76
Children: as workers, 27, 99, 161; clothing, 162, 171; servant's, 177-79, 185, 188-89; as social security, 188; as a means of survival, 221
China: propaganda in India, 159, 202; comparison of U.S. and Indian attitudes toward, 202-3
Communism: propaganda, 157; publications, 158-59; and sex, 159, 169; bookstores, 169; and youth, 161-62; in Kerala, 164-70, 173; vs. free enterprise, 166-67; and U.S. Department of State, 197. See also McCarthyism
Coorg, 82-88
Culture, Indian: attitude toward West, 19, 134-35; laborers, 59, 120-21; capitalism, 165-67; anti-Americanism, 169; touching, 172; faith, 237-40; impact on America, 241-43

Delhi, 41, 45-50, 62-69, 131-46, 177-89
Diplomatic corps: initiation, 11-12; life style, 132-39; and being a woman, 146

Festivals: Dussehra in Uttar Pradesh, 17; Holi in Bhilsa, 41-42; Janamasthami in Delhi, 36; Ga-

## Index

nesha Chaturthi in Coorg, 83-84, 87; Kumbh Mela, 232-33; of Jagganath, 233-34; of Gomateswara, 236

Hyderabad: 52-53, 55, 74, 153

Intelligence procurement. *See* Publications procurement

Jews and Judaism, 83-84, 114, 128-29

Kashmir, 147-56
Kerala, 161-73. *See also* Communism, Linguistic nationalism
Krishna: as idol, 36-38; as student, 43; as revelation, 44; as army captain, 46; as hunter, 60; as pilgrim, 229; as lover, 235; as Olympic swimmer, 240; as faithful married man, 241; as modernizer, 241; the hippie inversion, 242-43

Labor. *See* Culture, Indian
Lahore, 123-29
Languages: multiplicity of, 14; English, 52, 77-78, 96, 158; *Linguistic Survey of India*, 72; as basis of political organization, 72; Sanskritic and Dravidian, 73, 78; Hindi-Urdu-Hindustani, 75-76; changing speech patterns, 76; civil service standard, 79. *See also* Linguistic nationalism
Linguistic nationalism; Pukhtoonistan, 68; Andhra, 73-74; Reorganization of Indian States, 74; Bombay, 74; Kerala, 74, 164; not in Coorg, 82; and dictionaries, 88-89; and national unity, 89. *See also* Languages

McCarthyism, 194-97, 201. *See also* Communism
Marriage: changing concepts of, 30-31, 241; raising age of, 47; celebration, 60; and color, 102; wedding procession, 126-27; and foreign service, 144-46; Emmanuel's, 179-80; an Afghan instance, 223. *See also* Men and women

Men and women: travel arrangements, 18, 19, 213-14, 221; in crowds, 36; Radhakrishna, 43; Akbar's view, 61-62; in ancient sculpture, 92-93, 235; machismo, 110-11; in Afghanistan, 116-17, 219; nautch, 125-26; la chasse, 130-33; Dr. Radhakrishnan on, 143; across ceasefire line, 156; evils of coeducation, 157; a Chinese view, 159; two Americans, 175-76; a temporary merger, 206; chaudri use, 207, 216, 224, 218-19; woman as appendage, 211; chivalry, 215, 225
Mosques: Jamma Masjid, 62; Nizamuddin, 65; Mazar-i-sharif, 220. *See also* Temples
Music: of Tan Sen, 35, 186; in a tomb, 65; of the courtesans of Lahore, 125; of the nautch girls of Karachi, 125-26; at Maidens, 130; among the Quilon planters, 172; abroad the *Almirante Saldanha*, 176; Methodist hymns, 181; folk, 181-82; Bengali nautch boy, 182-85; in an Afghan tea house, 224

Nehru, Jawarhalal: deposes Lion of Kashmir, 155; acquiesces in Chinese takeover of Tibet, 192; mentioned, 13, 142-43, 193

Pakistan: and Urdu, 75-76; and Bengali nationalism, 79-81, 88-89. *See also* Bangladesh
Partition, 54, 55, 59, 64; aftermath at Lahore, 124; of Kashmir, 152-54
Pathans: way of life, 111-21; status of women, 116-17, 207, 219; Pukhtoonistan, 68, 113-14. *See also* Afghanistan
Pepsu, 56-59
Photography, 62, 247
Publications procurement: assignment, 11-14; in the bazaars, 20-21; railway publications, 28; telephone directories, 32-33; rationale, 32-33; dam specifications, 59; ephemera, 68; dictionaries, 70-71; palm leaf manuscripts, 91; Pukhto dictionary, 123;

250

## Index

gazetteers, 124; forestry reports, 149; communist propaganda, 158-59, 161 ff; government reports, 187; folk songs, 187; newspapers, 190-91; and intelligence, 194-96, 198; censorship, 198; in Afghanistan, 217
Punjab, 45, 56-57

Raj. See British Raj

Sherpas, 91, 103-4
Shiva: as a souvenir, 22; glimpsed in temple, 23; decapitates his son, 83; recollected, 239-40
Sikhs, 45-50, 57-58. See also Punjab
Sikkim, 203-5
Slocum, Harvey, 59
Souvenirs, 22, 40, 119, 215-16, 170, 193, 246

Temples: of Banaras, 23; difficulty in ascribing, 36; in Old Delhi, 36-38; in countryside, 38; Jain, 39-40; of Love at Banaras, 92-93; of Madurai, 174; Lakshminarayin, 178; of Kali, 231; of Jagganath, 234; of Khajuraho, 235, 239; in Ajmer, 242. See also Mosques
Tensing, 105-7
Tibet, 192-94

United States Congress, 197-201
United States Departmen of State: impact of McCarthyism, 197; and Congress, 197-201; competition with Department of Defense, 200
Untouchables. See Caste
Uttar Pradesh, 16-19

Vindhya Pradesh, 33-36

Weavers: of Banaras, 26-28; of Sikkim, 204
Women. See Men and women; Diplomatic corps

251

## Author Note for Reprint of Krishna Smiled

The author, one of the few women to be commissioned as a United States Foreign Service Officer in the 1950's, was assigned to publications procurement in India, Pakistan, Afghanistan, Myanmar and Sri Lanka. *Krishna Smiled: Assignment in Southeast Asia* is a memoir of her experiences as a 21-year-old footloose in Asia.

After two years in London as US vice consul, the author returned to the United States, married Sol Elkin, a labor arbitrator, and entered academia. Judith Laikin Elkin (Ph.D., 1976, the University of Michigan) is an associate of the UM Frankel Center for Judaic Studies and founding president of the Latin American Jewish Studies Association (LAJSA). She is the author of *The Jews of Latin America*, co-editor of *The Jewish Presence in Latin America*, and has served as consultant to exhibits and films on this subject. The mother of two daughters and four granddaughters, Dr. Elkin lives in Ann Arbor.